PLAYING TENNIS

95ª

PLAYING TENNIS

LIKE A PRO

WILLIAM RALSTON

ROBERT HALE • LONDON

First published in 2016 by
Robert Hale, an imprint of
The Crowood Press Ltd
Ramsbury, Marlborough
Wiltshire SN8 2HR

www.crowood.com

www.halebooks.com

British Library Cataloguing-in-Publication Data
A catalogue record for this book is available from the British Library.

ISBN 978 0 7198 1330 6

Typeset by Eurodesign

Printed and bound in Malaysia by Times Offset (M) Sdn Bhd

In loving memory of Andrew Charles Ralston.

This is for you.

Contents

CHAPTER FOUR

CHAPTER FIVE

CHAPTER SIX

Acknowledgements

No piece of creative work is the result of just one individual. Writing this book has been a great challenge for me both personally and professionally, and it simply would not have been possible without the continued support and understanding of my friends and family, all of whom have stuck by my side every step of the way.

Particular mention must go to William Gray, Thomas McKelvey, Simon King and Henry White for their patience and understanding, and James Barabas, the most generous and selfless person I have ever met, for his incredible support to my whole family. Special mention must also go to Charlotte Abroms, the most inspirational person I know, for her incredible shows of support through strongly worded emails, and Chuck and Oliver East for always being there to bounce ideas off. Thank you also to my wonderful cousin, Alex Hendrickson, for being a constant source of encouragement, and Jackie Poate, the world's greatest godmother, for her creative input.

I would also like to thank all those players, coaches and key figures who have spoken with me at length as part of my research for this book. In no particular order, these include Mike and Bob Bryan, Nick Bollettieri, Patrick Mouratoglou, Dick Gould, Brian Boland, Galo Blanco, Jez Green, Richard Gasquet, Jordi Arrese, Laura Robson, Dominic Inglot, Alexandr Dolgopolov, Nikolay Davydenko, James Ward, Filip Peliwo, Jonathan Stark, Peter Gilmour, Raleigh Gowrie, Colin Triplow, James Allemby, Roger Dalton, all those at the International Tennis Federation (ITF) and The Lawn Tennis Association (LTA), Calum Loveridge, Andrew Kean at First Point USA, Raphael Maurer, Juan Carlos Báguena, and the great team at the Barcelona Tennis Academy.

Last but not least, I would like to show the most sincere of appreciation to my dearest family: Dad, Mum, Tom, and Millie. I must begin by extending a brief apology to my brother and sister for deserting them when they needed it most, before thanking them both for their help and support through my days in tennis and beyond. We may not talk so often, but just knowing they are there is enough.

Words escape me to describe how important my parents have been in my development. As clichéd as it sounds, it really is not until you lose someone that you become aware quite how fundamental they were in your contentment. My father was a silent strength in our lives whose single greatest pride was seeing his three precious children flourish under his watchful guidance. Not only do I want to thank him for looking after my wonderful mother, the love of his life, I must thank him for allowing me the opportunity to play tennis, for supporting me every step along the wonderful journey and for keeping my feet firmly on the ground. It brings me the greatest of pain to know that he will never see the fruits of his support, but I need to express my appreciation for the joy and happiness he brought to us all.

They say opposites attract and my mother is the great antithesis of my father – whilst he was the stabilizer, a rational thinker, keeping us all secure, my mother gives anything and everything to ensure that we have the chance to enjoy each opportunity that life has to offer. From thrusting a tennis racket into my hand as a youngster to proof-reading each and every draft of this book, she has always encouraged us kids to pursue our wildest passions and still been there to catch us if things aren't quite working out.

Together my parents have provided the most secure of environments to allow us kids to flourish without the burdensome worries that so very often hold people back. Without them, not only would I have lacked the courage and confidence to pursue the avenues down which I have ventured, but I simply wouldn't have had the opportunity to even consider them at all.

Finally, I should also add my thanks to:

- Ella Ling, for providing photos.
- Tara Wallace, for her illustrations.
- my editors, Alexander Stilwell and Lavinia Porter, for their patience.
- Pierre Capel, for translating.

To you all – thank you for making this possible.

William Ralston

Introduction

This is not a book about regret. This is no time to reflect on paths not taken or mistakes made. This is the extensive map for players out there with similar aspirations to those that filled my mind for all those years, a medium through which I communicate the multitude of lessons learned during my years in the world of tennis. This book is about giving you, the reader, the benefit of my knowledge to assist you on your journey to become a highly skilled tennis player. In short, this is the book I wish I had five years ago.

The day was 5 October 2011. That was the day it collapsed. The day all faint hope of a successful on-court career stopped with my father's last breath on that sunny autumn morning. That was the day I hung up my rackets, the day I realized I had to pursue one of life's more convenient careers. My time was up. And as easy as it would be to blame my athletic shortcomings on this catastrophic event, I was already late. I was already behind the curve. The pressures of competitive tennis were disrupting my relationships as I chased the impossible dream alongside thousands of other 22-year-olds. My time was already drawing to a close and my father's passing was just a catalyst for the inevitable.

I wouldn't even blame it on a lack of talent – and there was certainly no absence of effort. My parents supported me the whole way. They gave me anything and everything I needed to develop professionally and athletically. For that I am eternally grateful. But

while hitting a fluffy yellow piece of rubber over a three-foot-high net sounds like child's play, the real challenge of the game comes in picking your way along the infinite number of paths that may or may not lead to the very pinnacle of the beautiful game.

As much as I felt confident in my ability on the court, the most challenging part of the whole experience was making decisions off it. It was like navigating myself through a never-ending maze with a list of conflicting directions. Should I go to college in the USA? Am I too old? How do I become 'professional'? How do I pick an academy? How do I select my rackets? What strings should I use? And this is just a speck on the shorts of something far, far bigger – and this bigger world is one where decisions count and choices do matter. The shelf life of a tennis player is so extremely short and all these decisions can make or break a player's career in the sport they call their own.

And the time is now. There is no other sport that has experienced the kind of changes that tennis has over the past fifty years. The original grass courts have been replaced by a plethora of more economical alternatives, the 'Western' grip has taken over the modern game and what was once considered a gentleman's sport has transformed into a game where force trumps finesse – where players are more likely to arrive at the net to shake hands rather than to win the point. While the same rules apply, a different game is being played.

The globalization of the sport has given players more options and choices than ever before. The year 2011 was the first where the WTA's top ten players hailed from ten different countries. In 1985 the top 100 men and women in the rankings hailed from twenty-nine and twenty-four distinct countries respectively. Both numbers have now climbed to more than thirty-seven. The growth of the sport has been nothing short of seismic, and the result today is that tennis academies in Florida are no longer the only option. Natural gut strings no longer monopolize the market. Grass is no longer the surface of choice. While superb news for the average player, it means that working your way to the top is now more complicated and confusing than could ever have been anticipated.

It all sounds so simple. Tennis is a game played on a rectangular court by either two or four players who have to hit a ball back and forth over a net. The ball is only allowed to bounce once on each side and players must return the ball back over the net and into the opponent's court. Failure to return the ball means the opponent scores a point. But reality tells an entirely different story, one where intelligence and decision-making can be the difference between failure and success.

I want to share with you, therefore, a concise collection of knowledge I have gained, with invaluable input from some of the game's greatest talents. In the following chapters, I will provide a detailed analysis of the important decisions to be made, discussing the techniques, tactics and equipment used in the modern age alongside extensive support and advice from some of the leading players and coaches in the sport, all of whom have found their formula for success.

I have no doubt it would have accelerated my development as a competitor.

I hope it will yours, too.

Author's Note

I have been driven to write this book to share my knowledge with players who, like my former self, have a goal to succeed as a professional tennis player. They say that you learn more by losing than winning and, while I did not achieve all I set out to do, I was compelled to explore why it is not always the most talented players that break through. Out of curiosity and for self-peace of mind, I needed to find the reason why some people make it and others do not. Having researched all aspects of the development of a player from my own personal experience, this is what I found, and I would like to help any young tennis players about to set off on a similar journey.

CHAPTER ONE

Understanding the Coach–Player–Parent Relationship

Hindsight is a wonderful thing. Although I reflect on my time in tennis with a great sense of pride, I cannot help but think about a number of choices I made with a lack of knowledge. I spent copious amounts of time choosing my equipment and the tournaments I was going to play, but one consideration I feel was often overlooked was my choice of coach.

As naive as it would now appear, I was under the impression that all coaches could develop my game, independent of who they were, and it was not until I began working with an Argentinian named Martin Cejas that I realized how important the coach–player relationship is in development. We gelled almost instantly – he understood me and I understood him – and this close-knit relationship of complete trust and confidence allowed my game to develop faster than ever before.

It happens all too often that players overlook the important factors when finding a coach, basing their decision on costs or convenience rather than what really matters. At the higher levels, whether choosing a college, an academy or a full-time coach to travel with, the coach–player relationship is extremely personal; what works for one player will not necessarily work for another, and it is important that the player commits the time to find the right person for them as an individual at that particular stage of their development.

Great strain, too, was put on my relationship with my family. At all times, whether it be on court or off it, there remained an unnerving sense of guilt in the back of my mind, firmly based on the fact that my parents had sacrificed so much, both financially and emotionally, to give me the opportunity to play the game. And make no mistake – my parents struggled, too. As all parents do, they just wanted to see their child succeed, but there were always doubts as to the extent of their role in making this happen.

Understanding the role of the coach and the parents is the first step in overcoming these hurdles. Of importance, too, are considerations of the fundamental factors in a healthy coach–player relationship.

Achieving the Ideal Coach–Player–Parent Relationship

With over sixty years in the game, there are few people better placed to determine the role of the coach and the parents than tennis legend, Nick Bollettieri. Widely credited for his work with many of the world's top players, including Tommy Haas, Maria Sharapova, Jim Courier and, most notably, a young Andre Agassi, Nick Bollettieri knows what it takes to mould a champion. I spoke with him to discover his thoughts on these issues.

According to Bollettieri, the role of the coach and the parents in player development should be inextricably linked. 'Both should play an incredibly important role,' he says. 'They must communicate and work together to create the right environment to allow the player to develop.'

Bollettieri goes on to describe how the relationship is like a pyramid: 'The player is at the top with the parents at the bottom right and the coach at the bottom left. Everybody must know their role because if the whole team does not work together then the team will fall apart.'

With this in mind, we must now understand what these roles are.

Nick Bollettieri's pyramid shows how the roles of the parents and coach in player development are inextricably linked

The Role of Parents in Player Development

❝ The parent–child relationship can be damaged irreparably if the parents do not understand their role in the child's development. ❞
NICK BOLLETTIERI, *Coach to ten World Number Ones*

Parents play an extremely important role in the development of a junior player. 'They have the greatest influence of everyone,' says Jordi Arrese, former Spanish Davis Cup Captain. Despite this, however, there is actually very little guidance about the tremendous role they play, and coaches are always looking for the best way to educate them about their role in the development of their player.

As illustrated so beautifully in the development of Chris Evert and Michael Chang, parents can become a very positive influence on their child's development, but their impact can quickly become negative should they not understand the scope of their role. 'Parents must get involved in the development of their children but *how* they get involved is so important,' says Bollettieri.

One of the biggest mistakes that parents can make is putting their children under too much pressure to succeed. This pressure, of course, may stem from the financial sacrifices made by the family, or even from parents who want their children to succeed where they have not. Pursuing tennis as a career can put the family under 'tremendous strain', says Bollettieri. 'There is no escaping the fact that it costs a lot of money. Parents no longer are saying "I love you" when their child comes off court; they are asking what the score was.'

This, too, is a view shared by Arrese. 'Too many parents put unnecessary pressure on their children instead of actually enjoying the sport and instilling the right values in them. The most important thing should be enjoying the sport and learning from it, but many parents focus their dreams on their children and this is damaging,' he says.

The parents' role is to support their children as much as possible. Inevitably, this support will consist of financial aid, but parents must also support their child emotionally and with making decisions. This support will also include psychological guidance and ensuring that the child is getting enough rest, eating well and showing commitment away from the court.

Of great importance, however, is that the parents do not involve themselves in any tennis-specific work – an aspect of player development in which the roles of coach and parents can easily become confused. 'The support from the parents must be outside the court and outside of tennis completely,' says Juan Carlos Báguena, former ATP Player and Director of Barcelona Tennis Academy. 'When the player is on court he is working on developing his tennis and that is his coach's job,' he says. 'This is where the line must be drawn.'

The unfortunate truth is that this line is crossed only too often. Coaches, as professionals of the game, recognize that parental influence on tennis-specific matters can have a negative effect on a child's development, but are forced to meet the demands of overly pushy parents because they are the ones paying the wages. While it is the responsibility of coaches to prevent parents overstepping the mark, parents must also be careful to respect the wishes of the coach.

Communication, too, is an important aspect of the parents' role. 'The parents must have regular meetings alone with the coach to give as much information about their player as possible,' says Bollettieri. In order to touch a player's game, the coach must know that player extremely well, and the parents play an important role in communicating with the coach exactly how the player is feeling or behaving to ensure that the coach can adapt his or her methods as necessary.

The Role of the Coach in Player Development

The coach today must control everything. They must know what makes the player tick, their idiosyncrasies, their superstitions. Being a coach is so much more than teaching the player to hit a forehand.
NICK BOLLETTIERI, *Coach to ten World Number Ones*

Patrick Mouratoglou (*left*) believes that the coach must take complete responsibility for every aspect of the player's development

Before we can discuss the necessary ingredients for a successful coach–player relationship, it is important to consider why players need a coach – what is their role?

Away from high-performance tennis, the responsibility of the coach is normally limited to regular on-court tuition with focus on technical and tactical progressions. Intermediate players, for example, will work with a local coach or 'club pro' a couple of times a week to develop a specific technical skill in their game. Towards the higher echelons, however, the role of the coach becomes far wider and stretches well beyond the realms of on-court technical and tactical training.

Patrick Mouratoglou (coach to Serena Williams, Jeremy Chardy, Marcos Baghdatis, and Laura Robson) explained to me that the coach's role at competitive level is all-encompassing and wide in scope. 'The role of the coach is to make the player win. That is the single purpose and responsibility,' he says. 'The role of the coach at these levels is not simply to run practice sessions or organize fitness training because all this would be completely irrelevant without the ultimate goal of winning.'

The coach has a responsibility to 'find solutions to solve any problems the player may have,' he says. These problems may be mental, physical, technical or tactical, but the coach must work to solve everything. 'There are *always* solutions,' says Mouratoglou.

Although Ivan Lendl (*right*) did not drastically transform Murray's technical and tactical game, he gave the Scot the mental strength and discipline needed to become a champion

Andy Murray, for example, employed Ivan Lendl more for his mental support and shared experience of having lost his first four Major finals than for his technical and tactical acumen. Over the course of a relationship that produced an Olympic Gold, a US Open title and a Wimbledon victory, Lendl brought a distinct discipline that allowed Murray to perform better when it mattered most. The world saw a quieter Murray on court, mentally more tuned in than ever before, but there were very few immediately obvious tactical or technical changes to note. Murray already knew how to play tennis.

Similarly, Roger Federer and Novak Djokovic, arguably two of the most technically gifted players of the Open era, began working with the great Stefan Edberg and Boris Becker respectively for a plethora of reasons besides actual stroke improvement.

While Edberg, known for his wonderful attacking repertoire, brought Federer two feet closer to the baseline and encouraged him to take risks to finish points early, he was also taken on board for his great experience and knowledge of the game. Any technical or tactical progressions in the Djokovic game are worked on with long-term coach, Marián Vajda; Boris Becker, known for his ability to win 'big matches', was hired to share his experience and knowledge at a time when the Serb had lost five of his last six Grand Slam finals.

'Where he helps me the most is from a mental point of view,' said Djokovic. Following his 2014 victory at the All England Club, the Serb praised Becker's influence in giving him the mental strength to get across the line: 'There were a few things that were important but most of all it was the mental toughness and the self-belief. He believes in my game.'

According to acclaimed coach Galo Blanco (coach to Milos Raonic, Jurgen Meltzer, Marcel Granollers and Filip Peliwo), the role of a coach at these levels is to ensure that the player has every aspect of performance to allow them to succeed on the court. As Blanco points out, the technical development of competitive level players is normally completed at a very early age. 'By the time players reach an advanced level, they will already be technically proficient and the coach must work only to tweak or fine-tune these strokes,' says Blanco.

In this way, Blanco believes that the role of the coach in technique development is just a small element of a far wider programme, stating instead that a large part of his work is actually carried out behind the scenes in off-court practices: 'It [the role of the coach] is to teach the player everything' and 'control everything on the court and off the court to ensure that the player reaches their goals,' he says.

Boris Becker (*left*), known for his ability to win big matches, was brought on board by Novak Djokovic to share his knowledge and experience with the Serb

Stefan Edberg (*right*) has worked with Roger Federer to both help him be more aggressive and finish points off at the net

Choosing a Coach

> ❝ It is people who play tennis, it is not machines. I treat my players as Formula One cars that need very special, individual treatment instead of cars that you can buy in the shops that are all the same. ❞
> PATRICK MOURATOGLOU, *Director of Mouratoglou Tennis Academy, Paris*

Dick Gould's journey started in autumn of 1966 when he was appointed the Head Men's Tennis Coach at Stanford University. These were the days before 'Open' tennis: the professional tour consisted of Jack Kramer playing one-on-one

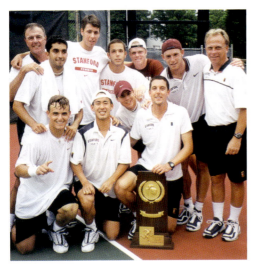

Under the guidance of Dick Gould (*top left*), Stanford University Men's tennis became the top team in the USA

A well-stocked Stanford University Men's Tennis trophy cabinet

Gould (*left*) honed the talents of some wonderful players in his time at Stanford, including Nick Saviano (*seventh from the left*), Roscoe Tanner (*middle, with jacket*), and John McEnroe (*right of Roscoe Tanner*)

matches across the USA and the only other people making money were enthusiastic amateurs taking payments under the table to appear in tournaments – later labelled as 'Shamateurism' by Kramer himself. Partly driven by the chance to defer military obligations by continuing education, almost everybody was driven towards a collegiate education.

After representing Stanford himself, Dick returned to take the reins of the men's programme in 1966 as a 'nobody', he says. Stanford had always had strong teams, but rivals USC, UCLA and Trinity of Texas were the leading tennis schools in the country. Gould worked tirelessly to build the programme and proposed a National Training Camp be hosted on campus after the introduction of 'Open' tennis in 1968. As the host of the camp, Gould built up a reputation with the best high-school players in the country and just six years later had developed enough credibility to attract the most talented players to his college. By 1972, Stanford had become one of the top teams in the country.

Stanford won its first NCAA Championship in 1973, seven years after Gould's entry on the scene, and the rest, they say, is history. Over the course of his thirty-nine-year tenure, Gould and his team won anything and everything that college tennis had to offer, including seventeen

NCAA Team Championships, two 'Coach of the Decade' awards and nine NCAA singles titles. Fifty of his players were selected as All-Americans, fifteen of whom went on to be ranked among the top fifteen in the ATP World Singles rankings. His list of alumni includes the likes of John McEnroe, Bob and Mike Bryan, Roscoe Tanner, Tim Mayotte and Jonathan Stark. His team of 1998 is widely regarded as the best college team ever, finishing with a perfect 28–0 record with the loss of just two singles matches. Fourteen of Gould's students became top ten doubles players in the world.

Short-lived success can come too easily but it is the sustained success of Gould's tenure that makes his achievements so astonishing. He created eight generations of successful intercollegiate teams during his reign, stepping down with an 84 per cent winning percentage. Put simply, Gould is the most successful coach in the history of US collegiate tennis and even today, his programme at Stanford remains the yardstick by which other top collegiate tennis programmes are measured.

Similarly, Brian Boland's name has been synonymous with success for nearly two decades. Installed as Head Coach at Virginia in 2002, Boland has taken Men's Tennis at Virginia from mid-tier to the most elite programme in the country. His list of personal achievements includes a National Coach of the Year award in 2007 along with ten Conference Coach of the Year and five ITA Regional Coach of the Year awards. His career win percentage sits at approximately 85 per cent – well among the greatest the collegiate game has ever known – and he is widely credited with moulding the likes of Somdev Devvarman, Dominic Inglot and Treat Huey into players fit for competition on the ATP Tour.

His 2013 season ranked among one of the greatest years by any programme in the history of collegiate tennis. Reaching the very peak by lifting the NCAA Championship trophy, Boland and his team went 30–0 and became the only tennis school to combine these achievements with the ITF National Indoor Championships title in the same year. After such unparalleled

Brian Boland has moulded the likes of Somdev Devvarman, Dom Inglot and Treat Huey into players fit for competition on the ATP Tour

successes at the helm of Virginia tennis, Boland has not only fixed himself as one of the premier modern-day coaches in collegiate tennis, he has created himself such a legacy to ensure that he will go down as one of the greatest collegiate coaches in history.

Despite their incredible achievements, neither Boland nor Gould simply walked into their success; Virginia University was approximately seventy-five in the country when Boland took over and Gould's Stanford was far from a spearhead of the collegiate tennis scene. I doubt whether there are two better coaches in world tennis who have achieved such sustained success. What, I ask, did they do differently? What was this common denominator that allowed them to turn their respective schools into pieces of collegiate tennis history?

Brian Boland, here celebrating another victory, is highly committed and takes complete responsibility for shaping his players' games

Commitment

The answers become evident following conversations with them both. I was immediately struck by their humanity and humility when accepting my questions. Open and honest at all times, even after decades talking about tennis all day long, they were both so passionate and willing to discuss their respective experiences. They spoke with such warmth and excitement in their voices that it became obvious that coaching tennis to developing juniors was by no means their job; it was very much their lifestyle – and they absolutely loved it. 'His passion and commitment goes into absolutely everything that he does,' says Jonathan Stark, who played under Gould before going on to be the Number One Doubles player in the world, winning Grand Slams in both mixed and men's doubles.

Gould (*centre*) went to great lengths to recruit the Bryan brothers

This unparalleled dedication and commitment of Gould is illustrated by the lengths he used to go to prepare his teams for success. Besides playing tapes of songs with the word 'Georgia' in on repeat for the fortnight before travelling to the NCAA finals in Georgia, Gould used to 'hire' a team of rowdy 'frat-boys' to heckle and distract his players in training for many weeks leading up to the event – the pinnacle of collegiate competition. Gould believed that this was an important element of preparation for the atmosphere that would present itself down in the Deep South. But

Gould's incredible passion for success is perhaps best illustrated by his recruitment of Mike and Bob Bryan to the Stanford University programme in 1996.

The Bryan brothers enjoyed extensive success as juniors in the USA. Victories in the 1991 USTA National Boys Under-14 Championships and the 1996 USTA National Boys 18 Championships had guaranteed them a highly sought after spot on the USC roster by the time they reached the age of eligibility. Wayne Bryan, Mike and Bob's father, was great friends with the USC Coach, Dick Leach, and the scholarships 'had been in place for nearly a decade,' says Bob.

Gould wanted the Bryans, one of the hottest properties in collegiate tennis, on his roster and was determined to make it happen. With his reputation as a legendary collegiate coach growing each year, Gould would use

Dick Gould moulded Mike and Bob Bryan (*above*) into the finest doubles pair the game has ever seen

this to lure the Bryans into his system. 'He would show us around the Stanford trophy room, take us for rides in his car with the number plates "NCAA1", and write lists as to why Stanford was the school for us,' Mike said to me of Gould's efforts to recruit him and his brother. On the day of signing, Gould offered to drive nearly six hours to Camarillo to push the deal through if the Bryans were having second thoughts.

Speaking to Dominic Inglot, a graduate of the University of Virginia, it becomes apparent that similar qualities can be found in Boland. 'The reason Brian [Boland] is so successful is his passion for the game,' he says. 'He lives, breathes and sleeps the sport and he is unique in that sense. Brian, through his passion and commitment for the game, creates an incredible, professional-like programme for his players and that, for me, is the reason behind his success.'

'I am always totally and completely invested in each and every player,' says Boland of his own programme. 'It is not a job in the formal sense; it is a lifestyle. Days, hours, weeks – what do they mean? It is what I love to do with my time and I really feel I am making a difference. What a privilege it is for me to be in a position to provide these resources for these athletes as they go through one of the most important periods of their lives.

'No matter how much I know about the game and no matter how much I love this game, until that athlete knows that I care, it really does not matter what I know,' adds Boland.

None of this is to say that commitment is the only necessary ingredient of a successful coach–player relationship, but its importance cannot be underestimated. You only have to visit a modern tennis training facility

Brian Boland chats with his player during a training session

Gould (*right*) stresses the importance of connecting with his players

today to see that there are too many coaches who are just looking for a quick payday and their commitment to a player's development is relinquished the moment the training session is over. This, quite simply, just does not cut it in the competitive world of tennis.

Professional tennis training is a full-time job and the responsibilities extend well beyond the white lines and around the clock. Just as players must make sacrifices to allow them to be at their best, successful coaches, too, must be willing to make the development of their players their priority, providing continuous support in both on-court and off-court practices.

'A coach's role is twenty-four hours a day 365 days a year,' says Nick Bollettieri. 'Coaches must be willing to make sacrifices too. They must be willing to suffer with the student,' he adds.

Individual Attention, Trust and Respect

Remarkably, there are actually very few similarities between the programmes implemented by Boland and Gould. While Boland incorporates a very individual programme with a maximum of two players on court at any time, Gould was not afforded this luxury and so set aside two and a half hours a day for team practice. One fundamental aspect that is common in both arrangements, however, is a willingness to get to know the players and their games on a very detailed level.

Individual attention is important from both a tactical and psychological perspective. The tactical and technical flaws in a player's game become smaller as gradual improvements are made and these will go unnoticed where the coach does not focus on these idiosyncrasies. It is simply not possible for a coach to touch a player's game in the necessary detail without individual attention.

'Players are all different. They all think differently. They all feel different and they all have very specific needs. These needs are mental, physical, technical and tactical. The only way to get the best out of players is to be connected with them. When I say "connected", I mean that you have to know them really well. You need to know them and get their full trust. Only then do you learn how to click the right buttons to make them give their best,' says Patrick Mouratoglou.

While Gould could not offer private tuition for his students, he made sure he planned his practice sessions with the upmost precision and used the time on court wisely to get to know his players' games and personalities inside out. 'When it came to training, he was very specific to each player and he would spend time with each one of us to work on our specific needs,' says Jonathan Stark, former World Number One Doubles player and 1994 French Open Men's Doubles Champion.

'I had a very personal relationship with each one of the players,' says Gould himself. 'I was working with them three hours a day, six days a week – that is more time than their parents spent with them. I got to know them very well and they were all different. For me, it is like having your own family; they all have their own different traits, interests, talents, possibilities, and a good coach must be able to appreciate that and help develop that.

'You can watch a player play a match and you can see strengths and holes in their game and you want to keep working to make the strengths stronger, and improve the weaknesses. You do not have to know the players well do to do that, but to get the best out of them in competition you have to know what buttons to push. As with your own children, each child has a different button which will help them compete and rise up at the right time and coaches need to know the players personally in order to do so. You only learn that by knowing the players and spending time with them.'

This incredible personal relationship has not been lost despite the miles travelled and great successes of his alumni. There remains a joke between the Bryans and coach Gould about the on-going tradition for their names to be engraved on the number of Stanford Monuments that rest outside the tennis hall on the Californian campus. At a cost of US$500 for each inscription, the Bryans have single-handedly cost Stanford University more than US$22,000 in engraving fees alone.

The Coach and the Importance of Adaptation

An important aspect of the coach–player relationship becomes adaptation. If the coach is to 'control everything' and 'find solutions' for the player to win, they must learn to adapt to the specific needs of the player. Although Galo Blanco describes himself as a 'highly disciplined' coach, he explains how he must 'adjust to his players' if he is to maximize their performance.

According to Patrick Mouratoglou, there are two phases that must be completed 'before the deep work can be started and the results will begin to show'. Phase one is getting to know the player completely; phase two is getting the trust and confidence of the player, ensuring that he or she will follow the coach completely. Sometimes the coach needs up to eight months to complete these first two phases and only then can the work really start. 'As the coach, I must tell the player what to do and they must trust me because everything I do has a reason behind it. Only with complete respect for me will they follow my instructions.'

Mouratoglou discusses how he once took a player from Number Sixty in the world to a career-high ranking of fifteen in just over eight months, a span that included victories over the top five players in the world at the time. With this particular player, Mouratoglou had to give her a complete game plan before each and every match she played. 'I told her where she has to serve, where she has to return, where she plays, how she has to play, and that if she respects the plan then there is no way that she is going to lose.'

Although Mouratoglou is 'not naturally a dictator' or someone to give strict instructions as exactly how to play a particular match, he knew his player well enough to know exactly what she needed. 'I was so tough and so demanding with her that it made her feel like a great player and it gave her so much confidence,' adds Mouratoglou. 'But I knew it was the right attitude to have with her.'

For this reason, it is important that the coach spends time with the player off the court, getting to know them as an individual and not just as a player. This is the only way to develop a relationship of trust and confidence, and also for the coach to learn exactly what he needs to do beyond the general technical and tactical work to maximize that player's performance.

'In order to really help a player, you must know them inside-out,' says Nick Bollettieri. Only too often do developing juniors become suffocated by the pressures of competition, and this can only hinder their progress. 'Let the player talk. Give them space!' he says. 'The coach must regularly meet with the player alone to discuss progress,' adds Bollettieri, before pointing out that training the great Andre Agassi 'made me a better listener'.

As a player, you must be wary of committing to any tennis training programme where you do not have a healthy, open relationship with the coaching team or where the coaches are not committed enough to put in time off the court to gain an understanding of who you really are.

There is a very fine line to be drawn, however, in developing this off-court relationship with players. The danger, according to Patrick Mouratoglou, who explains how he regularly plays PlayStation with his players, is that coaches must not become friends of their players.

'There must be a very close connection but you cannot be friends,' he says. 'My players know me, they trust me and I want them to do well, and they know that I am willing to do anything to help them succeed and I will find a way to help them be the best that they can be. They know they can rely on me and they know that if they have a problem then I will find a solution. But I am not their friend because the coach needs authority, and if he is a friend then he has zero authority.'

This finely tuned balance is just one more area where Gould excelled. 'He created an environment of complete mutual respect. He was very open and this created a great relationship with each one of us,' says Jonathan Stark. 'He reads people so well; he knew when it was time to lay the heavy hand and knew when it was time to lighten up and that is why he got the best out of his players.'

Finding a Coach

The modern tennis world is not blessed with too many 'Goulds' or 'Bolands' and very few players will be privileged enough to play under them, but lessons can be learned from their respective successes. What these two greats have achieved in the collegiate game is simply astounding and studying their attitudes towards player development offers a unique insight into the important aspects of the coach–player relationship.

The unfortunate truth is that there are just too many coaches out there who simply are not committed enough to their roles and, as a result, will fail to understand the player sufficiently to know which problems they have to solve to maximize performance. They will, in short, never learn which buttons to push.

It will not be easy, but you must commit the time to find a coach who will be completely committed to your needs as an individual player and will take full responsibility for carrying your game forward. Consider all these important aspects of the coach–player relationship and make changes as you grow and develop as a player. Make no mistake: choosing a coach is one of the most important ingredients of success because tennis development will always be a two-way street.

CHAPTER TWO

Continuing Your Development

> College was the best two years of my life.
> I have never had so much fun playing tennis!
> MIKE BRYAN, *Stanford University Alumni, London 2012 Olympic
> Champion and winner of over twenty-three Grand Slam titles*

I love academia and I enjoy studying. But as much as I relished the rush of competition and the thrill of perfecting a tennis stroke, I wanted to continue my education for as long as possible.

The discussion came on my return from Melbourne where I had been competing for the past year. Sitting there in my parents' bedroom as a boy of nineteen, a family debate ensued as to whether I should take my place at Law School in Nottingham or hop on a plane to Barcelona and compete full-time. After weighing up the pros and cons, we eventually chose the former. As much as I wanted to be *on* the court and not *in* the court, I was well aware this attitude would likely be reversed as time eventually caught up with me.

It was a painful decision to make. The British university system is not renowned for fostering great athletic talent and I saw this as the end to any real sporting aspirations I continued to hold. I knew it was the right decision, but the taste of bitterness existed well beyond my university years. If only there were an option to combine full-time tennis and education.

The answer presented itself in my second year of study when I was contacted by a number of US college coaches who wanted to take me onto their team. I jumped for joy; I polished my rackets; I rang my parents. As much as this seemed like the solution to my great dilemma that continually hung heavy around my neck, I was led to believe that a US education just could not match that of which I was already the fortunate recipient. It was as if accepting a scholarship to the USA would have re-ignited my athletic dreams but drawn a close to any meaningful career thereafter. In light of this, I politely declined.

It would be wrong to label my decision as a 'regret' because my Law degree has taken me to great places. I do wish, however, that there had been more information available at an earlier age on an American collegiate education because, in all likelihood, if I had known the full extent of the opportunities available, I would have jumped on a plane that very day.

This is what I wish I had known then.

The US Collegiate System

Collegiate tennis in the USA has grown to become a great option for players from all around the world, including many British hopefuls who wish to continue their full-time athletic development whilst studying for a degree. Offering places to international students reflects well on the college itself and allows them to cherry-pick the leading talents from all over the world. Spending up to four years at college can allow you to reach your academic and athletic potential without having to choose between one or the other and if, as a junior player, you have shown talent on the court and in the classroom, a tennis scholarship can allow you to attend at a heavily reduced price – sometimes even for free.

The level of competition in the USA does vary, but the best schools are brimming with international talent, many using their time to get vital match experience before joining the professional tour. College is a base where they can develop their skills, mature professionally and test themselves before they join the game's elite.'The professional game is so much more physically and mentally challenging than the junior circuit,' Marton Fucsovics, the 2009 Wimbledon Junior Champion, told me, and only the very best are ready to make an immediate step to senior level after a successful junior career. While Nadal, Djokovic and Murray would all have wasted their time in collegiate competition, they are 'freaks of nature and almost all players will need more time to mature,' says Daniel Kiernan, Director of SOTO Tennis Academy.

If you are a player with a good body of competitive results, it should be quite easy to find a US college to accept you, and there are hundreds of online agency companies who will manage the whole process for a reasonable fee. These 'agencies' do tend to be very selective with whom they work, so only players with a strong academic and athletic background are advised to approach them.

Although you can approach US colleges independently, it is advisable to use an agency with experience in the industry because the whole process of determining eligibility can be confusing. College tuition fees tend to be very expensive and agency companies will also be of great help when it comes to negotiating the size of any scholarship.

Collegiate Divisions

There are five different divisions of college sports in the USA, all of which vary in size, structure and sporting prowess. Because divisions are sorted according to other factors besides performance, the standard of tennis varies greatly and overlaps between divisions.

NATIONAL COLLEGIATE ATHLETIC ASSOCIATION (NCAA)

The NCAA houses three different collegiate divisions:

NCAA Division 1 schools represent the largest public universities in the USA and are the pinnacle of any college career, requiring both elite standards of academic and athletic ability to attend. UK applicants must normally have a minimum LTA rating of 4.1 and many players will have to build up a reputation in the lower divisions before transferring to a Division 1 school later in their student–athlete career.

NCAA Division 2 colleges are smaller than those in Division 1 and have a greater range of abilities. These schools offer scholarships to players who have shown particular promise at junior level, but they normally have fewer academic regulations for applicants. The leading Division 2 schools can be as strong as the weaker Division 1 schools, but UK applicants will require a minimum LTA rating of 5.2.

NCAA Division 3 schools tend to be small, private institutions with more focus on academics. Under NCAA regulations, these schools are not permitted to offer athletic scholarships, but international student grants are available and athletic ability will be a key factor when determining a student's eligibility.

NATIONAL ASSOCIATION OF INTERCOLLEGIATE ATHLETICS (NAIA)

The NAIA adopts slightly less stringent academic and sporting eligibility requirements and, for this reason, is full of extremely talented athletes who could not satisfy the rigid academic criteria required by the NCAA. The average level of tennis lies somewhere between NCAA Division 1 and Division 2, but the top NAIA schools tend to be amongst the very best schools in the country. The greatest difficulty lies with funding: coaches' budgets tend to be lower than those in the NCAA and most players will have to support themselves to begin with before increasing their scholarship based on their academic and sporting performance over the year.

NATIONAL JUNIOR COLLEGE ATHLETICS ASSOCIATION (NJCAA)

The NJCAA consists of community colleges running two-year courses. Colleges are designed for athletes who do not have the academic results for the NCAA or NAIA but who have shown particular promise on the tennis court. The top NJCAA schools rival NCAA Division 2 and NAIA schools in terms of standards and most NJCAA athletes will transfer to a four-year course in the NCAA or NAIA, assuming they meet the academic criteria. The LTA advises that players will need at least a 3.1 rating to receive a scholarship to the NCJAA.

A Player's Journey: The Benefits of College

To gain a greater understanding of the benefits of college, I spoke to three experts, all of whom have had experience of the collegiate structure in the USA.

Dominic Inglot, World Number 32 Doubles Player and University of Virginia Graduate:

Going to college was the best decision I ever made. I actually went on the understanding that it was the end of my professional career; I only had three ATP points at the time and I went to get an education and to see what happened with my tennis. It took the pressure off me because I was studying at the same time. I quickly realized that college offers many advantages that going straight on the tour does not.

College gives players the time to mature without the pressures of the circuit. Competing week in week out can break players as they try to gain ranking points. It can be so hard. I was training with seven guys who were playing at a high level, so I had great variety, access to fantastic facilities and coaches who worked tirelessly to develop my game. Unless the player is lighting up the world at junior level, I would recommend college to him or her.

Daniel Kiernan played at Louisiana State University as part of one of the most successful college teams before playing on the ATP Tour for three years:

I can without question say that I played the best tennis of my career at college. The collaborative environment of being in a team really bene-fited my development. We were pushing each other every day, we trained as a team and everybody needed everybody. It was an abnormal feeling because playing tennis before that had always felt lonely; I had always felt like I was on my own.

If it wasn't for the collegiate system, I would have given up tennis when I was twenty. I could not have joined the tour at that age; I wasn't ready emotionally or physically to handle it and college gave me the infrastructure to keep on going, to get some experience and to mature as a person and as a player. I definitely went further in my tennis because of college than I would have if I hadn't gone to college.

My rule is that if you are not making semi-finals and finals of Futures events on a regular basis by the time you are eligible for college, then college is the option for you because you need this time for development. And the same applies to girls; I would still advise a lot of girls to go to college, although the women's game is a younger, speciality sport and often requires less time to mature.

The ages of 18–22 are apprentice years. If you cannot travel with a coach and do it properly, you end up not training properly, not getting the right advice and not being professional enough in preparation for and when training for these events. It is therefore very difficult to reach

Developing players can really benefit from the collaborative environment of being in a team at college

One of the greatest advantages of collegiate tennis is that players can talk with their coach throughout the match

your potential, and that is why college in America is such a great option. You can go over there and play hundreds of matches without the pressures of having to prove yourself by picking up [ATP] points and getting caught up in the negativity that surrounds the ITF Futures Circuit.

Dick Gould, Head of Stanford University Men's Tennis 1966–2004, winner of seventeen NCAA Men's Championships and the most successful college coach in history:

The biggest advantage of college tennis for me is that coaches are allowed to talk to their players in a match. When you are teaching a kid something new, the kid is the last person to have confidence to try it in a match. But if I am telling a guy who has never served and volleyed that I want him to serve and volley on a certain point then he has no choice; he has to do it. And so I am the guy who takes responsibility; the player gets let off the hook. It is a great way to be able to teach and it is a great way for players to develop.

The College Application Process

Many colleges adopt a rolling admissions process that allows players to enrol at any time, but most student–athletes will enrol in either August or January. The application process should begin approximately eighteen months before enrolment, which normally means looking at the beginning of your penultimate year of higher level study.

'The process begins with the player,' says Stanford legend Dick Gould. 'Players should log onto the [ITA] Intercollegiate Tennis System website [http://www.itatennis.com/] and look at the rankings of the current players and of the school to see which colleges are within their range. Players should then look at the specific school's website, which will provide a background.'

You must both satisfy the specific entry requirements as set internally by the college itself and the student–athlete eligibility as determined by the NCAA or NAIA. 'All players should have completed their SAT [see below] at least twelve months prior to their enrolment,' says Andrew Kean, founder of First Point USA Athlete Recruitment Agency.

In the year prior to enrolment, you should be receiving your scholarship offer along with admission acceptance.

College Academic Requirements

Almost all applicants will be required to sit a standardized admissions test if they are to attend college in the USA. Although there are a few colleges which do not require any admissions tests, most institutions accept both the SAT reasoning and ACT for undergraduate admissions. To determine which colleges accept which tests, it is best to check the webpage of the specific college. If in doubt, contact the college directly.

In the case that the college accepts both the SAT and the ACT, choosing which one to sit will come down to personal preference. Although both tests serve the same purpose in the admissions process, the exams themselves are both quite different and you are advised to choose the test that best suits you and your academic skill-set. This can normally be determined by considering the structure of each test and by comparing the results of the various sample tests that are made available on both the SAT and ACT websites.

SCHOLASTIC APTITUDE TESTS (SAT)

All NCAA Division 1 and 2 colleges, and most NCAA Division 3, NAIA and NCJAA colleges accept the SAT. The exam can be entered via www.college-board.org and comprises three parts: Critical Reading, Mathematics and Writing. In the UK, the test is held at test centres across the country six times per year between October and June. As an applicant, you can sit the SAT as many times as you want.

The specific SAT requirements will be dependent on the college, all of which make their SAT data public on their respective websites.

AMERICAN COLLEGE TEST (ACT)

The ACT tests focuses on four subject areas: English, Mathematics, Reading and Science Reasoning. There is also an optional Writing section which will be required by the most competitive US institutions. Although the ACT is not as readily available in the UK, it is preferred by students with a strong grasp of Science and Maths for two reasons: the SAT does not include a Science section and the Maths section is at a higher level (Trigonometry) in the ACT than in the SAT.

You can register for the ACT via the website (www.actstudent.org).

The importance of the SAT/ACT cannot be underestimated by applicants. As schools will claim to offer a holistic approach to their decisions, these tests hold significant weight in both admission and any merit-based scholarships because of their numerical nature. As a result of this, you are advised to thoroughly prepare for each test by reading around the subject areas and reading one of the many specialist SAT/ACT textbooks available. In addition to the SAT/ACT, some international students may be required to sit an English Language Proficiency Exam.

Negotiating Your Scholarship

An important aspect of this process is negotiating the scholarship money received. The average cost of tuition alone in public US schools is close to £14,000 per annum – almost double that in the UK. This figure rises to approximately £19,000 for private institutions and it becomes difficult to complete one year of study in the USA for less than £30,000 when you factor in living costs, including books, travel, accommodation and food – over £10,000 more expensive than most British universities. Tuition and fee rates can vary significantly, but almost all international applicants will need financial aid or a scholarship. 'Deals can always be negotiated,' says Kean, and the size of the scholarship will be largely dependent on your results as a junior.

You can receive either a full or partial scholarship. Partial scholarships are the most common type to be offered by coaches. An example would be where a college coach offers to pay US$40,000 of the total cost of US$55,000 for you to attend the institution and play tennis there. From the coach's perspective it is still a fantastic offer and a significant sum of money for them to invest, but the remaining cost of US$15,000 is still something for you or your family to fund.

'Full-rides' – 100 per cent scholarships – are 'unbelievably difficult to obtain and very rare,' says Kean. These scholarships cover tuition, accommodation, food, books, and most things related to the sport. This is obviously a huge financial investment by the college and it expects an excellent performance from those athletes fortunate enough to receive this level of funding. What is not covered within the scholarship is the cost of flights, health insurance (approximately £400 per year), student visa fees, and money for a social life – 'not that you'll have time for one,' jokes Kean. Most scholarship deals can be renegotiated before each year once the coach has seen what you can do.

According to Brian Boland, Head Coach at the University of Virginia, negotiating a scholarship is about compromise. As a recruiter, he thinks it is important that players make some sort of financial commitment. 'I look for the player and his family to make an investment in us as much as we make an investment in them, because I find that if there is an investment on both sides, that is when both parties really feel like they are benefiting from the experience,' he says.

To understand more about the recruitment process from the view of the coach, I asked Boland to share his thoughts with me:

I spend a fair amount of time keeping myself abreast of tennis results and begin recruiting student athletes by identifying them as early as 14– 15 years old. I will do this by looking at their national and international rankings and I will then try to speak to coaches in that particular area to learn as much as I can about that particular player. As these players then become closer to reaching college, I will then reach out to coaches in that area and eventually, if the coach has not initiated contact with me, I will then try to initiate contact with them.

I will always ensure that the individual places some value on academics before considering them; student–athletes must want to further their education and they must have an understanding that college is about education. I also look for a passion in tennis development and assurances that they are willing to put in the kind of work to really play at the next level. They must be interested in what this whole process is about. I also want to investigate what kind of character the player has because I believe that to build a strong tennis player, you need character.

Finally, there is a certain threshold of tennis results that I require. I will look at each and every one of a player's results, from juniors through to ITF to determine whether they can compete at this level. I am most interested in live competition in a real tournament and I have little interest in the videos that candidates send in.

Selecting the College

With over 5,000 US colleges to choose from, there is an incredibly diverse range of opportunities for all players who have excelled both academically and athletically in their junior years. Most colleges will offer a vast array of information about their programmes on their sites, but applicants can use the Princeton Review (www.princetonreview.com) and US News World Report (www.usnews.com/rankings) to look at the unofficial collegiate rankings.

Depending on your results inside the classroom and on the court, not all colleges will be available, but it is important to choose the best college available to you. So what are the important factors to consider?

THE COACH

You are advised to engage with the college coach before any commitment is made. You attend college to further develop yourself both athletically and academically, and it is essential that you look out for a coach who will provide you with as much support as possible to graduate.

THE EDUCATION

Make no mistake: you can receive a very strong education in the USA. However, as with any education system, there are a number of lower-quality institutions where the education received may be poor. The strength of the education along with the academic reputation of the institution must be an important factor when it comes to deciding which college to attend.

PUBLIC V. PRIVATE

In the USA, public colleges are owned and funded by the state whereas private colleges are supported by endowments, tuition fees and donations from alumni and friends. The most obvious public colleges are the 'flagship' colleges that exist in most states across the USA, e.g. Ohio State and University of Texas, but most states will also have smaller public colleges.

The most viable difference between the two is the cost of tuition, which tends to be higher at a private college. While this cost of tuition will inevitably be an important consideration for most applicants, it should not be the deciding factor – initially, at least. The higher tuition fees mean that most private colleges have greater budgets for financial aid and scholarships, and you should refrain from basing your decision on financial factors until any financial aid has been factored into the equation.

Public colleges are generally not as prestigious as private institutions, yet with their bigger budgets, wonderful facilities and diverse populations, they do attract the leading athletic talents. From an academic standpoint, prestigious private institutions generally offer smaller class sizes and student–teacher relationships but it is the public colleges which have the strongest tennis programmes.

Other factors to bear in mind when choosing a college:

- **Location**: How easy is it to access? What is the climate like?
- **Size of campus**: Is it large, medium or small?
- **Scholarship availability**: Does the coach have money to spend and space available on his or her roster?
- **Ranking (athletic and academic)**: Does the school have a reputation for producing strong athletic and academic talents?

The Collegiate Education

‘ Let us not forget that college is a place to continue education. Too many times athletes will forget this. Some people will gain a tremendous advantage in life from going to college and players should only consider going to college if they are serious about continuing their education; they must feel that going to college will be of some value downstream that not going to college might not afford. If players are going to college just to continue their athletic career, then they are there for the wrong reasons. It will be a waste of the player's time and a waste of the college's money. ’
DICK GOULD, *Head of Stanford University Men's Tennis (1966–2004)*

The quality of the education received in the USA is a subject of great debate and students have been known to forego the collegiate opportunity because they believe they can receive a better education in the UK. But just how does the US system compare with that in the UK?

The US liberal arts education allows you to keep your options open by requiring each student to learn a broader curriculum. You are not required to declare your major until the end of your second year, and even then you can take extra subjects. The premise of this is to cultivate a rounded individual; you are not fully developed in your skills and intellectual interests by the age of seventeen, and this structure gives you the space to explore and catch up on any skill gaps.

In comparison, degrees at UK universities tend to focus on the practical aspect of the profession, requiring students to concentrate their efforts on a single chosen subject area from the beginning of their enrolment. For this reason, the education system in the United Kingdom is particularly highly regarded for specialist subjects such as Medicine, Law and Architecture.

'I tried to recruit a student a while back, but he wanted to be a lawyer,' says Dick Gould, talking about his time as Head Coach at Stanford University. 'He didn't want to come because he could start studying law immediately in his home country, but he would have had to wait four years at college before attending law school in the USA.'

For long periods, there has been a general feeling that the US system lacks depth of focus, but the opportunity to enrich a degree with a greater breadth of subjects is actually growing in popularity. US colleges are growing in reputation and, according to the *Times Higher Education* rankings, almost half of the Top 100 global universities are based in the USA. While there are many other league tables of the world's universities, this was the first to go on purely reputation alone, further increasing the credibility of a US college education and increasing job prospects.

However, the real benefit of the US system lies somewhere beyond the classroom, deeply rooted in the all-round programme enjoyed by student–athletes as they work hard to combine high level sports and academia. As Brian Boland explained, the organizational and team-work skills developed in college alongside the international experience and high-level sport are all highly-valued skills by recruiters:

I really believe that there is nothing more important during the ages of nineteen, twenty and twenty-one than learning how to manage your time, deal with adversity, apply yourself when you least want to and adapting to being uncomfortable at times. College forces student–athletes out of their comfort zones; they learn to deal with adversity, to think creatively, to focus and study when not interested in the particular discipline – and these are the exact same ingredients that are required for success both on and off the court in the future.

There is so much opportunity both on and off the court to develop and grow in the collegiate environment that by the time you leave college to pursue any other career, you are so much further ahead than peers who didn't have similar opportunities. Collegiate student–athlete graduates have already learned how to manage their time effectively, to focus on a

Collegiate tennis gives players the time to mature and develop their skills without the pressures of the professional tour

Somdev Devaarman, pictured celebrating here, used his time at the University of Virginia as a springboard to success on the professional tour

goal and work in a team that they don't have to learn this when they have left – they've already got it!

Turning Professional: College

❛There is a step between professional level and the junior ranks. That level is college.❜ MIKE AND BOB BRYAN, *winners of over forty-six Grand Slam titles*

'The physical difference between junior and men's tennis is unbelievable,' says tennis legend Nick Bollettieri. The sport has become more physically demanding with the advent of high-tech rackets and strings, the influx of top-flight athletes from around the world and more sophisticated training methods. The days of young teens winning Grand Slams have become a thing of the past.

The collegiate system gives those players who are not quite ready for professional competition time to mature and develop mentally and physically under the guidance of a highly skilled coach in a comfortable environment without the pressures or negativity of the ITF tour. That is not to say that all players will turn professional, but the stronger athletic programmes in the USA can provide a foundation for players to develop into a highly-tuned physical athlete fit for professional competition.

It is important to note that it is possible for collegiate players to compete as an amateur in professional events before they have actually completed their studies. In this way, college represents the best of both worlds: you can gain experience of professional level events, earn a ranking and then review your position before making a decision about the following year. If you do then successfully break through to the tour and want to turn professional, you can. If not, then another year of college offers you a chance to develop further whilst always testing yourself on the professional circuit to determine when you are ready.

How College Prepares you for the Professional Tour

Let's leave the last word to a British player who knows the US collegiate system from experience.

Dominic Inglot, Top Thirty Doubles player and University of Virginia graduate:

There are a lot of players who can go to college as the unfinished article and leave a tough, physically fit, fighting machine; they just learn to play matches. John Isner had very little success before he went to college and quickly went into the top fifty after graduation. Steve Johnson went to USC as a walk-on because he didn't warrant a scholarship and has recently broken the top 100 in the world, too. Not everyone will come out as a great tennis player, but college allows players the opportunity, for those willing to work hard enough, to grow into a great tennis player.

Dominic Inglot (*above*) believes that his four years at the University of Virginia prepared him well for life on the professional tour

On the flip side, many players enter college after a successful junior career and realize that professional tennis is not for them, so it also gives players the time to decide what they really want to do with their careers, be it on a tennis court or elsewhere. This, for me, is particularly valuable.

I found the transition from collegiate level to professional level quite easy. Playing tennis at college, I was allowed to be 'normal'; I could be a regular teenager and still develop on and off the court. I had fun, I went out, I had girlfriends – I did it all. As a result, when I turned professional I didn't feel the pressure to have enjoyment on the road because I had already done that. I was then ready to knuckle down and focus on my game as a professional tennis player.

College also toughened me up for the professional tour – not so much technically, but the idea of working hard, being focused and disciplined. Then when you go and play on the road, it is not that bad. People on the ITF Circuit complain about hostile environments, tough crowds and poor facilities, but this is nothing compared to what you can have at college.

The University of Virginia celebrates another NCAA title

UK Universities and High-Performance Tennis

'There are some incredible programmes in the USA but I also believe that universities in Britain are often ignored or undervalued by many.'
– RALEIGH GOWRIE, *Sports Performance Manager, University of Stirling*

Opportunities for players to compete at a high level whilst remaining in the UK have expanded through the British Universities Performance Programme, which takes place at four universities: Bath, Loughborough, Leeds Metropolitan, and Stirling. Programmes at these institutions normally have an international-level coaching team in place, fantastic facilities and approximately 18–20 hours of training a week available for those highly skilled players enrolled.

Scholarships for top players are available and selected scholars will receive up to £5,000 per annum to subsidize travel and other sports-related costs. Squad members can compete on the British Tour and 'Pro' series events along with the British Universities Championships and various other national-level competitions throughout the UK.

It sounds great, right? So why, if such a strong system exists in the UK, do thousands of students flock across the Atlantic each year?

Marketing, without doubt, is a major factor. The glitz and glamour of the collegiate lifestyle in the USA is so appealing to these young players; these institutions are thirty years ahead and already know how to attract the best talent. Availability in the UK is also limited and many players are forced to go abroad where colleges can accommodate a greater range of academic abilities.

This, however, only gives half the story. US collegiate programmes have enjoyed considerably more success in producing top-quality talent than their UK counterparts, and while the USA can happily count the likes of Jack Sock, John Isner and John McEnroe on its growing list of noteworthy alumni, the UK can account for just one world-class player: Colin Fleming.

The big advantage of the US system is its strong and competitive programme. The players at these top colleges are regularly competing against the best and this raises the bar and the standard of tennis continually each year. In the UK, however, there are just not the same opportunities because competition between universities outside the top four is almost non-existent. As a result, it could be argued that the competitive culture within these British institutions does not naturally breed players who are mentally and physically prepared for the challenges of the professional game.

Undoubtedly, the UK university system represents a great opportunity for you to continue your development and if you are committed enough then you may find a way to rise to the top – Colin Fleming has proven that. But it is not yet a legitimate stepping stone to the professional game and this will continue to be the case until the LTA overhauls the UK competitive structure.

Other UK Universities and Tennis

Outside of Bath, Loughborough, Leeds Metropolitan, and Stirling, almost all UK universities will have a tennis team in place and will compete in one of BUCS (British Universities and Colleges Sport) Team leagues. Although the facilities and training are generally more suitable for players who do not harbour professional aspirations, the level of play will still be competitive and scholarships may be available.

To find out more about this, including eligibility and membership enquiries, you are advised to contact the specific university directly.

Tennis Academies

You talk academies and you talk colleges and you think of the best way to go. Who knows? Some players just aren't college material academically and should be in an academy. Even for very intelligent kids, academies offer them some wonderful opportunities.
DICK GOULD, *Head of Stanford University Men's Tennis* (1966–2004)

Having achieved some of the best results for one's division, a highly qualified coach and fitness trainer is the natural progression in any player's development. Indeed, Andy Murray, Grigor Dimitrov, Maria Sharapova, Andre Agassi are all results of a disciplined training regime, whether it be at the IMG Bollettieri academy in Florida or one of the numerous academies nestled throughout mainland Europe.

Academy attendance is by no means an alternative to a collegiate education. It is quite common for academy-based players to move on to study in the USA, while others will remain at the academy to continue training with a view to earning enough ranking points in ITF Pro Circuit events before joining the professional tour.

Many top players, including Grigor Dimitrov (*pictured*), trained at a tennis academy as a junior

Academies undoubtedly offer some great opportunities for talented individuals, even beyond the quality training and support network. James Ward, British Number Three, was schooled in Valencia under the guidance of Juan Carlos Ferrero and feels that the Spanish academy was fundamental in his development. 'I just couldn't have received that level of training in the UK,' he says.

When Ward was attending, however, the academy option was the lesser-known route and the situation has changed dramatically since then. The rapid growth of the game and the globalization of the sport have created a huge market for tennis development and, as businesses of the modern age, these academies will make decisions based primarily on business logic. The leading academies today are filled with players from all over the world, supported primarily by their parents who are looking to fund the development of their children into the next tennis champion. Full-time attendance is not cheap and there is no guarantee of quality training or future success.

'The difficulty with modern academies is that if you are not very good at a young age, then nobody seems to care,' says Ward. Academies can certainly provide the required training but that rarely comes without either a great expense to buy it outright or a proven ability on the court.

Having players join the professional tour is a fantastic advertisement for their programme and so almost all academies will adopt some sort of 'scholarship' system under which the most talented players are accepted at a highly discounted rate. In this pyramid-like structure, the lesser-talented players can become neglected, viewed as little more than sources of income used to fund the training of the scholarship players. In these cases, it is only the 'scholarship' players who will be given sufficient time and individual attention to succeed in the game.

It must also be noted that the life of an academy student is not for everyone. Hitting tennis balls and lifting weights may sound like fun, but the reality of an academy is actually far less glamorous. Academies are designed to produce world-class players, and this requires dedication, discipline and hard work. The goal of all parties involved is to maximize a player's athletic potential. Life in an academy will consist of repetitive drills and the whole process becomes almost robotic causing many players to quit before they have even started.

'I like the idea of an academy but I would always be wary before sending my children to one,' says Dick Gould. 'I want them to enjoy a normal childhood – the high school, the prom, the football – I think these are all important parts of growing up and academies can often suck the fun out of these activities.'

Choosing an Academy

> Being in a big academy makes you feel like another mouse on the wheel. It's a good experience, but only for a short time.
> JAMES ALLEMBY, *ITF Futures player*

Once you and your family have made the decision to attend an academy, it can be difficult to choose the right one for your development. There are many factors to consider: the size, the coaching staff, the facilities, and the price – not all academies suit all players.

Visiting the academy is important because the facilities play a major role in your development. Is there a well-equipped gymnasium? How many courts are there and what is the surface? Are there indoor facilities? Are the balls well-stocked? How many students are there on a court? Do all players have individualized programmes? All these factors can make a difference in this highly competitive sport.

One of the most important factors to consider when choosing an academy is the coaching team. As discussed earlier, individual attention and complete commitment from the coach are fundamental ingredients in overall player development, and it is important that you choose an academy that will offer this. Read the attendance contracts very carefully to ensure that a healthy player–coach ratio (i.e. 1:4) is guaranteed. Many academies will promise, but few will actually offer it.

It is also important that a good level of communication between the coaching team and the player is maintained at all times. Nick Bollettieri, the man credited with nurturing illustrious talents including Agassi, Courier and Sharapova, advises that parents should hold regular 'conferences' with the coaching staff and their child to ensure progress is monitored at all times.

Although tennis academies can accelerate your development, the training and lifestyle can be gruelling and lonely

'Of course, to produce good players, academies and coaches must get to know their players,' says Patrick Mouratoglou, founder of the Mouratoglou Tennis Academy in Paris and one of the most celebrated coaches of the modern era. 'Since I started the academy twenty years ago, I said that my system must be a human system where every player is treated as a person and is known as a person. It is imperative that every player gets exactly what he or she needs to improve their game.'

Steer clear of academies backed by business investors because it is likely that these will be driven solely by meeting financial targets as opposed to actual player development. Researching and reviewing the coaching team and structure is similarly important: many academies will base their marketing around the endorsement of one-big name former player who will rarely, if ever, actually step onto court with the players. Ask yourself: Who is really responsible for player development?

Modern-day academies are filled with players from all over the world, all looking to develop their game

The facilities of the Mouratoglou Tennis Academy in Paris are world class and have been used by many of the world's leading players

Look closely for academies with a team of coaches who have a proven track record of success; this team will know what it takes to develop a professional player and they will normally impart their knowledge and experience to create a strong, well-rounded programme fit for player development. Finally, be wary of academies that advertise in an overly-aggressive manner for these tend to rely on a fast-turnover of players to compensate for a lack of quality in the programme.

To learn more about variation in academies, I spoke with Jordi Arrese, Raphael Maurer and James Allemby, a former attendee of Sanchez-Casal, one of the most publicized academies in the world:

Jordi Arrese, 1992 Olympic Silver Medallist and former Spanish Davis Cup Captain:

I really do not believe in large academies. Academies must either be small or have a high number of trainers; otherwise they are charging a lot of money for absolutely nothing. Coaches will struggle to spot your talents in a large academy, whereas in smaller, more focused academies, coaches can spot and correct any faults.

James Allemby, ITF Futures player:

For most of my career I've been part of a team or group situation. I was at Sanchez-Casal [in Barcelona] for three years, the Catalan Tennis Federation for three years, and with a couple of smaller groups in between. After living through so many different situations, I would say that the most effective is an individual one-on-one situation or a very close-knit academy with limited numbers of strong coach-player relationships.

In a group, there are a lot of distractions. Many of these places are just money-making factories that actually stop a lot of people playing

tennis. They advertise people like Andy Murray as their alumni but in reality Murray trained under the private guidance of Pato Alvarez and so was rarely involved in the group programme.

Many players go to these large academies and become so sick and tired of the same mind-numbing drills each day, and the general lack of interest from the coaches who are motivated by the pay-cheques rather than any player development. From my class of twenty players, only two of us still play. This is ridiculous considering that these places are designed to promote – not destroy – the game.

Raphael Maurer, Director of Barcelona Tennis Academy (BTA):

I am a firm believer in creating a family-like training environment. I have spoken to players and coaches at these large, factory-like academies and they complain about a lack of personal touch and collaboration. Smaller academies, where players can have a personal programme tailored around their specific needs, are the best way to ensure development. Each player's progress should be closely monitored by the coaches and this is only possible in a small, close knit environment found at smaller, specialized schools.

The brute physicality of the modern baseline game means that there are very few teenagers competing as a touring professional, and both academies and the US Collegiate system offer junior players the opportunity to continue maturing and moulding their games individually until they are fit for professional competition. Almost all players will attend an academy at some point in their development, and some will go on to join the professional tour without needing an extra four years in college. Other players will not be quite ready and can attend college to give them more time to mature and finely tune their game.

Either way, it is important to acknowledge that the globalization of the game has led to more opportunities for you to continue your development than ever before and making decisions on what is the best way forward can be a challenging process. There is no time to waste; choosing the wrong academy or spending four years at a college where there is not enough focus on your game can prevent you from reaching your potential.

Tennis is a dynamic game; different players develop at different rates and it is impossible to write a formulaic plan as to what is right for each individual player. The above, however, offers you a greater insight into exactly what opportunities are available allowing you to make informed decisions based on your individual needs.

CHAPTER THREE

A Guide to Competing on the Tour

W e're haemorrhaging money,' my old man used to say. And understandably so. Tennis is an expensive sport, one that requires great investment for very little return – in the early days, at least.

My competitive career was draped in uncertainty. As I struggled to navigate my way through the tournament structure, it always felt like an uphill battle. I had posted some strong results as a junior in Australia, largely without any view to pursuing any career in the sport. I also had some reasonable results in Barcelona and France where I had played some events, but I had very few results on a domestic front, primarily because the fast indoor courts did not suit my predominantly topspin game. While I knew – in myself and after confirmation by coaches – that I had the ability to be competing regularly at a professional level, I had no strict record to back it up.

I was totally unprepared for this first stage of professional competition. So much uncertainty, so much jargon. The 'sign-in' deadline. The 'freeze' deadline. The entry fees. How do I arrange a practice court? When do the courts open? What balls do they use? The atmosphere so severe, the structure and organization so precise; it was a completely different world to anything I had become accustomed to previously and there was no support to guide me through.

I blamed my first few defeats on mental fortitude. I was adapting, I thought, but that was only half the battle. My first taste was a 6–1,6–1 defeat to an Australian talent I had beaten just a week prior in a warm-up event. He had all the strokes but so did I; he was just better prepared. He had experience; he knew how it all worked. Similar results ensued and it took me a while to notice why. While I was practising with slow, heavy Wilson US Open balls on hard courts, fast, light Babolat balls were being used in the tournaments. I also failed to take proper advantage of the on-site practice courts. As a result, I had no 'feeling' and struggled to hit the ball in the court with any conviction. Power and penetration were mere luxuries – but I now knew why.

This became a recurring theme. Each tournament I entered, I learned something valuable to improve on in the next event. Without a strong national ranking, I learned to enter as an 'On-Site Alternate'. I learned that the practice courts are open for all players on the day of sign-in. I learned that ball type is published on the ITF website weeks prior to the event. I quickly learned that the range of abilities at these ITF Futures events is actually very small, and that the winner is often the person who is better prepared.

While players will inevitably learn the tricks of the trade by competing, here are some tips that will provide you with more than a mere head start.

The global governing body of professional tennis is the International Tennis Federation (ITF), which publishes the rules of the game and is affiliated with the 210 full and associated national member federations across the world. Together, these bodies cooperate to provide a clear, layered system of international competition that allows players to climb the ranks of professional tennis.

The governing body in each country is responsible for the selection of teams and training programmes for all categories, age groups and levels of play in that nation. As a player you will normally begin training and competing at club and local level before moving up to national competitions if your results so allow. Once you have achieved success on a national level, you can then begin to consider international competition on the ITF Pro Circuits – the first tier of professional tennis competition.

Professional male tennis players today compete on one of three tours and professional females compete on just two. Both men and women will typically begin their professional careers in ITF Pro Circuit events before progressing to the ATP Challenger and WTA Tour events respectively. Men who gain enough ranking points on the Challenger tour will then progress to the highest tier of professional men's tennis: the ATP World Tour.

Climbing this ladder is extremely challenging and the lifestyle at the lower levels is notoriously tough on both the players and those around them. It is important to recognize that tennis is an individual sport, a dynamic process of growth and development in which players progress at different rates. As such, you must make decisions based on what will suit you as an individual and as a player.

National Competition

‘ It is important for all players to begin competing at an early age; I would say approximately thirteen or fourteen years old is the perfect time. Players can begin competing a little bit earlier, but focus before these ages must be on perfecting tennis strokes and developing a tactical understanding rather than just winning. If you become too competitive too early, it can turn you into a worse player because you become too defensive. ’
JORDI ARRESE, *1992 Men's Olympic Silver Medallist and former Captain of the Spanish Davis Cup Team*

Before joining the ITF Pro Circuits, you must first prove your talents on the national stage. The governing body that exists in each member state will organize a rating or ranking system that is implemented via local, county/district, regional and national tournaments over the course of the season. The LTA has incorporated a rating style system for many years, using the 'British Tour' as the highest level of national competition, but each organization has a different structure and it is best to contact the specific governing body directly for more details on how to enter tournaments, earn a rating and gain a national ranking.

Competing abroad is a great way to gain valuable match experience and is easily done. Tournaments in France, Spain and Germany, for example, are played with far more regularity and often benefit from a greater depth of field and larger money pots than tournaments in the UK. Players in Germany have been known to earn more than €50,000 per year through national competition alone. You can contact the relevant national body for further details on entry requirements and procedures. This will normally involve the purchase of a national competition licence.

The primary purpose of competing on foreign shores is to gain match-play experience by competing against a wider variety of players with different game styles in differing conditions. For this to be achieved, it is important that these matches are played against athletes of a similar, or higher, level.

The difficulty with competing abroad in national competitions is that it can sometimes be difficult to enter higher-tier events without first establishing a rating/ranking with the relevant national body. You are therefore advised to hold on to proof of ranking or a signed letter of recommendation from a licensed coach to ensure that your results are recognized by and successfully transferred to overseas tennis governing bodies. This problem does not occur with competition on the ITF circuits because results and rankings are governed by an international governing body: the International Tennis Federation.

Problems with the UK Competition Structure

The difficulties with British tennis are highlighted by the fact that Andy Murray remains the only British player to regularly reach the first weekend of Wimbledon. This, of course, is not the only measure of success – as Roger Draper, former Chief Executive of the LTA once said, 'If you judge British tennis on the first day of Wimbledon, that's your choice. But I judge it on the number of [British] people playing.' Ironically, in an attempt to dodge the bullet, Draper actually exposed the very root of the problem.

Figures from Sport England's Active People Survey indicate that only around 400,000 people in the UK play tennis once a week. But this is not for lack of trying: the LTA has invested approximately 10 per cent of its income into developing participation over the past couple of years and there is continued effort to work more closely with local authorities to further raise these numbers.

The problems, however, are far greater. Outside of the LTA National Tennis Centre in Roehampton, the costs of hiring a tennis court in the UK can reach over £30 per hour – hardly a fee that can fit comfortably into the average budget. Despite Andy Murray's great rise to superstardom, in Britain tennis remains very much a minority sport compared to football and rugby, just as in the USA with NFL, NBA and NHLA. While these sports both form a key part of the sporting curriculum at established schools across the country, tennis training and competition must normally be sought outside of the academic infrastructure at a cost that many families just cannot absorb. Tennis is just not as accessible in the UK as in France, Germany or Spain and if we want success, players must be given the opportunity from a young age.

In a piece written by Jonathan Overend for BBC Sport, the tennis correspondent tells the story about a couple of talented ten-year-olds who were refused entry to a 12-and-under competition because the LTA competition framework does not advise ten-year-olds to use the regular yellow tennis balls. 'Every child is different and if the coaches believed the time was right for these particular kids, common sense surely should have prevailed,' says Overend.[1]

Inevitably, this overly regimented system can actually begin to hold the good players back because they are unable to progress and challenge themselves: 'The competition can stop stimulating them, because they can't move on,' says Judy Murray in a piece with Kevin Mitchell of *the Guardian*.[2] As Overend points out, Andy Murray, the very model of British success, moved up from the soft, red balls used by under-12s at the age of just seven.

A valid illustration of the flaws in the UK competition structure this most certainly is, but it is also just a speck on the shorts of something far, far bigger. For those who play the game, it is no secret that the opportunities to compete in the UK are far more limited than throughout Europe and even further afar. British players are also forced to travel long distances to tournaments if they want to compete, and this comes at a considerable cost of accommodation, food and transport. In the same piece, Judy Murray suggests that the key is to have 'better competition locally'.[3]

To learn more about how the competition structure in Spain encourages player development, I spoke with Jordi Arrese, 1992 Men's Olympic Silver Medallist and former Captain of the Spanish Davis Cup Team.

As Arrese points out, the annual tennis budget in the UK is no less than in countries like Spain or France, but the money is being spent very poorly. 'We [Spain] do not necessarily have teenagers who are more talented than other nations, but the structure of competition allows us to produce champions,' he says. 'If you want to see how

Jordi Arrese (*centre*) won the Davis Cup with Moya (*left*), Nadal (*middle left*), Robredo (*middle right*) and Ferrero (*right*)

good you are at tennis [in Spain], you have competitions from the age of eleven at regional, national and international levels. This means that players can compete at the very highest level in their own country. This gives players the feeling when they are at that age that they are competing at a professional level. You also do not even need a lot of money to compete.'

This structure just does not exist in the UK; there is just not this level of competition. From grass-roots tennis to the highest national level events, competitions in the UK just do not happen with the same frequency as in France or Spain. Additionally, players aged thirteen to sixteen are restricted from playing 'Open' tournaments, whereas in Spain 'Open' tournaments exist allowing developing players to compete against a wider range of players of different ages and game styles. 'This accessibility improves players so much,' says Arrese.

'It is normal that there are not many tournaments in December, but throughout the season players must be playing lots of matches against different players because this is how you create a champion. In my opinion, therefore, the total failure of the UK is the total fault of the Federation. The Federation is completely accountable.'

For these reasons, junior players are strongly advised to research and test themselves in competitions abroad.

Turning Professional

‘ There is no luxury on the ITF Circuits. It is a lot of hard work, lots of sketchy places with dreadful facilities, very low prize money and few [ATP] points to be earned. It is about as far away as possible from what outsiders perceive as the life of a professional tennis player. ’
FILIP PELIWO, *former Junior World Number 1*

Comprised of the Men's Circuit (termed 'Futures') and Women's tournaments, the ITF Pro Circuits are the minor leagues of professional tennis. As the entry point to professional tennis, life on the ITF Pro Circuit tour is not easy; players do not have many of the benefits that the top guys enjoy and there is virtually no money to be made. It is here that all rising stars must begin their journeys and, just like the lower leagues of any sport, it is ferociously competitive.

The circuit is a mixture of young, aspiring, confident professionals looking to break through to the higher levels and these cynical, older 'has-beens' who are not really doing it professionally but just have a lot of experience and know-how. Instead of trying to pass through and move on to the next level, these older journeymen pros try to play psychological games to belittle the newcomers, creating a highly competitive, sometimes hostile environment.

Funding Life on the ITF Tour

'The main problem for players on the ITF tour is money. Tennis is their profession, but they just do not make any money from it,' says Raphael Maurer, Director of Barcelona Tennis Academy. The prize money at this level of competitive tennis is still low, and you will need complete dedication if you are to survive. As a result, players competing at this level are forced to cut corners in their preparations by, for example, sleeping on floors and eating poorly.

Almost all players will need support from their families to get started, and many will supplement this by looking for sponsorship or through competition in the European leagues (see 'Inter-club Competition' on page 61). Any money earned from competing will have to be reinvested in their development. It is of no surprise that financial problems are one of the major causes for players dropping out of the sport early.

'My parents were paying a lot of money to keep me playing because it was what I wanted to do, but I was not really earning anything back,' said James Ward, the British Number Three, in our conversations together. 'It is a difficult life and the expenses weigh on you,' he adds. 'The financial pressures are really tough.' Players can also ask for donations or work as sparring/hitting partners in academies to help support themselves.

Rule Changes

In 2014, the ITF undertook a full review of the ITF Pro Circuit structure to fully understand the current situation and how best to improve entry onto the performance pathway, increase prize money, raise event standards and ensure developing nations have the best opportunity to produce world class players. It was concluded not only that the prize money levels need to rise, but that the number of those competing on the Pro Circuit are unsustainably high. In 2013 there were almost 14,000 male and female players competing, of whom over 6,000 failed to earn any prize money.

With this in mind, the ITF Board of Directors has approved an extensive programme of prize money increases for the ITF Pro Circuit, with phased introductions planned for early 2016. On the ITF Men's Circuit, $15,000-category tournaments will be increased to $25,000 in 2016, while the lower-level $10,000 tournaments will be increased to $15,000 in 2017. Additional rises are currently planned for 2018 and will be announced in due course. The ITF Women's Circuit, which currently includes tournaments between $10,000 and $100,000, will see the elimination of the $15,000 category in 2016 with the view that these tournaments will offer $25,000 in prize money. In 2017 prize-money levels will rise to between $15,000 and $125,000, ahead of further proposed increases in 2018.

In addition to an increase in prize monies available, the proposed changes also include the introduction of a new entry to the professional player pathway. This new level of tournaments looks to ensure adequate levels of opportunity for emerging players by offering qualifying or merit points to players before enabling them to progress on to the Pro Circuits.

The new entry level is yet to be finally approved, but is on course for 2017.

For long periods, the prize money available on the Pro Circuits has been the main problem for players competing at this level. It is advised that these changes could go a long way to supporting these players as they look to break into the higher levels of professional tennis.

PLAYER FUNDING IN THE UNITED KINGDOM

For long periods, the leading British players were eligible for the LTA's training programme under which they would receive up to £48,000 per year to cover travel and expenses. Following a decision in 2013, and adjusted in 2014, this funding was severely cut making it even harder for British players to compete on the professional tour.

Under the scheme, the LTA decided that in-house coaching support, instead of cash, would be offered to those leading players who meet their age-related ranking targets. Only a few world class players would be permitted to use the LTA's support to fund an overseas coach. Elite players outside of this system continue to have access to support provided at the LTA headquarters in Roehampton, alongside the stringently applied Bonus scheme under which they can have their winnings supplemented by the LTA. All others are forced to support themselves.

While these cutbacks will inevitably make it more difficult for British players to compete at the lower levels of the professional ladder, many believe that these cuts were needed to help British tennis. Following her first round 2013 Wimbledon victory, Naomi Broady, an outsider to the LTA system after losing her backing in 2007, stated how she has become hungrier after being forced to go it alone. 'It makes you fight harder because if you don't fight and you don't win, then you can't afford the next tournament,' she said.

Players competing in Spain, Serbia and France, three of the most successful nations when it comes to tennis, are not funded at all. In the Spanish Tennis Federation (RFET), for example, the player support network is limited to a technical team of five coaches working with a hand-picked number of players in Sant-Cugat. Is it really a coincidence, therefore, that Spanish players are known for their tenacity and work ethic, and there are more Spanish players inside the top twenty than the UK has in the top 100? 'If you give them too much to eat then they become accustomed to not being hungry', says Jordi Arrese, 1992 Olympic Men's Singles Silver Medallist.

Choosing to enter the LTA system is a big decision for any player in the UK, and many will be forced to enter the programme for financial reasons if they are to continue playing the sport. If you do choose to go it alone, or are simply not invited into the LTA programme, it is still possible to compete at the higher levels, but it will require a great deal more fight and motivation than simply having it all provided by the LTA.

Life on the ITF Tour

To find out what life is like on the ITF Tour, let's find out from a player who knows:

James Allemby, a Futures player, describes life on the ITF Circuit:

Life on the Futures circuit is extremely challenging. There is an inherent lack of respect towards the players from officials even though we [the players] are the mainstay at the lower levels of the game. We normally have very small time-slots to hit during the day. Normally practice or warm-up consists of sharing a court with three other players while four others breathe down your neck, forcing you to get off as soon as your half-hour allocation is up.

The facilities and conditions at these events can also be extremely poor. I've been to clubs that would make your eyes water and you just have to wonder how these clubs are approved to host a professional sporting event when there is no bar or restaurant and the side-fence is pretty much glued to the doubles line. I've even been to places where one service box was about a foot larger than the other, and in 2009 I went to an event in Lanzarote where the facilities were so poor that the main draw players just refused to play!

Bribery, although rare, continues to rear its ugly head and it is not uncommon for players to be offered over €1000 to lose a match. Wild cards for the Main Draw for these events are sometimes available to buy for approximately €800, although there is room for negotiation and they can sometimes be purchased for as low as €500. This is why there are a lot of fictitious results lying around.

The governing bodies must ask themselves why this is happening. It is no surprise given how poorly Futures players are paid. Even if the player is regularly winning these events, the lifestyle is still poor. The hotel, food and travel costs all add up making it almost impossible to make a living at this level. I have a friend who won an ITF event in Egypt and still ended up making a loss for the trip!

I really enjoy the competition and the process of training, improving and going to events all over the place. It has a lot of ups and downs, but the positives make it all the worthwhile. Many of my friends have bought caravans and park at the tournament's parking lot for the week, use the showering facilities, cook their own food, charge low rates if other players need a place to sleep and they can also string rackets for less than the tournament to make more money. It is no easy life, but it is an unreal experience!

With the exception of the odd qualifier, all players competing at ITF level are highly skilled and extremely dedicated to their sport. When starting out, enter the lower level ITF events (i.e. US$10,000) and, while not a necessity, extensive match-experience and success on a national level is advised. If in doubt about the level of these tournaments, you can always visit to watch free of charge.

Cracking the ITF Pro Circuits is no easy feat and will test even the most talented players' resolve. ITF events are normally heavily oversubscribed and almost all players will have to begin their careers by battling into the Main

Draw by passing the Qualifying Draw. You must be realistic about your goal when entering because you will have to win between two and four matches to reach the Main Draw, and only the very best will do so on the first attempt.

As Raphael Maurer, Director of BTA Tennis Academy, says, 'There are no easy matches at this level.' These players are willing to fight and battle on the court for as long as they need to win and, even with all the talent in the world, most players will need time to adapt to the environment, become match-tough and learn to really grind out the victory before they taste any success.

As a player, you are strongly advised to travel and train with a group. Not only will this allow you to minimize expenses by sharing any costs with others, it also creates a support network – a feeling of stability and comfort in the very brutal environment of professional tennis. It is a lonely old world doing it for fifty-two weeks a year, and it is for this reason that the top players in the world all have a very constant, stable team around them.

Be it their physiotherapist, physical trainer or their girlfriend, this is their 'family' as they travel from country to country on tour, and it is important to understand that besides the obvious work that they do, they also provide a comforting, supporting environment for their player so they can feel relaxed in the ever-changing surroundings as they travel from tournament to tournament.

Entering an ITF Pro-Circuit Event

The rules and regulations governing ITF Pro Circuit events are incredibly detailed, precise and accurate. Before entering, you must take the time to gain an understanding of these rules because they are unlike anything at national or regional level.

While the following will provide the basic information required for starting out on the ITF Tour, you are strongly advised to read the ITF Pro Circuit Regulations for full details of the rules and regulations as well as the 'ITF Pro Circuit Organisational Requirements' for supplementary information, including tournament/on-site/logistical rules and procedures. Both can be found on the ITF website.

SIGN-UP

There are over 1000 ITF circuit tournaments held annually worldwide and entry is based on merit without discrimination except that minors under the age of fourteen (based on a player's age as of the first day of the tournament draw) are not eligible for entry. The online calendar is updated on a quarterly basis and can be found on the ITF Website (www.itftennis.com) along with all entry regulations, recent results and other important information.

To compete, all players are required to purchase an International Player Identification Number (IPIN) from the official IPIN website (https://IPIN.itftennis.com/). This must be renewed at the start of each calendar year and so, from a financial perspective, the best time to make the purchase is in January. Once registered, you can then sign up for events online, by fax or in person.

All tournament information is provided on fact sheets on the ITF website several weeks in advance of the tournament. Complimentary hospitality is provided at tournaments where indicated (+H). Online entry is done by logging into the IPIN website and locating the tournament(s) you wish to enter. Alternatively, you can submit an Official ITF entry form via fax or post, but entries cannot be officially accepted over the telephone or via email. The entry deadline for all ITF events is 1400 GMT on the Thursday eighteen days prior to the Monday of the tournament week.

You will be either accepted directly into the Main Draw or Qualifying Draw by virtue of your rankings, international or national, under the applicable 'System of Merit'. ITF rules dictate that those with an official ATP computer ranking (below) are given preference over all other entries and are selected according to their ranking as of twenty-one days prior to the Monday of the tournament week. Preference will then be given to all top 500 nationally ranked players as recognized by the ITF. All lower-ranked, or nationally unranked, players are then drawn at random for a position in the Qualifying Draw. Those who do not make the cut-off will be entered onto the waiting list as an 'Alternate'. The complete list of entrants will be listed on the ITF website after the entry deadline has passed.

WITHDRAWAL DEADLINE/ONE TOURNAMENT PER WEEK

The standard Withdrawal Deadline for ITF events is 1400 GMT on the Tuesday thirteen days prior to the Monday of the tournament week. Any withdrawal after the 'Withdrawal Deadline' will be deemed 'late' and subjected to the provisions of the Code of Conduct. Players on the 'Alternate' list can withdraw at any time.

Many players will sign up to an event without having their plans confirmed because it is easier to enter the tournament and withdraw than miss entry altogether. This is particularly true of foreign players who enter and withdraw when they see they have not made the Qualifying Draw cut-off and do not want to risk the outlay of flights, accommodation and food without guaranteed entry. Many others will withdraw due to injury and illness.

You are permitted to register for up to six tournaments in any given week but must state a priority at the time of entry. You will be withdrawn from all except one tournament event according to your indicated priority at the time of entry, although any Main Draw acceptance will be given automatic priority over Qualifying Draw. This system allows you to have a back-up, i.e. if you do not gain entry into one event, the ITF allows you to enter a tournament running elsewhere the same week in which you may have gained direct entry.

Once you are accepted into the Qualifying or Main draw of a Pro Circuit tournament at, or any time after, the Withdrawal deadline, have signed in for Qualifying, or have applied for a Wild Card or Special Exempt, you are then committed to that tournament and are not permitted to compete in any other tournament in that same tournament week (before or after said tournament), except in few specific circumstances, unless released by the ITF or other governing body.

Player commitment and 'one tournament per week' are key principles of professional tennis (all circuits/tours) and if you break these rules, you will be penalized heavily. Therefore, only choose to submit entry into tournaments that you are actually prepared to go and play.

'FREEZE DEADLINE'

At 1400 GMT on the Thursday preceding the tournament week, you cannot move up the Qualifying or Main Draw acceptance list, even as a result of any 'late withdrawals' by other entered players. This is known as the 'freeze deadline'.

Accepted players are then committed to play the tournament and 'Alternates' will not gain entry other than through 'On-Site Alternate' sign-in (see below).

HOW TO WITHDRAW

You can withdraw online from any event at any stage prior to the 'freeze deadline'. Alternatively, you can fax a completed and signed ITF Withdrawal Form to the ITF Office, or send it as an email attachment. No withdrawals will be accepted over the phone or via email at any time. You can only withdraw once the 'freeze deadline' has passed by faxing a completed and signed ITF Withdrawal Form to both the ITF Office and the ITF Supervisor on-site.

Any withdrawal after the 'withdrawal deadline' is considered 'late' regardless of the reason for the withdrawal. Players are excused three 'late withdrawals' in any calendar year provided that each withdrawal is submitted prior to the relevant 'sign-in deadline' (see below). Withdrawals due to injury are treated differently in that only the first withdrawal will be considered 'late' provided that a valid ITF Medical Certification Form is submitted by the last day of the tournament.

Vacancies in the Main Draw after the commencement of the Qualifying competition will be filled by 'Lucky Losers' – players who lost in the final round of Qualifying, selected at random. Vacancies in the Qualifying Draw at this point will be filled by 'On-Site Alternates' who have signed in as 'Alternates' on the day of competition. Players on the 'Alternates' list should always withdraw to avoid incurring a fine if moved into the 'Qualifying Draw' at late notice.

If you have 'committed' to an event and do not show ('No Show'), you will incur a fine that must be paid in full before you can submit any appeal.

TOURNAMENT SIGN-IN

If you are accepted into the Qualifying Draw prior to the 'Freeze Deadline', you are required to sign in at the tournament site the day before the commencement of the Qualifying event. Sign-in begins at approximately midday and closes at 1800 local time – the 'sign-in deadline'. All players must be present with photo-identification and the tournament entry fee in cash (US$ or local currency) – debit/credit cards are not accepted at the majority of sites and it is not possible to sign in on behalf of another player. The entry fee varies between events.

SIGN-IN PREPARATIONS

A quick signature, an exchange of money, and the sign-in day is complete – for an amateur, perhaps. However, experienced competitors will make full use of the day as they look to ensure peak performance on match day.

The practice courts of the event are open for you to practise on sign-in day and ITF rules dictate that the tournament is obliged to make three of the official match balls available for practice per day, free of charge, to each player accepted into the Main Draw and/or Qualifying Draw from the day prior to the commencement of the respective draw until he/she is eliminated from the tournament. At this level, performance can be heavily influenced by the playability of the particular court which will, in turn, be dependent on the official ball of the tournament.

After having a practice on sign-in day, you can then make the necessary adjustments according to your feel of the court. There is a tournament stringer on site to assist but you must provide the strings. A number of courts will also be reserved throughout the tournament for players to warm up, practise and cool down, but it is always best to book these courts early because they can get very busy.

During the Qualifying and Main Draw, it is a requirement at all ITF Pro Circuit tournaments that transportation is made available free of charge for all players between the official hotel and the tournament site on the day of competition, and this can be booked in advance via the tournament director. Rackets can be picked up from the official tournament stringer and the practice courts will be available as previously arranged.

'ON-SITE ALTERNATE'

ITF rules dictate that all vacancies in the draw from the Qualifying Sign-In Deadline until the commencement of the Qualifying competition are to be filled by entered players who have signed in for the Qualifying event according to the 'applicable System of Merit'.

This allows those players who failed to make the Qualifying cut-off, or simply failed to sign up, to be entered into the Qualifying Draw. Alternates must sign in with the ITF Supervisor on-site prior to the Qualifying sign-in deadline to be eligible for any vacancies in the Qualifying event. If you are such a player, to continue to be eligible, you must sign in at 'at least half an hour before the scheduled start of play' each day that the first round is played. There is no guarantee that any spaces will be available but it can be worth making the trip if the site is within a reasonable distance from home.

Priority for all 'On-Site Alternates' will be given to ATP-ranked players over nationally ranked players. Unranked players will be drawn at random.

PLAYING DOUBLES AND SINGLES

All players are permitted to enter both the doubles and singles competitions of the same event in any given tournament week. Entering doubles events is recommended because it allows players to gain experience by competing against Main Draw players and it also offers another potential avenue to a long-term career in the game. It is not uncommon for players to earn an ATP Doubles ranking point well before they taste success in Singles events.

All team entries for the doubles competition must be made in writing and received by the ITF Supervisor by 1200 noon (local time) on the day before the singles Main Draw is scheduled to commence.

ITF Junior Tour

Running alongside the National Associations' developmental programmes, the ITF Junior Circuit Tour is a core vehicle used by many international junior players as they look to progress to the ITF Pro Circuit tour and beyond. The circuit allows junior players competing at a national level to test their standard against the very best players from other nations and provides them with great experience of international competition before they join the professional tour.

There are over 400 events held annually in over 120 countries on the ITF Junior Circuit and the level at these events is very high. You should not consider entering ITF Junior Circuit events without having first tasted success at National or Regional Junior level, for example through 'Tennis Europe'.

To be eligible for competition on the ITF Junior Circuit, the player must have turned thirteen prior to the first day's play in the Main Draw and be aged eighteen years and under (i.e. they can play to the end of the year in which they turn eighteen and become ineligible to play from 1 January of the year they turn nineteen years of age). The entry procedures are very similar to those required for ITF Pro Circuit events; while national federations and their affiliates operate the event, all entries are done via the ITF IPIN system.

There are six categories of events on the ITF Junior Circuit Tour: Grades A, 1, 2, 3, 4 and 5. Grade 5 offers the lowest number of ranking points to the players, while Grade A – which includes the four Junior Grand Slams – represents the pinnacle of the junior game. Grade A, 1 and 2 tournaments constitute the 'High Performance' and Grade 3, 4 and 5 the 'Development' sides of the Circuit.

An ITF Junior World Ranking will almost certainly be necessary to be accepted into Grade A, 1, 2, and 3 tournaments. Entry into Grade 4 and 5 tournaments is based on a player's ITF Junior World Rankings to an extent, but with more opportunity for unranked players to be accepted especially if they are from the host country or the region in which the tournament is held. The Junior ITF office only accepts the national rankings of the Top 150 aged 18 or under players who do not hold a Junior ITF world ranking. Players outside of this list are drawn into their position on the acceptance list in random order.

Your ranking is determined by your best six singles and six doubles results over a fifty-two-week period and the ITF will crown a boy's and girl's Junior champion at the end of each season. Junior players who end the year ranked in the top ten all qualify for the ITF Junior exempt project under which they are given automatic access to certain ITF Pro Circuits events with a view to facilitating the integration of junior players into the professional tour.

More details on entering these events alongside the tournament calendar and the Junior Exempt Project can be found on the ITF website.

The ATP Point and Climbing the Rankings

A prestigious talent and a genius on court, Chilean Marcelo Rios was a player like no other. Seemingly creating angles out of nothing and adding a rare artistic variety to the sport, Rios wowed the world with his own unique array of shots and is perceived by many, including Pat Cash and Nick Bollettieri, to be one of the finest talents ever to grace the game. But as exceptionally gifted as Rios was, he never once won a major singles title. How, then, did he hold the Number One ranking for six weeks in 1998?

Tennis players are not ranked simply by their wins and losses, nor does a judging panel gather to give their thoughts on who is better than whom. Instead, the ATP or WTA ranking of any player is determined using a complicated points-based system, which applies once a player has achieved his or her first ATP/WTA ranking point right through to the top players in world tennis.

Under this fifty-two-week system, players accrue ranking points with each Main Draw victory and their cumulative points total determines their ranking over the course of the season. Different tournaments are given different values with regards to the number of points on offer. Factors such as the opponent and the scoreline are not taken into consideration.

The answer, therefore, is consistency. While Rios did not win a Grand Slam title, he earned his World Number One ranking because he had posted the most consistent results of the calendar year up to that point. In other words, he had accumulated more points than any other player by playing consistently rather than winning just one major title.

DEFENDING POINTS

Confusion often lies with the idea of 'defending' points. When you win a point, it does not last indefinitely. Points earned in any given tournament are 'dropped' from your total points when the tournament is held again the following year. You must therefore 'defend' your points each year.

Suppose, for example, that you win the ITF US$10,000 event to pick up eighteen ATP ranking points. You will lose those points by the time the tournament is played the following year. Assuming you enter the same event the following year, successfully defending your title will not affect your points tally, but if you lose in the quarter-final round, you will then only pick up two ranking points with a resultant loss of sixteen. Conversely, you will earn points by improving your result in the following year.

'Defending' points does not, however, require you to enter the same event each year. You, for example, may have won eight points by reaching the semi-final of a US$15,000 Futures fifty-two weeks ago but continued to build your ranking thereafter. You are now playing Challenger level tournaments so would not return to the $15,000 this year, but you would still be 'defending' your eight points during this tournament week.

'BUYING' THE ATP POINT

The standard of tennis and depth of competition varies from country to country. All ITF Pro Circuit events will have a number of high-quality, seasoned professionals, but this number will be smaller in some places than in others. For example, Pro Circuit events in Africa and Asia will normally have a smaller number than in Western Europe.

While it is not possible to 'buy' points in the strict sense, some players will travel to the remote corners of the globe to maximize their chances of success – a process known as 'buying' an ATP point. These players can then return to Europe with an official international ranking and gain direct entry to qualifying draws because the governing bodies do not factor in where a point was actually earned.

You can further maximize your chances by choosing the right time to play an event. Entering a tournament at Christmas time in the likes of Iran or Pakistan is likely to generate a more favourable draw than an event in Barcelona in the peak of summer. It is a question of sacrifice, intelligence and luck, and players who invest enough time and money can normally find success down this avenue.

Winning a first Main Draw match and earning an ATP Point is a huge step on the pathway to a professional career because it will give you preference over all unranked players in ITF Pro Circuit events in the future (if you defend it).

STAY FOCUSED ON YOUR GAME

Breaking through this first stage of the professional circuit is one of the most challenging steps for any player, and you must work hard to avoid getting stuck at this level by breaking through onto the higher tiers of professional tennis as quickly as possible. You may find that you take more time than others, and one of the great dangers is that you may become disheartened by comparing yourself to other players.

Mediocrity always tries to bring excellence down to its level and, as a starter on the tour, you may be tempted to lower your standards and become unprofessional like the many seasoned pros who have failed to break through this level. One thing that spurs improvement is playing against someone who forces you out of your comfort zone; this makes you raise your game and push yourself to the next level. Getting caught on the Pro circuit will slow down any development and you must keep focused on your own personal game if you are to break through to the higher tiers of professional competition.

Inter-club Competition

More and more players are becoming part of tennis leagues emerging in Italy, France, Switzerland, Belgium and Germany. These leagues are played in parallel to the professional circuits and have become a major source of income for players competing on the ITF and ATP/WTA World Tours. Each club is sponsored, usually by local businesses, and this money is used to take professionals under contract to boost their chances of success. Clubs in the top leagues have been known to have a budget of between €700,000 and €1million each season.

The inter-club system is brilliant for two reasons. Firstly, these leagues give players the opportunity to fund their own tennis. Daniel Kiernan, now Director of SOTO Tennis Academy, earned more money as a player by competing for eight weeks in the winter inter-club season and six weeks in the summer than in a full year battling out on the ITF Pro Circuits. Secondly, they are incredible ways of meeting other players at a similar level to travel or train with outside of the inter-club season.

The money in the higher divisions can be very good and it is guaranteed, whether you win or lose, although bonuses are awarded for victories. As a result, the paralysing pressure of losing ranking points does not exist.

Seasonal salaries are normally determined by your ranking. A top 1000 ranked player can earn over €500 per match, a top 100 player will earn approximately €5000 per match, and there are stories of top 30 ranked players earning over €12,000 per match. There is no non-slam ATP tournament that pays this well. Together with the German Bundesliga and the Italian Seria A, the top tier French leagues pay the highest sums of money and are also the hardest to get into. The crowd turnout is often high, the atmospheres electric and the stadiums overfilled.

Although clubs in the lower divisions will not normally have the budgets to pay international players to play, they represent a great opportunity for players to go and get some match experience abroad in a team environment. These smaller clubs will normally pay for flights, accommodation and food, and will sometimes offer players to opportunity to earn a wage by coaching the younger players on the team.

If you are interested, contact the relevant national federations or specific clubs, which will be able to provide more details, although it is advisable to do so months before the season begins to ensure the best chances of signing a contract. It is not uncommon to be 'scouted' at tournaments and 'agents' do exist to facilitate the process. If playing and competing enough at the right level, you will normally meet the right person, although it might not be in the league you want immediately.

As a player, your contract will normally be renewed each year provided that you have had a good season and managed to blend in with the team and local way of life.

Moving on from the ITF Pro Circuit

The most talented players will use the college/academy infrastructure as a springboard to success on the professional tour. The common misconception is that tennis is all the glitz and glamour that fills our television screens around the country during the Grand Slam events. In reality, that is the very pinnacle of professional tennis and beneath this wonderful world where the air is fresh and money-pots deep lies a long road comprising two less glamorous tiers of the professional game.

Men who accrue enough ranking points on the ITF Futures Circuit will move on to the secondary tier of men's professional tennis – the ATP Challenger Tour, formerly known as the ATP Challenger series. These events are regulated by the Association of Tennis Professionals (ATP), which is affiliated to the ITF and is the governing body of men's professional tennis. Challenger events are a step below the ATP World tour and feature players ranked between approximately 50 and 350 in the world. It is not uncommon for players to compete on both the ATP and Challenger tours. Players at this level are more clinical and more ruthless.

Women are not eligible for the ATP Challenger tour. Instead, after earning sufficient ranking points at the US$10,000 Future level, women will become eligible for US$25,000 ITF events. Above this level are then US$50,000/US$75,000/US$100,000 ITF events, where players in the main draw usually range between 50 and 400 in the WTA rankings. These players will then look to progress to the 'International Events', which are governed by the WTA (Women's Tennis Association) and make up the WTA Tour – the highest tier of women's professional tennis. The WTA is the governing body of women's professional tennis and, like the ATP, works together with the ITF.[4]

The ATP and WTA both hold a series of tiered events throughout the season. The top tier of men's professional tennis is the ATP World Tour and the best women in the world compete on the WTA Tour, of which the Grand Slam events (the Australian Open, the French Open (Roland Garros), Wimbledon and the US Open) are the most prestigious individual competitions in tennis.

While all those hours on the practice court and many more in the gym will help you on your way to success in tennis competition, so too will making informed decisions about which tournaments to play and when. Playing intelligently, using the Inter-club system and gaining valuable match experience abroad can all help prepare you for the challenging path that lies ahead.

CHAPTER FOUR

Adapting Successfully to the Court

I don't know where I got it from, but I possessed a heavy topspin game. A big 'kick' serve was my weapon, and I loved to slide – far from the hallmark of a traditional British player. Indeed, if it were not for my curly blond locks and strong English accent, I could easily have been mistaken for a well-trained Spaniard drilled from a very early age. On many occasions, I was.

My results were great on clay. I tasted success in Australia as a youngster and, though intermittent, I posted some strong results on the European continent at sporadic moments in my career. But problems came with transferring these skills to domestic shores.

The high cost of maintenance and the rainy climate mean that clay courts are far less prominent in the UK than in mainland Europe. Year after year, I would test my skills against Britain's best in the indoor arena and come unstuck. I remember losing to one player 6–2, 6–2 on a hard court, beating him 6–0, 6–1 on the clay. My game just didn't work; my topspin sat up and balls flew past me. My weapons were neutralized.

It didn't take me long to learn why, but it was something I wish I had known at an earlier age. I could then have made the adaptations at the dawn, rather than the twilight, of my sporting career.

This is what I wish I had known.

Court Factors

While the official document detailing the rules and regulations of the beautiful game are specified to the finest degree, at times obsessively so, there is one enormous oversight that has largely shaped the modern game as we know it today. To give an example: court must be 23.78 m (78 ft) long and 10.97 m (35 ft) wide for doubles; 8.23 m (27 ft) for singles. The balls, too, are heavily regulated: they must be yellow or white, all seams must be stitchless, and their weight must not exceed 59.4 g (approx. 2 oz). There is, however, absolutely no stipulation as to the surface on which the game must be played.

Slow-motion cameras indicate that the ball is only actually in contact with the racket for approximately five milliseconds on each hit. In other words, the ball actually spends less than one per cent of the time on the racket. Ninety-nine per cent of the time, the ball is travelling between the players or bouncing off the ground. In other words, the ball actually spends less time than one per cent of the time on the racket – this is the only time when the player is actually in physical control of the ball. The rest is controlled by physics, but 'the physics of tennis – those impersonal forces shaping every shot – are not constant,' writes Jonah Lehrer in his piece for *Grantland*.[1]

Instead, the trajectory of the ball through the air following the bounce is completely dependent on three separate factors determined by the court surface: (1) speed, (2) vertical rebound, and (3) bounce height.

Speed

The horizontal speed of a tennis ball is reduced as it interacts with the court surface. If the surface has a great impact on the speed of the ball following the bounce, the court is referred to as 'slow'; if the influence is small, the court is said to be 'fast'. The speed of the court is determined by its coefficient of friction (COF), a measurement of the abrasive force between the surface and the ball, in a direction parallel with the surface.

The speed of a tennis court is officially calculated with the 'Court Pace Rating' system, which measures the ball–surface interaction. The test involves firing a ball at the surface and recording the reduction in the horizontal component of the post-impact ball velocity, and the vertical restitution, which is determined by the time between successive bounces. On test completion, each court is given a 'Court Pace Rating' (CPR) and classified into one of five categories.

CATEGORIES OF SPEED

CPR: $\leq$ 29 = Slow
CPR: 30–34 = Medium–Slow
CPR: 35–39 = Medium
CPR: 40–44 = Medium–Fast
CPR: $\geq$ 45 = Fast

The unofficial speed of a court can normally be judged by the number of 'aces' and 'winners' in a match. Well-struck balls will be harder to return on a fast surface with a low COF (High CPR) because they will stay low and maintain a faster speed following the bounce. As a result, there are a higher number of aces and winners on the grass courts of the All England Club than on the slow, abrasive clay courts of the French Open.

The speed of a tennis court is officially calculated with the 'Court Pace Rating' system, which measures the ball–surface interaction

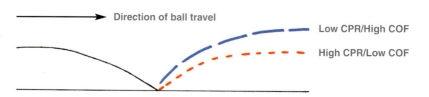

Vertical Rebound

The Court Pace Rating (CPR) also gives the best indication of the bounce height of the outgoing ball because the ball is being fired in at an angle rather than a simple vertical drop. It is important to note that there is a link between the COF and the vertical rebound height of the ball: the higher the COF, the greater the vertical rebound height. This is because the abrasive nature of the court increases the friction pushing against the ball's horizontal path, 'redirecting' the forward momentum of the ball upwards at a steeper angle. This, in turn, leads to a higher vertical rebound on the outgoing ball.

The vertical rebound angle is actually more important in determining the perceived speed of the court then the actual speed itself. As Howard Brody, physicist at the University of Pennsylvania, noted in his book, *Science for Tennis Players*, 'The eye and brain are much better at gauging an angle than observing a slight change in ball speed. If the ball comes off the court at a low angle after the bounce, you conclude that the court is fast because you must act faster.'[2] The higher the vertical rebound angle, therefore, the slower the player perceives the court to be.

Bounce Height

The vertical bounce properties of a surface (i.e. how bouncy the court is) depend on the 'coefficient of restitution (COR)', and each court is classified as a low, medium or high bounce depending on the results.

While the COR will not influence the horizontal velocity of the ball (i.e. court speed), it will have an impact on the vertical velocity of the ball after the bounce. Courts with a low COR will, however, normally be perceived to be faster because the ball bounces off the court at a lower angle and players have less time to react.

Generally speaking, the lower the COR (i.e. the softer the court), the lower the ball bounces – except on clay. The clay builds up in front of the ball as the ball slides through the court and this results in a steep angle of reflection and extremely high vertical rebound despite clay's soft nature.

The Importance of Footwork

Though not a factor in determining the path of the ball, the surface does affect the way players move on the court and this variation can have a big impact on results. Some surfaces, such as grass, are slippery and require you to lower your centre of gravity and use small steps, while others, such as acrylic, offer you high-level grip and prevent you from sliding into the shot.

The Different Types of Court Surface

Different Surfaces

Until the early 1970s, almost all tournaments were played on grass, including three of the four Grand Slams. Today, the situation has changed dramatically: Wimbledon remains the only one hosted on the sport's original surface and the French Open in May is the only Grand Slam event held on traditional European red clay courts.

The Australian and US Open events are both strictly classified as hard court tournaments, although the hard, 'Plexicusion' courts in Melbourne are much slower than the hard 'Decoturf 2' courts in Flushing Meadows. Almost all other professional events are played on one of these three surface types.

Outside of these professional events, the International Tennis Federation (ITF) officially recognizes over 150 varieties of surfaces suitable for tennis competition, including carpet, artificial grass, clay, wood, and gravel. All surfaces are subject to a rigorous testing procedure before they can be approved as an official surface, key considerations being the friction, energy restitution, topography, and consistency.

The ITF identifies nine generic surface types into which all other officially recognized surfaces are classified. An exhaustive list of all officially recognized surfaces and their respective categories can be found on the ITF website (http://www.itftennis.com) where players can also type in the name of a surface to discover its court pace rating and classification.

The Homogenization of Court Surfaces

> There are a lot of factors that can affect the court pace, especially if you start tinkering with the composition.
> JAMIE CAPEL-DAVIS, *Senior Project Technologist, ITF*

The 2001 decision of The All England Lawn Tennis Club to replace grass with a slower rye-seed alternative proved unpopular with players who had shaped their games to suit the traditionally fast surface. Former British Number One, Tim Henman, bemoaned that the grass was becoming 'increasingly slow, heavy and high bouncy', while Frenchman Michael Llodra expressed preference for the clay courts of Roland Garros, which were 'much faster' than the lawns of SW19 when dry. The BBC famously broadcast a comparison of two Federer serves: one hit in 2003; the second in 2008. Both were clocked at 202 km/h (approx. 126 mph). The latter serve bounced higher and came off the grass travelling 14 km/h (approx. 9 mph) slower.

Traditionally considered a fast hard-court event, the US Open used to play more like Wimbledon than the Australian Open. In 2011, however, the annual Grand Slam event was the centre of great controversy with many players complaining that more sand had been added to the acrylic paint, causing the ball to come off the court slower than ever before. Although the dimensions of a tennis court have historically remained constant, the tennis surfaces on the professional tour have gradually become more uniform.

The ITF does not have a comprehensive audit of court pace across all the events and its official statement is that there is no evidence of systematic and deliberate manipulation of the court pace. But the court speed across the events can be inferred from the pile of statistics granted to us by the ITF itself.

Although the average serve speed has started to plateau since 2010, it has been gradually increasing since about 2004. Over the same period, however, the number of aces has not really changed, suggesting one of two things: either the returning has improved or the surfaces are slowing the balls down more than ever before.

It may well be that the returning has improved; it is of little doubt that players have adapted to the new power play, either by increasing footwork or reading more advanced cues from the server. Over the same time period, however, the first-serve percentage has increased quite dramatically, indicating that players are moving away from just speed and are beginning to favour accuracy, possibly as a result of the slower surfaces. While only hypothetical, 'the figures do support the theory,' says Jamie Capel-Davis, Senior Project Technologist at the ITF.

At this point, it is easy to point the finger at the ITF because its motive appears obvious. Through a combination of technological development and enhanced physical training, today's players are hitting with more spin and more power than could ever have been anticipated and there is a growing feeling that the game will soon become unplayable if it continues to evolve at the current rate.

Rafael Nadal is able to generate over 3,200 revolutions per minute on his forehand – almost twice that of Sampras and Agassi. In 2012, Andy Murray broke the record for the fastest forehand ever recorded with his 199 km/h (approx. 124 mph) inside-out forehand winner against Mardy Fish in Cincinnati, just eight months before Australian Samuel Groth broke the serve-speed record with a 263 km/h (approx. 163 mph) rocket in South Korea. This would just not have been possible a decade ago.

The signs are there for all to see; the game is evolving and it will eventually reach a stage where the equilibrium between striker and receiver is lost, at which point the game will become unplayable. It is this fear that motivated the great John McEnroe to cry out to the ITF in his *Serious* autobiography and it is this concern that lead to his collaboration with Martina Navratilova and Björn Borg to pen an open letter demanding a reduction in the size of the rackets.

Many believe that these changes have been the ITF's response to this significant pressure applied by tennis' elite, while others believe the changes are designed to promote a beautiful baseline game and longer matches with a view to captivating a wider worldwide audience. Both would be just causes; it is no secret that five-set thrillers like Nadal's 2010 Wimbledon victory or Djokovic's 2012 triumph in Melbourne have been fundamental reasons behind the dramatic growth of the sport over the past decade, but questions remain as to who is actually responsible for the slowing of the courts. The ITF only sets limitations as to the speed of the court; it is actually the tournament officials themselves who determine the speed itself and their motives are far slower to represent themselves.

It may be that the court pace has been tweaked without the ITF's involvement, but this homogenization is beginning to cripple the game. The unfortunate truth remains that the game today is just not as varied as it once was. Whether it be Nadal–Federer, Sampras–Agassi or McEnroe–Borg, diversity of style has been the common denominator for the sport's greatest rivalries and the game today is just not quite the same without it.

Unfortunately, the 'Court Pace Rating' is the source of the problem. While the system operates to measure the speed of the court on any given day, it fails to monitor the actual manufacturing process of the surface when the court is being laid. This allows tournament bodies to manufacture the court as they see fit; they can vary the composition of the surface each year by including more or less sand, adopting a smoother finish or choosing a different particle in the mixture. As a result, the 'CPR' measurement is overridden by the desires of the tournament officials who are at liberty to lay down a surface to play as they wish.

The result is that these changes are going to have a serious influence on the future of the game and the issue will be a source of continued debate until a time when the rules are changed. There lies no easy solution besides regulation and enforcement of stricter limitations, preferably via an external governing body.

Before an important Davis Cup tie in 2010, the French famously laid an ultra quick surface to favour their countrymen, most of whom were comfortable serve-volleying. The ITF has placed strict boundaries on Davis/Fed Cup ties to prevent home nations from manipulating the court pace too far in their favour.

It is important that these restrictions are soon applied to all areas of competition to ensure consistency across the board with any particular court surface.

Understanding How the Surface Affects Your Game

Success in tennis at any advanced level requires an ability to tailor a game-plan to an ever-changing set of surface conditions. Going from one surface to another can be a great challenge for even the most advanced players, and one of the biggest difficulties faced by the modern-day professional is the tiny gap between the second and third Grand Slams of the season. Players are given just a few weeks to adapt their games to the idiosyncrasies of the fast grass courts after six weeks on the slow clay courts of central Europe.

The very nature of the game requires you to anticipate how the ball is going to react off the surface; only then can you properly position your feet and time your swing to connect with the ball in the strike zone. Without a grasp of how different surfaces affect the trajectory of the ball and how to adapt your playing style to suit the surface, you will struggle to find success in the game.

In order to make the necessary tactical adjustments, you must first develop a careful understanding of how the different surfaces 'play'. How do you move on grass? How do you move on clay? How does the ball react to each surface? Although players do not have time to think in the midst of a point, the best athletes will normally win because they can play more intelligently.

It is to these questions that we now turn.

Adapting Your Game to Clay Courts

After gaining popularity in the 1950s, clay courts have become very prominent throughout Europe. Clay courts consist of a base layer of crushed stone covered with a layer of rough particle material such as crushed brick. The following is applicable to clay and artificial clay courts, both of which are classified as either 'Slow' or 'Medium Slow.'

Play: Slow/High Bounce

Clay tennis courts are notably slower than all other surfaces and the balls bounce higher than on hard and grass courts. The resistance generated when the ball bounces causes a build-up of clay, which forces the ball to slow down and rebound at an extreme vertical angle. Their abrasive nature slows down the bottom of the ball without influencing the velocity of the top and this disparity forces a vertical impact with the court, pushing the ball upwards at a greater vertical angle than on a faster, smoother surface.

To a certain extent, you must also adapt your style of play according to the condition of the clay. Clay courts, when wet, become incredibly slow, especially when the balls pick up moisture, and hitting a winner becomes almost impossible. In these conditions, clay court tennis becomes a war of attrition as to who will break first – you or your opponent.

Comparatively speaking, dry clay courts on a warm summer's day play more like a hard court; the ball fizzes off the surface, 'kicking' up high above head height. Rafael Nadal has publicly spoken about his love for the drier clay courts, primarily because they exaggerate the effect of the quite astounding amounts of topspin he is able to generate.

Due to the slow nature of clay courts, you are forced to work hard if you are to generate great pace on the ball, especially when the ball 'kicks' up high outside of the comfortable hitting zone.

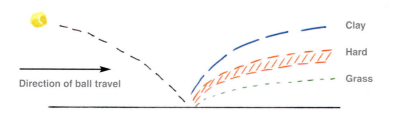

Direction of ball travel

Clay

Hard

Grass

The friction of clay courts results in a higher bounce and slower ball than on hard and grass courts

Rafael Nadal jumps in the air in celebration after hitting a winner past Andy Murray at the 2011 French Open

Because of this, if you are a player who relies on brute force, you will tend to struggle. Instead, the surface favours those who are comfortable hitting consistent, deep groundstrokes from the baseline and so you must learn to construct the point (see page 147, 'Consistency') if you are to be successful. As a result, such points are usually longer and more physically gruelling than on any other surfaces.

Importantly, you can normally determine whether a ball was in or out by checking the mark on clay – something unique to this particular surface. This can be especially useful at the lower levels of competition where there are no line-judges on court.

Game Style

On 9 May 2013, Rafael Nadal sealed his place in history as the greatest clay court player of all time. A 6–3, 6–2, 6–3 victory over his compatriot David Ferrer in the final saw Nadal become the first ever man to win the same Grand Slam title eight times, and took his astonishing record at Roland Garros to fifty-nine victories out of sixty matches. Rafael Nadal is a phenomenal tennis player on any surface, but on his beloved clay he is the most dominant the sport has ever seen. What have been the keys to the Spaniard's unparalleled success?

Generating an incredible racket head speed and topspin to 'kick' the ball above his opponent's head, the Spaniard possesses perhaps the best forehand in the history of the game. Using slow-motion video cameras, it has been determined that the Spaniard can generate close to 5,000 revolutions per minute: twice that of his great rival, Roger Federer, and almost three times that of Pete Sampras and Andre Agassi.

Topspin (*red*) is produced by brushing the strings up the back of the ball. As the ball flies through the air, forward rotation pushes the ball down into the ground, allowing Nadal to hit with a higher net clearance in the assurance that his ball is unlikely to fly long. As a result, the Spaniard's groundstrokes are dropping from a greater height and so actually bounce higher (*see the diagram on page 71*).

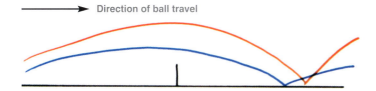

Direction of ball travel

Topspin (*red*) v. flat (*blue*)

Additionally, because topspin makes the ball descend at a steeper angle than a 'flat' or sliced shot, the resultant ball responds at a steeper angle (assuming the court plays consistently). This pushes the ball high above Nadal's head and out of the comfortable contact point, keeping his opponent uncomfortable and off balance. Not only does topspin allow Nadal to hit with greater consistency, it also allows him to hit with aggression and cause his opponent problems from almost anywhere on the court.

The clay surface actually works to maximize the potency of Nadal's forehand. Topspin shots bounce more steeply on clay because the ball digs a shallow hole into the court and is pushed upwards by the front slope of the hole as it reacts on contact with the surface.

The slow nature of the clay and the typical high looping groundstrokes also give Nadal more time to run around his backhand to reposition himself during a rally, allowing him to hit more forehands than on any other surface, further advancing his topspin advantage. Very often during rallies Nadal has the time and energy to run around his backhand to play from the forehand, and from here he can hit just about any angle on the court.

Rafael Nadal strikes his trademark lasso-like forehand on the clay courts of Madrid

Mental and Physical Toughness

Clay court matches tend to be long, gruelling affairs in which you have to work extremely hard to create just a single opportunity to win a point. The increased length of the points requires great mental and physical endurance because you must make more decisions per point and maintain focus over the course of a longer match.

Having grown up battling on the clay, Nadal has developed incredible mental strength and the resolute focus to allow him to fight up to the very last point and make these important decisions at crucial moments in matches.

For this reason, you are advised to take every opportunity to train and compete on clay courts.

The Advantage of Clay

' The French tennis schools are the best in the world. French players have the best technique but they play indoors and on fast surfaces. As a result, they never learn to fight. Spanish players, who grow up and train on clay, may not have the best technique, but they learn to win matches through sheer grit and determination; they become more combative. Players who train on faster surfaces are not prepared to hit ten balls in a rally because only playing on clay can prepare players for this. '
JORDI ARRESE, *1992 Olympic Silver Medallist and former Spanish Davis Cup Captain*

Court surface is a key reason behind Britain's undeniable failure to produce many tennis players capable of mixing with the game's elite. Looking at the number of clay courts by country, Spain and Germany have approx. 84 per cent, Serbia has 80 per cent, while approximately only 1 per cent of Britain's tennis courts are made from crushed brick. A coincidence it may seem, but there is a strong correlation between tennis success and clay court prominence – and the reasons are clear.

To succeed on clay, players must learn to construct points. From a very early age, players training on this surface develop a firm grasp of tennis tactics; they learn patience, grit, and determination, as they gradually grow into physical specimens capable of on-court dominance. Of importance, too, is that they develop a valuable repertoire of shot combinations because it quickly becomes apparent that they cannot win a point with one forehand or one big serve.

If you head to Spain or France, the proof really is in the pudding. The intensity, work-rate and concentration of the players on the Catalan coastline makes the training in the UK look frighteningly amateur.

'A big part of my job used to be working with all the High Performance Centres in the UK and one thing that struck me was the lack of intensity and effort in the training sessions,' says Duncan Callan, the Prince UK Brand Manager. 'I've been to Spain and there will be high-intensity, physical tennis on each court all day long but this work ethic does not exist in the UK. I think this is a major problem.'

It is not the players' fault. The fast grass, hard or astro-turf courts in the UK do not lend themselves to patience or point construction. UK players never learn how to move the opponent around the court – not because they do not want to, but because they do not need to. By the time they realize the importance of these skills, they are already well behind the curve.

Unfortunately, there is no end in sight. The gradual homogenization of the court surfaces has only compounded these grass-root problems by making all other surfaces more amenable to clay court practices. UK players are learning a brand of tennis that just does not transfer well to the modern professional game.

Indeed, it is no coincidence that Britain's only great success, Andy Murray, honed his skills as a junior on the clay courts of Barcelona, and there is a very strong case for developing juniors in the UK to train abroad.

Clay Court Tactics

> You have to work harder for a point [on clay]. You can't rush the point like a player who has grown up on a fast court who wants to win the point immediately because the ball will come back. To win [on clay], you have to be a more complete player; players must learn lobs, drop-shots and also be more physically strong.
>
> JORDI ARRESE, *1992 Olympic Silver Medallist and former Spanish Davis Cup Captain*

Clay is the most tactically demanding of all tennis surfaces: the slower court, increased rally length, footwork patterns and wider variety of shots required can really test a player's physical and mental resolve.

There exists a very rare breed of player who has conquered the secrets and mysteries of clay court tennis and the sport is littered with 'greats' who have not enjoyed similar successes at the French Open and other clay court events, including John McEnroe, Boris Becker, Pete Sampras and, in the 1970s, Jimmy Connors. Being a strong clay courter is very much an art within an art.

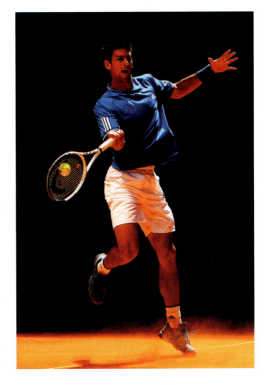

Novak Djokovic has become one of the few players in the history of the game to have mastered clay and triumphed over Rafael Nadal

Long rallies: You must be able to hit consistent, quality groundstrokes and learn to be patient when constructing the opportunity to win a point. You must also improve your endurance, strength, flexibility and speed because you must be willing and physically able to stay in each point for as long as it takes to win it.

Topspin: Topspin is a particularly potent weapon on clay courts and it is almost impossible to succeed without it. Not only will it increase your consistency by allowing you to hit with a greater net clearance, it also allows you to hit with a greater range of angles not available with a 'flatter' groundstroke.

Enhance repertoire of shots: Stroke variation pays big dividends on a clay court. Clay-courters tend to play in a semi-circle about 5–10 feet behind the baseline, which leaves them vulnerable to the drop shot and the

Clay courts require players to slide to reach the balls and are widely considered to be the most physically demanding

short angles. With the increased rally length, you will need to show a greater variety of shots if you are to win the point.

'There's no surface which takes a drop shot better. You need to work every rally before you can open up the court for a winner,'[3] says Andrew Castle, the former British Number One, for the BBC.

Rafael Nadal serving during his seventh straight Monte Carlo Masters Series tournament victory

Fight: The composition of a clay court allows you to track down more shots than on any other surface, and you must use this to your advantage by training yourself physically and mentally to never give up on a ball. Chasing a ball down and winning the point gives you a psychological boost and discourages your opponent.

Serve intelligently: Statistics show that Andy Murray loses approximately 11 per cent more service games on clay than on any other surface. A similar correlation exists for almost all of the top players, except Rafael Nadal, whose percentage of service games won actually remains fairly constant across all the different surfaces. Watch Nadal serve on clay, and the reasons become obvious: what he lacks in power, he make up for in intelligence.

First-serve percentage is particularly important because slow second serves are especially vulnerable. To keep this percentage high, Nadal uses a mixture of slice and 'kick' serves, both of which are also highly effective on the surface.

Go behind your opponent: Clay is surface that is inherently slippery to play on and it can be very difficult to change direction quickly. When

The tramline throws exercise, where the player is A and the dotted line indicates the sliding movement. Player A must slide out to stop the ball as thrown by the coach

playing, a good strategy is to aim shots behind your opponent because it is unlikely that they will have the time or agility to change direction and return.

Sliding: Most advanced players actually generate so much force with their legs that they actually take off the ground when hitting a groundstroke. If you do this on clay, you will continue to slide on landing and will be late changing direction to arrive in time for the next shot. Moving well on courts requires you to slide into the shot, slowing down sufficiently at the point of contact to allow you to push off and arrive in time for the next shot.

You must slide with your outside leg. For a right-hander, this means sliding with your right leg when pulled out on the forehand side and with your left leg when out wide on the backhand. For a left-hander, you must slide with your left leg on the forehand side and the right leg on the back-hand. It is also important that you learn to slide and hold shape; you must stay balanced enough to execute a stroke.

The easiest exercise to help you develop a good sliding motion involves you (A) standing at the 'T' in the middle of the court with your practice partner (or coach) at the net. Your partner bounces a ball across the court at an angle (*see the dotted line in the diagram top right*), which forces you to slide, cutting off the angle and catching the ball with one hand before it has bounced twice or crossed the tramlines. You should focus on main-taining form and balance throughout.

Another important aspect of the slide is the push-off on completion of the movement. To practise this, stand on the balls of your feet at the baseline and face the net. Your practice partner stands behind you and rolls two balls in the direction of the net. You must react and

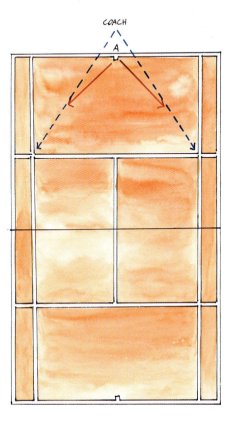

The sliding balls behind the body exercise, where the player is A and the solid line indicates the sliding movement

chase down the first ball, slide, stop and push to slide in to collect the next ball. The speed, height and direction of the feeds should be varied each time (*see the diagram at the bottom of page 75*).

This final exercise is designed to help you practise the complete sliding motion, including the recovery to the baseline. Standing approximately 6 ft inside the court from the baseline, your practice partner holds a ball in each hand with arms out wide. Without warning, your partner drops one of the balls, forcing you to move forward, sliding to catch the ball before it bounces twice. Following this, you must return to the baseline, continuing to face the net, split-step, and move forward to catch the second ball.

This will also help you to work on your explosiveness and first-step towards the ball.

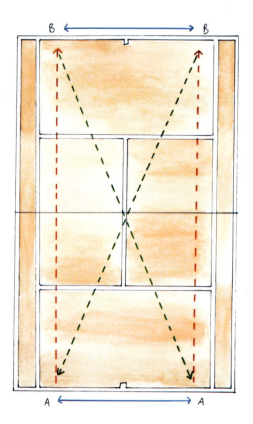

Clay court patterned hitting: here player A hits down the line while player B hits cross-court

Clay Court Training

Patience: You can use the following exercise to practise determination, consistency and patience. The set-up is simple: you and another player of a similar standard rally in the open court counting the number of times the ball passes over the net. The point is 'active' throughout the exercise but the number of points awarded to the winning player corresponds directly to the number of times the ball passed over the net. The winner is the first player to reach 100 points. Learn to work the point, probing and looking to create space into which you can attack.

It is important to note that you should maintain a solid racket head speed at all times in this drill. The fear is that intermediate players will gain nothing as they begin 'pushing' the ball over the net because they are afraid of making a mistake – make sure that you don't fall into this trap.

Patterned hitting: this involves hitting controlled patterns on-court and is a great way for you to practise the movement and racket head control you require on a clay court. The two most common patterned-hitting exercises are:

1. **Cross-Court/Down The Line** – Hit each shot down the line; your opponent must respond by hitting each shot cross court (*see diagram, above left*).

2. **Cross-Court/One Down the Line** – You can only hit cross court while your opponent must hit two cross court and one down the line. The feed does not count as a 'shot'.

See also the drills highlighted in Chapter 7 which are also applicable to clay court practice.

Serving

Slow second serves are particularly vulnerable on clay so you should work on consistently hitting a variety of targets with different types of serve. Place targets at three different positions in the service box, e.g. out wide, in the middle (body serve) and down the line (down the 'T'). Practise hitting each target using a flat, slice and 'kick' serve.

To increase the quality of the 'kick' serve, place a mini-tennis net across the court half-way down the length of the service box. The aim is to get enough spin on the ball to force the ball up and down fast enough to land deep in the service box beyond the mini-tennis net. This will ensure that the ball drops at a steep angle, landing deep in the box with lots of spin, maximizing the effect of the 'kick'.

Clay Court Conditioning

Clay court tennis is the most taxing on the body, requiring you to have perhaps the highest levels of physical fitness of all surfaces. Points and matches tend to be longer, forcing you to have incredible levels of physical endurance, and the slow nature will lead to you having to generate a lot of the pace for yourself. Flexibility is also greatly important because sliding can lead to an over-extension of the muscles. Exercises to develop these attributes can be found in Chapter 8.

The most challenging aspect of clay court tennis is the high contact point. Hitting with power and control when the ball is at shoulder height requires great strength in the shoulders, and this can be developed by attaching a resistance band to a fixed object about knee height. You must pull the other end of the band above shoulder height as if hitting a forehand or a backhand. This will develop the power and strength in the shoulder and help you to generate pace when the ball is up high. You must work especially hard to develop strength in your lower body and endurance levels to cope with the demands of playing on clay.

Developing shoulder strength using resistance bands

Adapting Your Game to Grass Courts

Grass courts are notoriously difficult to play on because they have a low COF and COR (see Chapter 5). As a result, the ball skids through the court faster than almost any hard court and considerably faster than all clay courts. The surface can also be very slippery and the bounces are rather unpredictable, largely due to the fact that the spin stays on the ball as it bounces. When playing on grass, you will have less time to prepare for your

Djokovic celebrates an emotional victory at Wimbledon 2014 following a breathtaking display of grass-court tennis

The unpredictable nature of grass courts requires players to finish the points off early with a volley

groundstrokes and the points are generally shorter, favouring fast, powerful players who play close to the baseline with 'flat', penetrative groundstrokes.

The 'play' of a grass court will actually change considerably depending on the weather, length of grass and, to some extent, the actual condition of the court. Grass courts at the start of the season tend to be softer because they have not yet been used. As a result, the bounces will be lower than at the end of the season when the grass is short and the surface has been hardened by the weather. Grass courts will actually slow down over the course of the season because the exposed dirt plays like clay. It is for this reason that Rafael Nadal's game becomes much more effective during the second week of the Wimbledon Championships, when the courts become harder, dustier and suit his topspin game while allowing him more grip to move.

The major disadvantage of the grass surface is maintenance: the condition of the soil and the length of the grass can affect the movement of the ball and so the surface must be constantly monitored and well cared for. As a result, AstroTurf or 'artificial grass' is often used as it is a cheaper and easier-to-maintain alternative to traditional grass in the United Kingdom. These courts are designed to mimic the 'play' of natural lawn tennis courts, although the balls tend to bounce slightly faster and higher on artificial than real grass.

Game Style

Grass courts today are not what they once were. Once upon a time, the serve–volley game as used by Boris Becker, John McEnroe and Pete Sampras was the hallmark of successful grass-court play. Spectators were fortunate to witness a single baseline rally at the All England Club in the 1990s and it was the area closest to the net, not the baseline, that became bald and worn over the course of the fortnight. The prevailing feeling was that only a few players could succeed on the rapid-fire grass surface: those with big first serves and good skills at the net.

In 2001, the All England Club ripped out the old grass and started to use ryegrass seed to increase the durability of the courts. This change marked the end of an era and the beginning of the end for traditional serve and volley tactics. The result is that all types of players can now enjoy success on the lawns of SW19, including Rafael Nadal, the perennial 'clay court specialist'.

While grass continues to remain the fastest commonly used surface in the world today, the serve–volley game has been replaced by one that is played predominantly from the baseline. In their 2002 Wimbledon final at the All England Club, neither Lleyton Hewitt nor David Nalbandian constructed a single serve–volley point despite a combined 150 notable opportunities.

Nonetheless, grass-court practices remain unique to the surface and you must learn to adapt your game style to the nature of the court if you are to succeed.

The Serve

Looking at their respective technical attributes, it is no surprise that Pete Sampras and Roger Federer are the most successful grass-court players in the history of the game. The serve plays an especially important role in determining the outcome of points on grass, and it is difficult to think of two players who have been more dominant on their serve than these two modern greats.

American legend Pete Sampras dominated the Wimbledon tournament in the 1990s largely as a result of his huge first service. Simply put: he was the model of serving perfection, possessing a consistent, fluid motion that generated great racket-head speed to hit with unparalleled power and accuracy. At times, Sampras' serve appeared unbreakable; he was broken only four times in 131 service games throughout his seven Wimbledon finals, and he frequently led the tour in terms of 'aces' hit. His second serve was equally, if not more, spectacular than his first, generating great amounts of spin and 'kick' to increase consistency and prevent his opponent from getting into any sort of rhythm.

Although not quite in the same league as Sampras', Federer's service is one of the most underrated shots in the game. His serve represents a foundation upon which the Swiss dominated the lawns of SW19 for over a decade. It is not the speed at which Federer delivers the ball, but the variety and disguise that make it impossible for his opponent to anticipate the incoming shot. Federer holds the record for most aces served in a Grand Slam final (2009 v. against Andy Roddick) and he uses his consistent, accurate delivery to set himself up to dominate the point.

One of the standout aspects of Murray's game in winning the 2013 Wimbledon crown was the quality of his first serve. He made 65 per cent of his first serves and won 79 per cent of points behind it throughout the tournament. Defending on grass is very difficult and the advantage lies firmly with the player dominating the point. You must use your serve to put yourself in an attacking position from the very start of the rally.

On grass, especially freshly cut grass, the ball stays lower than on other surfaces, causing the ball to slide through the court. The slice serve is particularly effective and can be used to provoke a short, defensive return. Players can normally find great joy by serving into the returner's body, especially with the slice serve.

Similarly, the flat serve, if it is hit hard and accurately enough, tends to slide through the court. Andy Murray, for example, changes his serve considerably on grass to go 'flat' down the 'T' more often than not. 'Kick' serves can be used to greater effect as the grass surface hardens and the dirt becomes exposed after some wear and tear.

The serve-volley combination following a slice serve

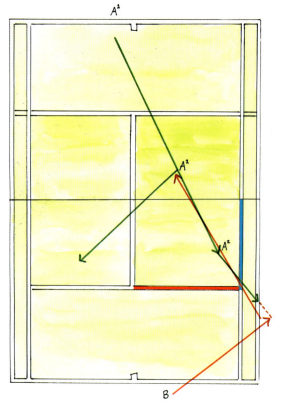

Serve–volley

Expelled from the modern game maybe, but the serve–volley combination can still have an important role to play in the outcome of a match, particularly on grass. Roger Federer, a serve–volleyer by trade, has used the tactic throughout his career as a surprise or to recover after a physically taxing baseline rally. Andy Murray, similarly adept around the net, uses the tactic to keep his opponents guessing.

The easiest way to practise the serve–volley is on a cross-court half-court where you (player A – the server) must serve–volley to your opponent (player B – the returner). Your practice partner will practise their cross-court return and you will develop your serve–volley skills under controlled conditions in which the ball is coming straight back in your direction. You are also advised to play conditioned sets in which you must serve–volley at least once each game or even play a complete set where you must serve–volley on each first serve.

A popular combination is to approach the net following a well-placed slice served out wide. If executed well, this will stay low, dragging the returner (B) off court (*red line*) and generating a weak return allowing you to move forward (A1–A2) to place the volley into the open court. The quality of the slice serve is largely determined by where the ball exits the court. A quality slice serve will actually cross the tramline (*blue*) as opposed to the end of the service box (*red*).

Movement

As BBC analyst Mark Petchey has said, 'Learning how to move [on grass] is an art'.[4] Grass courts are slippery and you must lower your centre of gravity using small, fast adjustment steps instead of one long slide to get into position for a groundstroke. These courts also tend to give uneven bounces and you will be forced to make quick final adjustments to swing pattern and footwork.

Proper physical conditioning goes a long way to developing this movement. The ball tends to stay very low and you will need to develop strength in your lower body if you are to bend at the knees while remaining stable at the core to execute a controlled groundstroke. You can develop this strength using medicine ball rotations, in which you hold a medicine ball in the lunging position (see Chapter 8) before rotating to the forehand and backhand side.

These movement patterns can also be practised by tying a piece of elastic cord around your knees to prevent your legs from coming too far apart when you move. Then, have balls fed slowly to either your backhand or forehand.

The idea is simple: the band encourages short, sharp adjustment steps by preventing you from lunging or stretching for the ball. With practice, you should attempt the same footwork pattern without the cord in place. Your aim is to develop a habit of using short steps in place of long strides.

The low bounce on a grass court forces players to bend their knees

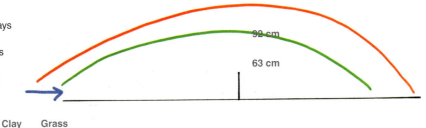

Rafael Nadal plays closer to the baseline and hits flatter on grass (*green*) than on clay (*red*)

Clay   Grass

Flat Penetrative Groundstrokes

The topspin game certainly reigns supreme in the modern age but players will 'flatten' their strokes to suit the characteristics of the grass court. Rafael Nadal, for example, will position himself about 1 m (approx. 4 ft) closer to the baseline and reduce his net clearance from approximately 92 cm (approx. 36 inches) to 63 cm (approx. 24 inches) when he moves from clay to grass between the French Open (*red*) and Wimbledon (*green*). This allows him to cut off the angles available to the opponent and hit groundstrokes that relate to the physical forces created by the court.

The skill of stepping up to the baseline and hitting a 'flatter' ground-stroke is most easily practised by placing a line of cones approximately 1 m (approx. 3 ft) behind the baseline, behind which you cannot step. This forces you to step into the court to take the ball on the rise, taking time off your opponent and helping you to naturally hit through the court with aggression. The position of the cones can be adjusted according to your level.

Advanced players can also place another line of cones running approximately 1 m (approx. 4 ft) inside the baseline. If your opponent's ball lands before this line (*red zone*), you must step forward into the shot and attack the ball on the rise. This battle – the topspin player hitting deep (Nadal) versus the player looking to pounce early on any short ball (Djokovic) – has been showcased most accurately in the long-standing Djokovic–Nadal rivalry.

You can practise hitting the 'flatter' shot by using this drill (*see below*).

The 'tempo' drill as detailed on page 145 can also be used to practise this skill.

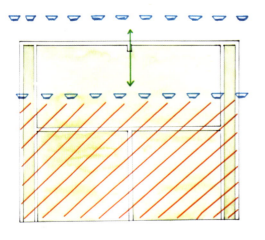

Stepping up to the short ball

DRILL: *Hitting a 'Flatter' shot*
Tie across the court a rope that runs approximately 6 ft above the net. Now practise hitting the balls beneath the top, while keeping the ball *above* the net.

Drop Shots/Drop Volleys

These can be used to great effect on the grass. The area closest to the net tends to be soft because players rarely use it. As a result, a well-placed drop shot will bounce very low, leaving your opponent with very little time to reach the ball. Combined with the slippery nature of the court, this makes drop shots a particularly potent weapon on grass.

Grass Court Training

Grass court tennis is about making your opponent react to you. The player with the initiative in a grass court rally should normally win the point, and the best players will be ruthless whenever they have an opportunity to attack the ball.

Rafael Nadal hits a forehand from on top of the baseline on the grass courts of SW19

When playing on grass you must look to win the point at the earliest opportunity by pouncing on returns and short balls as soon as there is a reasonable opportunity. The footwork and anticipation required to attack a short ball can be practised using the following drill.

DRILL: *The Mid-Court Ball*

With you (B) and your practice partner (A) positioned on opposite baselines, A feeds a short/mid-court weak ball to you to give you the opportunity to move forward and attack. At this point, your goal is to win the point as quickly as possible using controlled aggression to the corners, forcing A off balance.

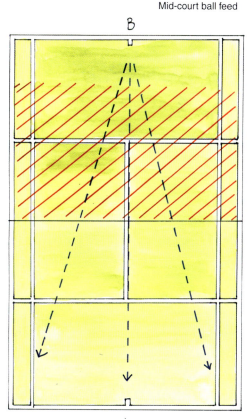

Mid-court ball feed

It is important that A adds variety with the feed, hitting with topspin and slice, some low, and some high, to ensure that you practise attacking a range of different mid-court balls. This drill can be executed on an open court, but skilled players can increase the intricacy by carrying out on a half-court, either down the line or cross-court.

An important consideration for you (B) is which type of shot you should follow to the net. In the past, 'flat' balls worked most favourably due to the slippery nature of the court, but topspin has become more effective as the court

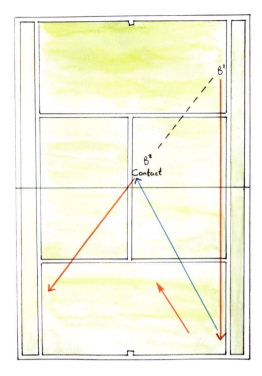

A nicely placed aggressive slice backhand down the line (*red line*) gives you time to get to the net (B1–B2) and cut off the angles

pace has slowed down. It is slice, however, that can be used to great effect because the evolution of the game has led to players adopting more extreme grips on their groundstrokes, making it harder to attack a low incoming ball. A nicely placed aggressive 'slice' backhand down the line (*red line*) also gives you time to approach the net (B1–B2) and cut off the angles (*see diagram, left*). Practise the 'slice' approach by adapting the Mid-Court Ball Drill on page 83 (i.e. you can only come to the net following a 'slice' ball).

The approach shot should almost always be hit down the line, especially on grass where it will stay low and slide through the

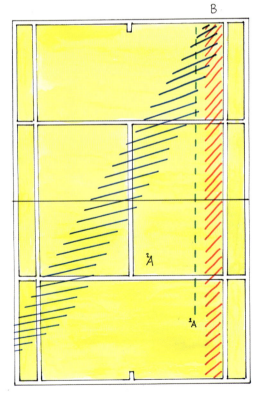

Approaching down the line (*red channel*) leaves your opponent with a tough passing shot (*blue channel*)

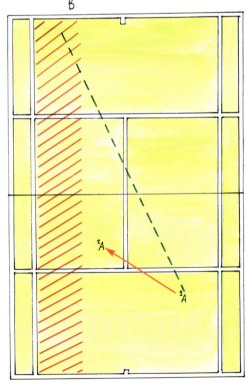

Hitting an approach shot cross-court gives your opponent lots of space to hit a passing shot (*red*)

court. The reason for this is simple (*see both diagrams at the bottom of page 84*).

Suppose that you (player A) hit a groundstroke down the line before following the ball to the net (*see diagram on page 84, below left*). Your opponent (B) can only pass you at the net, either by squeezing the ball down the line (*red channel*) or attempting to pass cross-court (*blue channel*), which necessarily involves the ball passing across your body at the net. Both options favour you (A).

Alternatively, should you hit the approach shot cross-court (*see diagram on page 84, bottom right*), you will leave a gaping open space for your opponent to hit into down the line (*red channel*).

Return of Serve

It is no surprise that there are fewer breaks of serve at Wimbledon than on the clay at Roland Garros. The fast nature of the grass court favours the server and it can be very difficult for the returner to do anything with quality service delivery. For this reason, neutralizing the first serve should be your priority as a returner on grass.

Neutralizing a fast, well-placed service is most easily executed using an 'open' racket face to 'slice' the ball back into court, similar to the technique used on a volley. The aim should be to place the ball as close to the baseline as possible in the centre of the court (*red zone*) to reduce any angles available to your opponent (*see diagram on right*). Returning a slow ball to the forehand or backhand side of the server will leave you as the returner vulnerable to more acute angles than returning down the centre of the court.

'Reading' the serve is a skill that you as a player cannot practise per se, but that will develop with match experience. It happens deep within your subconscious as your brain picks up on the small idiosyncrasies of the server's motion to anticipate the placement of the serve. Lower-level players may have a more obvious 'give', which allows you as the returner to anticipate the placement of the serve, but at the higher levels these adjustments will be too small to be registered.

However, you can work on your agility and reactions to improve your grass-court return. This is most easily done by reducing the time you have to react. To do this, your practice partner should serve at you from the service

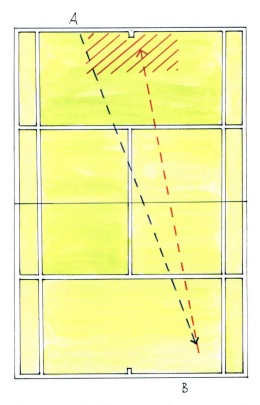

On grass, you should look to neutralize your opponent's first serve (*blue*) on grass by getting the ball deep into the middle of the court (*red zone*)

line from across the net. This will shorten the distance between server and returner and minimize the time available for you to react.

Over time, as these reactions develop, you can look to be more aggressive with these returns. You must also be aware of positioning yourself too far behind the baseline – a move that will work to neutralize the efficacy of the exercise. The best returners – Agassi, Djokovic and Murray – have trained their ability to take the ball early. Indeed, in his book *Open*, Agassi (perhaps the best returner the game has ever seen) describes how he honed his returns using a similar drill with help from the fearsome ball machine dubbed 'The Dragon'.

Shortening the Backswing

If you have a long, slow backswing, you can struggle for timing on grass because the fast nature of the surface minimizes the time available to complete your preparations. To adapt, you must work on increasing your racket-head acceleration and reducing the length of your backswing. The simplest drill to develop these skills requires the assistance of a coach or a willing practice partner.

DRILL: *Reducing the Length of Your Backswing*
Position yourself on the baseline as if to swing through to strike a shot. Your coach or partner must then drop ten balls consecutively out in front of you to your forehand or backhand side. The speed at which the balls are dropped depends upon your ability, but it is important that you are rushed in your preparations for the stroke. This drill forces you to speed up your backswing and execute an abbreviated groundstroke.

To develop the physical element of this shot, you can work on the fast-twice muscle fibres in your pectoral and shoulder muscles. This will ensure that the racket-head acceleration remains high despite an abbreviation in the racket-head take-back.

DRILL: *Accelerating Your Swing with Reduced Take-back 1*
Attach an elastic resistance band to a fixed object at approximately waist-to-shoulder height. Holding onto the other end of the band while standing in the forehand position, practise accelerating your swing with a reduced take-back.

It is important that you discipline yourself not to take the arm too far behind your body. Focus on developing a fast, powerful movement with a shorter backswing.

DRILL: *Accelerating Your Swing with Reduced Take-back 2*
On court or in an indoor open space, complete a fully executed swing with the head cover attached to your racket.

This will increase the air resistance of the racket and help you to develop the muscles used to drive your racket forward. Aim to complete this exercise before each training session.

Adapting Your Game to Hard Courts

Acrylic courts are the most common type of hard courts found today. They will play similarly to asphalt and concrete courts, and the following will apply to all courts of this nature. Hard courts are also the most used courts on the professional tennis tour and offer the most consistent bounces.

Play

Acrylic hard courts are made from a flat base of asphalt or concrete, layered with a shock pad/levelling coat of crushed rubber, sometimes from old tyres or ground-up tennis balls, then topped with one or more layers of acrylic paint mixed with sand. Not all hard courts are created equal, and the composition and application method of the acrylic material has a direct influence on the playing characteristics of any particular court.

Although some court manufacturers have softened and slowed down the common hard court, the speed at which the ball comes through these surfaces will normally sit somewhere between a clay and a grass court. While grass courts will slow down as they become used, hard courts tend to become faster as the abrasive surface is worn down by the soles of players' shoes. The height of the bounce is normally higher than on grass but lower than clay because the smooth surface does not force the ball in an upwards direction.

On this type of surface, you will benefit from a firm footing, allowing you to change direction far more easily than on the slippery grass or clay. As a result, it can be difficult to hit winners and matches are normally long, gruelling, physically demanding affairs.

Hard Court Tactics

'Hard' is very much an all-encompassing term and will include a wide range of courts with varying speeds and bounce heights. With this in mind, there is no universal approach applicable to playing on all hard courts because players are required to adapt their tactics to fit the specific nature of the hard court on which they are playing.

Players, for example, will employ different strategies at the Australian Open and the US Open even though, strictly speaking, these are classified by the ITF as 'hard court' events. The 'Deco Turf 2' courts at Flushing

Meadows are harder and faster than the luminous two-toned blue courts of the Australian Open, which traditionally play more slowly like a clay court, thus favouring players who construct the point. Using the Court Pace Rating system as detailed on page 64, the Melbourne courts average approximately thirty-four points, increasing to approximately thirty-seven after heavy play, while the 'Deco Turf 2' in New York hits closer to forty.

Generally speaking, therefore, hard courts tend to favour the aggressive baseliner. Almost all outdoor hard courts are too slow to win with serve–volley tactics and so most players opt for controlled, powerful groundstrokes and big serving to move their opponents around the court to either force an error or create the space for a 'winner'.

There is also a great emphasis on serve and return; serving well on hard courts can be a great source of cheap, easy points. Faster, smoother hard courts will favour a 'flat' or 'slice' serve while more abrasive, slower hard courts favour 'kick' serves. Indeed, a big part of Rafael Nadal's success on the hard courts has come after he worked hard in the off-season to increase his average service delivery from 100 mph to approximately 115 mph.

Drop shots on hard courts should be used less frequently than on grass and clay because the ball tends to bounce higher. The traction of a hard court allows you to push off faster and arrive at the drop shot more easily.

The hard nature of these courts make them very physically taxing on the body and you should work hard to condition your body for the stresses and strains of playing on this surface. Exercises to develop this strength and prevent injuries can be found in Chapter 7.

Inside-Out/Inside-In Forehand

The inside-out/inside-in forehand is an incredible weapon used by all the game's elite. Not only does it allow you to hit with a greater range of angles, you can also disguise the direction of shot until the very moment you actually strike the ball. The inside-out forehand is used to great effect on hard courts because most are sufficiently slow to allow players to work their way around the backhand, yet sufficiently fast enough for the shot to accelerate through the court.

The first thing to note with the inside-out/inside-in forehand is the importance of creating space between yourself and the ball. Striking a penetrative shot requires you to put your body weight through the ball and you must create space by moving accordingly.

Moving directly across the baseline (*green*) can leave you 'jammed up' and so you are advised to move in a 'C' shape to get behind the ball and create the necessary space (*blue*). This movement pattern is not necessary when moving into the court to a short ball.

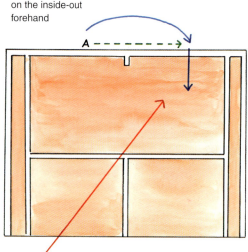

'C' shape movement on the inside-out forehand

Adapting Your Game to Indoor Courts

Having won an incredible thirteen Grand Slam titles and more than twenty-six Masters 1000 titles, Rafael Nadal has become one of the most successful players in the history of the sport. He is yet, however, to win his first professional indoor title. Indoor tennis is very different to outdoor tennis and the 'play' of indoor court surfaces does not match up with the Spaniard's finely-tuned weapons.

Tennis is an outdoor sport and it should be played outside wherever possible. It is inevitable, however, that circumstances will sometimes dictate that the game be played indoors or under a roof to avoid the elements.

Djokovic jumps to hit a backhand at the 2010 US Open at Flushing Meadows

Not all indoor facilities are the same; some are permanent structures with insulated metal walls and others are temporary, inflated structures commonly referred to as 'bubbles'.

These two indoor environments can differ from each other significantly. Common indoor surfaces include hard, carpet and wood, which further influences the 'play' of the particular court. There are, however, a number of important considerations to consider when adapting to indoor play.

Surfaces: Fast/Low Bounce

Indoor tennis is played on a variety of surfaces. 'Rubberized' courts consist of a thin piece of rubber stretched over piece of concrete. These courts and carpet are the fastest courts available, causing the ball to stay low and slide through the court, and you must adapt your game accordingly by stepping up to the baseline and taking the ball on the rise

'Topspin' players will find these courts almost impossible to play on because their fast nature neutralizes the spin, allowing their opponent to strike the ball at a comfortable height within their strike zones.

Indoor hard and clay courts tend to play a little bit more slowly, but noticeably faster than if they were located outdoors.

Court Space: Angles

The space on indoor courts is normally far more limited than on outdoor courts. Indoor courts are commonly divided by nets designed to prevent balls from rolling onto adjacent courts and you can use this to your advantage by hitting short, sharp angles to draw your opponent from the baseline. If executed well, these shots will normally hit the side-netting before your opponent can reach them.

Serve: Flat/Slice

Serve 'flat' or 'slice' with the first attempt and use a 'slice' serve for the second. These serves will slide through the court and drag the returner out of position. In contrast, the smooth surface does not lend itself to the 'kick' serve.

Groundstrokes: Flat

Fast indoor tennis courts favour the aggressor, and groundstrokes should be hit hard and 'flat'. Playing a consistent, topspin-based baseline game is almost impossible so you are strongly advised to end points with an approach shot and volley at the first opportunity.

That said, it is important that you find the right balance between aggression and consistency. Fast indoor courts do not give players the licence to hit winners off every ball so you must be careful not to 'overplay'. You should be consistent enough from the baseline to work the opportunity to attack and be aggressive enough to step to win the point when you have the chance.

Noise

Background noise becomes more pronounced and noticeable on indoor courts and it can be distracting. Focus on the match and use the techniques mentioned in Chapter 8.

Lighting

Different indoor courts use different forms of lighting, so allow yourself time to adapt to your environment.

You will rapidly develop a natural affinity to the court surface on which you grew up and this surface will also shape the style of play that you adopt. Spaniards, for example, tend to favour the Western grip to maximize topspin, which suits the clay courts that they grow up competing and training on. The French, on the other hand, tend to train indoors and therefore favour flatter, more aggressive shot-making.

While you must continue to develop your skills on your preferred surface, it is important that you also learn to adapt your game to different conditions. Adaptation, therefore, is key and the first step is learning how the different surfaces 'play'.

After reading this chapter, you should now be clear as to which changes need to be made to your game.

CHAPTER FIVE

Choosing the Right Equipment

Babolat to Dunlop; Dunlop to Tecnifibre; Tecnifibre to Wilson ... while I fully understood that the equipment I was using was influencing my performance, I was often overwhelmed by the advice offered by colleagues in the game.

'You should use this to get more spin.'

'Use this for more power.'

'This is the best string on the market.'

'He uses this string and racket – you should, too!'

Do shaped strings *really* add more spin to the game? Should I string higher or lower on clay? Am I using the right racket?

Some days I felt good, some days I felt bad. And it was so easy to place any blame on the equipment I had in hand because I never quite grasped a complete understanding of how weight, balance point and string tension impacted on my performance in the game I was trying to perfect. The wide variety and choice of tennis equipment can be bewildering, and a lack of confidence in the equipment I was using was actually damaging the game I was playing.

Some players will spend hours on court with a coach honing their forehand but will spend very little time selecting the right equipment to suit their game. But it is important to understand that tennis is a game of precision and the equipment you use can be highly influential on your performance. If you are going to take your tennis seriously, you must begin by also selecting your equipment seriously.

While the following information should certainly be used to guide your choice of equipment, it is important to recognize that you must go and find out what actually works for you personally. 'It's like cooking,' says Joe Heyott, professional stringer on the ATP tour, 'I cannot tell the player what feels good for them. They must find out what feels good for them: they must find out what their taste is. My job as a stringer is to finely tune it.'

The Key Factors When Choosing a Racket

The tennis racket is the most important piece of equipment for any player. The leading brands throw millions of pounds a year at marketing their products and paying the top professionals to appear on court as if they have selected one of the rackets that sit comfortably on the shelves at the average sports retailer.

However, the specific rackets used by the world's elite are not actually readily available to the public; each racket is individually tailored to suit a particular player and then painted to resemble one of the brand's mainstream rackets. Rafael Nadal's rackets, for example, have long been painted to resemble the then current Babolat AeroPro Drive Cortex model to drive sales of that particular frame. With this in mind, it is important that you select your racket according to what feels good for *you* on court, and not because your idol would appear to have chosen it.

Under many national coaching regulations, including those of the LTA, coaches are not actually required to understand racket and string technologies in order to qualify as a coach – and yet it is they who are advising the majority of players on which equipment they should use. To avoid being misinformed, you should go to a qualified racket technician who can advise on which equipment you should use depending on your individual playing style and preferences.

The modern market is scattered with a huge range of rackets of different specifications, the details of which can normally be found printed on the frame or on the majority of online tennis retailer websites. While you are advised to read racket reviews online or in magazines, you should bear in mind that the most important factor when selecting any racket is how it feels in your hand, and this is something that is completely unique to you as an individual. In short, there really is no substitute for actually trying the racket out on court.

There are several key specifications that you must consider when selecting a frame:

- Weight and balance point (swing weight)
- Head size
- Length
- Frame stiffness
- String pattern
- Grip size
- Width of frame

Weight and Balance Point

The two most influential attributes in determining the performance of a racket are its balance point and weight.

The balance point of a racket is the point where the racket is equally balanced between the head and the handle. The average length of a frame is around 27 inches (68.5 cm), which means that a tennis racket with a balance point of 13½ inches (34.2 cm) is evenly balanced in the middle of the racket frame. Tennis rackets can be classified as either 'neutrally balanced', 'head heavy' or 'head light', depending on whether the balance point is, respectively, in the middle of the racket, closer to the head or closer to the handle. The more severe the positioning of the balance point in either direction, the more 'head heavy' or 'head light' the racket will feel.

Weight is measured in grammes (g) or ounces (oz) and represents the weight of the frame, excluding strings and any other modifications. Contrary to what many believe and all other things being equal, heavier rackets are more powerful than lighter rackets because more energy is transferred to the ball on contact.

However, while this is true in theory, it is only partly true in practice, the caveat being that a player may not be able to swing a heavy racket as fast as a light racket. It takes more energy to accelerate a heavier frame and so, for out-of-shape, recreational players, a heavy racket may not actually allow them to hit the ball any harder. On the other hand, advanced players with sufficient conditioning to maintain racket-head acceleration will feel an increase in power should they switch to a heavier frame. Heavier rackets will also feel more stable when the ball strikes the strings.

It is also important to note that weight and balance point are inextricably linked because it is the distribution of said weight that influences how heavy a racket will feel when hitting a groundstroke. To give an example: you can determine the weight of a racket by pointing the head down to the ground. However, if you hold the racket parallel to the ground at the handle, a 'head light' racket will actually feel lighter than a 'head heavy' racket because the weight is distributed closer to the body. Generally speaking, as the weight increases, the more head light a frame will become.

With the above in mind, the most important factor when considering the weight and balance point of any particular frame is actually 'swing weight', i.e. how heavy does the racket feel when it is swung? Very

V Head heavy

13.5 Neutral

ʌ Head light

Weight and balance point are highly influential on the feel of a tennis racket

The swing-weight can be determined by swinging the racket

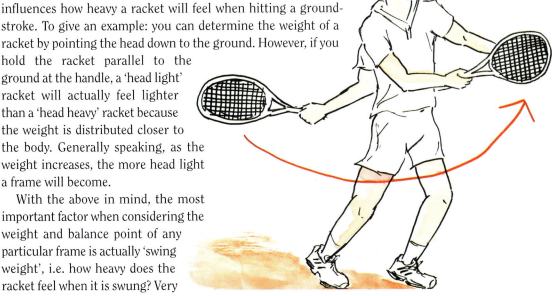

Stability

Power

Sweet Spot

Forgiveness

Big Head Size

Manoeuvrability

Control

The head
size affects the
performance of
the racket

Small Head Size

rarely is a racket's swing weight actually printed on the racket itself, but it can normally be found on the manufacturer's website or via online retailers.

Advanced players will normally select a head-light racket to maximize manoeuvrability in the knowledge that they can generate their own power with efficient stroke mechanics.

Head size

Roger Federer is unique, both in the way he plays and the equipment he uses. While the modern game has been shaped by light, over-sized frames used by many of the top players, the Swiss was celebrated for his continued use of a 90-inch^2 head (approx. 612 cm^2), by far the smallest on the professional tour. At the beginning of the 2014 season, it was confirmed that Federer had changed to a 98-inch^2 (approx. 632 cm^2) head for the foreseeable future to enable him to keep up with the ever-increasing power and spin that his peers are now able to generate.

The head size has a great influence on the performance of any particular frame. The rule is quite simple: a larger head makes it easier for you to hit the ball, offers you more rotational stability and marginally more power. The larger head also allows more forgiveness on any off-centre hits. It does not, however, actually increase the size of the 'sweet spot'.

The flip side of a large head size is that it can begin to compromise manoeuvrability and control. 'Most of the players feel that anything above 100 inches^2 (645 cm^2) causes the ball to fly off the strings a little too much and they begin to lose control,' says Colin Triplow, Master Racket Technician.

Advanced players are advised to choose a head-size between 95- and 100-inch^2 (612– 45 cm^2).

Length

The frame length, traditionally measured in inches, is the length of the entire racket (including the handle). The standard length of an adult racket is 27 inches but most manufacturers will offer a (+) option which is 0.5–1 inch longer than the standard model. The legal limit for tournament play is 29 inches. Interestingly, the 2012 Wimbledon Ladies' Singles Champion, Marion Bartoli, played with a 28-inch racket manufactured by Prince especially for her.

All other things being equal, a longer frame provides you with more reach on groundstrokes, added leverage on serves and slightly more power than standard length rackets. If you're an advanced junior, you may want a junior or youth-sized racket of 26 inches. If you are especially tall, you may benefit from the extra length.

Frame Stiffness

Measured in 'RA', frame stiffness is how much the frame flexes on contact with the ball and it affects three things: power, control and comfort. The majority of modern rackets fall somewhere between 57 and 72 RA (the higher the number indicating a stiffer frame). While the tension of the strings in the racket will impact the trajectory of the ball, the power of the racket is determined by frame stiffness.

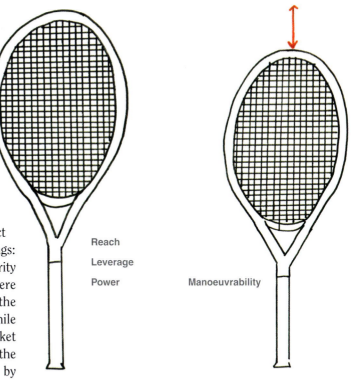

Reach

Leverage

Power

Manoeuvrability

For long periods, it was commonly assumed that the energy used to deform the frame on contact was actually transferred to the ball as it returns to its original shape – in a trampoline-like effect. But research using slow-motion cameras has indicated that the ball is not actually on the strings long enough for this to occur. Stiffer frames, therefore, are actually *more* powerful because less energy is absorbed in deformation when the ball and racket collide. As a result, more energy is directly transferred from the string bed to the ball.

Flexible frames are thought to offer more control. The theory is that because the ball and the racket are in contact for a longer period of time, you will normally enjoy a more complete 'feeling' on contact. In reality, however, you may prefer a stiffer racket because the bending of the frame influences the directional control and results in a less responsive sensation. It is a matter of personal preference and it is for these reasons that you must *always* test rackets with varying stiffness to determine your preference.

With regards to comfort, it has long been thought that players with a history of upper body injuries should select a flexible frame to soften any impact. In practice, however, the vibrations caused by striking the ball are larger and continue for longer with a flexible frame and so many players will actually protect their upper bodies by choosing a stiffer frame to dampen any vibrations. This, as with many other racket specifications, is a matter of what feels comfortable for you.

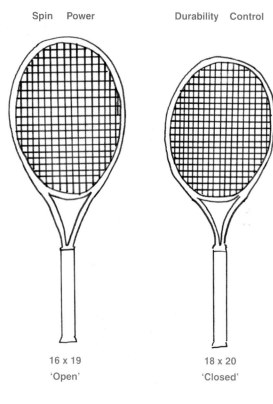

Spin   Power   Durability   Control

16 x 19   18 x 20
'Open'   'Closed'

An 'open' string pattern (*above left*) generally offers more power but less durability than a 'closed' string pattern (*above right*)

String Pattern

The string pattern of a tennis racket is how many 'main' (vertical) and 'cross' (horizontal) strings the racket has. An 'open' string pattern (i.e. 16 main × 19 cross) differs from a 'closed' string pattern (i.e. 18 × 20) in three ways: access to spin, durability and string bed stiffness.

SPIN

Rackets with an 'open' pattern generate more spin than rackets with a 'closed' pattern, all other things being equal. This is because the extra space in between the strings allows the ball to embed itself more deeply, increasing the friction as you brush up the back of the ball.

Frames in Prince's 'Extreme String Pattern' (ESP) range have a 14 × 16 or 16 × 16 string pattern designed to maximize this spin and, as the game continues to develop and players look to produce more spin, the average string pattern may become more 'open' still.

DURABILITY

The price you pay for spin is reduced durability. 'Open' patterns give strings greater freedom to move and 'rub' against each other, which causes them to weaken and eventually snap. This rise in breakages through selection of an 'open' pattern can substantially increase costs over the course of the season. You can minimize this expense by using a thicker gauge or more durable string material.

STRING BED STIFFNESS

Strung at the same tension, an 'open' string pattern will not feel as 'tight' as a closed pattern. This is particularly true when the ball is struck slightly outside the sweet spot. An 'open' string pattern will normally provide more power and less control by deflecting more on impact than an equivalent racket with a 'closed' pattern.

Although a factor worthy of consideration, you must be cautious of using string pattern as an alternative to technique development. With good technique, you should be able to hit with control and spin using a 'closed' string pattern, but should select an 'open' string pattern to maximize the effect. 'An open string pattern will maximize and complement a topspin game, but it will not do it all for you,' says Colin Triplow, Master Racket Technician. 'If you have a flat game it won't magically develop topspin.'

Grip Size

The grip size is the circumference of the handle and can normally be found printed on the bottom of the racket or inside the racket throat. Although this will have a very obvious impact on the 'feel' of any particular frame, it is normally one of the last specifications to be considered when selecting a racket to use.

On European shores, rackets come in seven recognized grip sizes (0–6) while in the USA the sizes range from 4 inches to 4¾ inches. These are, in fact, exactly the same. The European numbering system corresponds to the number of eighths of an inch above four inches. For example, grip size 2 is 2/8 (¼) inches, grip size 3 is 4 and 3/8 inches, grip size 4 is 4 and 4/8 (½) inches etc.

Choosing a grip size is a matter of personal preference. Developments in the game over the past decade have seen players switch to smaller grip sizes to increase the manoeuvrability of the frame. If in doubt, you should always elect for the smaller option because the grip can always be made larger. Prolonged use of a grip that is too small can cause problems with your elbow and upper arm.

The grip size can normally be found on the bottom of the handle – players today are moving towards rackets with smaller handles

Width of the Frame

The thicker the width of the frame, the higher the power and the lower the control. Advanced players tend to choose a thinner frame to maximize control because they can generate their own power.

Selecting a Racket

So, just how exactly are you supposed to find a racket that suits your game? The answer is trial and error. This information will not choose the racket for you, but it will naturally help limit the number of options and will allow you to make informed decisions as to which frames will suit you, based on how different specifications affect the play of a racket. Selecting a tennis racket is a big commitment and the most important consideration of them all, beyond all the numbers printed on the throat of the racket, is 'feeling'.

'What matters most is that the player feels comfortable with the racket in hand. It doesn't matter what the racket is,' says former ATP player, Daniel Kiernan. 'I switched to the newer model of my racket at one point in my career and it was only when I switched back that I was successful again. I just felt comfortable with that racket in my hand, and that is what matters.'

Most specialist tennis shops will have a racket demo programme available. It is important that you check the strings in the demo racket because a low-quality or overly-used string-bed will give a very poor representation of how the actual racket will play. Each racket should be tested over at least four training sessions before any decision is made because it can take a while for the body to adapt to any new frame.

You must also bear in mind that the racket can be 'customized' (see below).

Maintaining and Replacing Rackets

Tennis rackets are expensive pieces of equipment and you must take care of them to ensure peak performance and longevity. Racket care is mostly common sense: for example, avoid throwing when frustrated, install fresh grips or over-grips as necessary to prevent it slipping out of your hand, and keep it out of the sun when not in use. Rackets should always be replaced at least once a year for competitive players, as even with proper care attention the frame will naturally become warped and worn.

Racket Customization

❛ We have over 300 players on our international team but no two players' rackets are exactly the same. They choose the basic frame and then we go on court with them and we make different prototypes depending on their 'feelings'. When we have the exact specifications that suit the player, we send the details off to Belgium and we customise, we change grips; whatever the player wants, we do it. ❜
GUILLAUME DUCRUET, *Sports Marketing Manager, Tecnifibre International*

Customization allows players to have their rackets tailored specifically to their individual needs. On a very basic level, it refers to selecting a string, but many players will take this further by changing the handle shape and altering the actual specifications of the frame itself. 'I am constantly looking to improve my game and this inevitably involves looking to add weights, remove weights and change my string bed to maximize my "feeling" on striking the ball,' says Dominic Inglot, World Number 34 Doubles player.

Which Modifications Should You Make?

The most commonly used methods of racket customization are:

- Weighting: increasing/decreasing weight
- Balancing: modifying the swing weight of the racket
- Grip shaving: increasing or decreasing grip size and the shape/size of the butt cap
- Grommets: replacing the plastic 'bumpers' on the frame to prevent unnecessary string breakages
- Vibration dampeners/racket protection

Some aspects of customization can be done very easily: replacing the grip, adding over-grips and fitting a vibration dampener do not require any professional expertise. Altering the specifications of the frame can be a lot more difficult and players should normally seek professional assistance. Racket technicians normally charge a flat fee for the work and advice they provide. As you become more experienced, you will normally be able to determine which modifications are required by the 'feelings' you have on the court. These alterations can void the warranty of the racket and cause irreparable damage to the frame if done incorrectly.

WEIGHTING

At the beginning of the 2012 season, Rafael Nadal reportedly decided to add weight to his racket, the Babolat Aero Pro GT. In its stock iteration, the Aero Pro Drive is 320 g (just over 11 oz), but the Spaniard added more weight with a view to increasing the speed of his service. From increasing torsional stability, raising the racket's sweet spot or counter-balancing a head-heavy racket to make it more head light, adding weights to the frame can be a vital modification for a player's game.

Adding Weights: Method

Lead tape is available in half-inch and quarter-inch widths. One inch of half-inch-wide lead tape weighs 0.5 g and 1 inch of ¼ inch lead tape weighs 0.25 g. You are advised to keep strips to a maximum of 6 inches in length,

You can add lead weights at 3 o'clock and 9 o'clock to increase the torsional stability of your frame

adding more layers if you wish to increase weight further. Pete Sampras, for example, was known to use 4–5 layers of lead tape positioned at '3 o'clock' and '9 o'clock' on his Wilson racket. The quarter-inch wide tape is recommended because it fits nicely between the existing grommets at the frame edge. You should always add tape to both sides of the racket to prevent an imbalance of the frame.

Applying weights is a reversible procedure and you must feel free to experiment with the placements and quantities of weights because it can take some time to find the desired specifications that suit you at a given time. However, you are advised to limit any modifications to small increments of 5 g to avoid injury or any damage to the frame.

Adding weights to the handle of the racket is more challenging because, with a small screwdriver, you must remove the grip and butt cap of the racket by dislodging the staples holding it in place. Although lead tape can be placed inside the handle, many players prefer

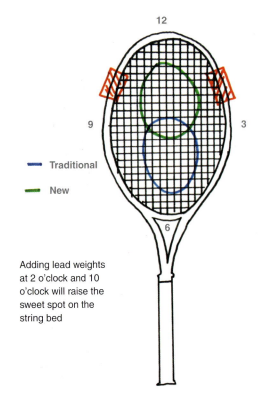

Traditional

New

Adding lead weights at 2 o'clock and 10 o'clock will raise the sweet spot on the string bed

to use fishing weights. These come in various shapes and sizes and can be purchased from specialist tennis shops or most fishing retailers. They can be inserted and held in position with foam, cardboard or another stuffing material.

Adding Weights: Position

Torsional stability (3 o'clock and 9 o'clock): Positioning lead weights at 3 o'clock and 9 o'clock on the frame will minimize your frame twisting on off-centre hits by pulling the 'sweet spot' out to the sides. Although your racket may feel less manoeuvrable, you should find an increase in power. Avoid adding weights at this position to manufactured 'head-heavy' rackets (*see diagram top left*).

Raising the sweet spot (10 o'clock and 2 o'clock): The sweet spot of a tennis racket is a small point, not an area, of the string bed where there is zero vibration when the ball strikes it. Many players will actually miss their sweet spot when striking the ball because traditional rackets have their sweet spots located in the centre/lower-centre of the string bed. This will result in irritating frame vibrations and low-power shots. You can check this by locating the green 'fuzz' after a training session with new balls or by stencilling to strings to find the wear pattern.

To amend this, you can raise the 'sweet spot' by positioning lead weights at 10 o'clock and 2 o'clock on the frame. Your shots hit high in the string bed will then become much more solid.

Increasing swing weight with minimal added weight (12 o'clock): You can increase the swing weight without any substantial increase in the overall weight of the frame by adding weights at 12 o'clock on the tip of your frame. Positioning weights here will also draw the sweet spot up the string-bed, making the racket more head heavy.

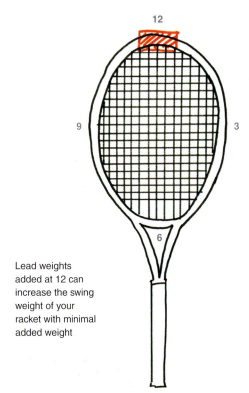

Lead weights added at 12 can increase the swing weight of your racket with minimal added weight

Increasing weight without changing balance (6 o'clock):
Adding weights at 6 o'clock or on the throat of the frame increases the weight of your racket without altering the balance point. This will increase swing weight, power and stability with only a minimal reduction in manoeuvrability. It is important to add weight gradually because this modification also has the effect of drawing the sweet spot down the string bed.

Increasing the weight without increasing swing weight (handle): To increase the weight of your frame without increasing swing weight, add weights in the handle of the racket. Swing weight remains the same because the weight is applied below the axis of rotation where swing weight is measured, but your frame will become more 'head light'. Most players will also report an increase in manoeuvrability.

OTHER RACKET MODIFICATIONS

You can further finely tune your rackets by tweaking the size of the grip and the butt cap. It is also common for players to select a frame with a smaller grip size to allow space for an over-grip because this provides extra moisture absorption, comfort and cushioning.

Reducing the size of the butt cap is supposed to increase the manoeuvrability of the frame and can be done by filing it down with a rasp. This modification is especially popular amongst players who play with a single-handed backhand. French top ten player, Richard Gasquet, for example, builds up the size of his butt cap because he prefers the solidarity it offers when changing from forehand to backhand and vice versa. In both cases, the grip must first be removed and then reinstalled.

Vibration dampeners can be added to the string bed to reduce the vibration transferred up through the player's arm, and most players will also note a change in the 'feel' of the racket on contact. It is a matter of personal preference: some complain of a lack of 'playability' when a dampener is installed, while others cannot play without one. Andre Agassi used to use his own personal version of a vibration dampener: an elastic band tied around the two central main strings of the rack.

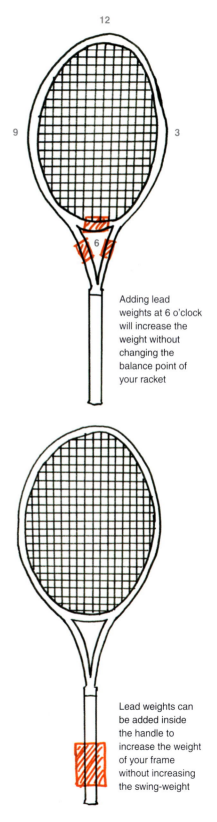

Adding lead weights at 6 o'clock will increase the weight without changing the balance point of your racket

Lead weights can be added inside the handle to increase the weight of your frame without increasing the swing-weight

Racket Matching

'If my racket is half a gramme off what I am used to, I can feel the difference; I am so sensitive to the feel. The difference in my game was immediate and obvious once I started to match my rackets. It felt great.' – DOMINIC INGLOT, *World Number 34 Doubles player*

Ever wondered why two supposedly 'identical' rackets somehow feel 'different'? When the manufacturer first makes the mould for a racket, it is fresh and free of any cracks. The first rackets to come out of this mould are the ones they give to their contracted players. But as production continues, air pockets are created and the rackets coming out of the mould become less and less consistent. As a result, 'identical' rackets sold at most retailers actually differ in their composition, and most manufacturers allow up to 5 per cent (15 g or 0.5 oz) difference on weight, swing weight and balance point in their frames. Only the stiffness of the frame remains constant.

As a competitive player, you must be sure that all your frames are exactly the same in their specifications. Racket-matching requires expensive, complicated equipment and is best done via a professional racket technician. The equipment does all the work by taking precise measurements of several racket and string specifications, including weight, balance, stiffness and swing weight. Once the figures have been accumulated, the necessary modifications can be made to ensure that the rackets are identical, i.e. they match. Although it is theoretically possible to racket-match without this specialist equipment, the process is extremely time-consuming and can lead to inaccuracies.

Strings and String Tensions

'The strings are responsible for at least 60 per cent of the performance of a particular racket frame. The racket is like the steering and the strings are the engine. It doesn't matter which frame a player chooses if they do not select the right strings to be used.' – ROGER DALTON, *Head Stringer at the Wimbledon Tennis Championships*

A well-chosen, quality frame with some personalized modifications is sure to improve your performance, but the tension, material and gauge of the string-bed will perhaps have an even more profound impact on your game. It is the combination of string and racket technology that produces maximum effects.

Almost all competitive-level rackets will come un-strung from the retailer. However, in the case that you purchase a racket with strings already installed, arrange a re-string because the tension will be unknown and the extreme temperatures in transit will have alienated the strings' performance characteristics.

String Performance Characteristics

Broadly speaking, there are three important performance characteristics that must be considered when selecting a string to use in your frames: 'playability', durability and tension stability.

Playability

'Playability' refers to how the racket 'feels' – or how the string 'plays'. Does the string feel crisp and firm or soft and spongy? The 'playability' will be determined primarily by the material of the string, the gauge and the construction.

Durability

'Durability' refers to how long the string will last before it snaps, and is usually sacrificed for 'playability'.

Tension Stability

The tension of a string-bed will reduce over time. Strings with high-tension stability hold tension better than strings with low-tension stability.

The String Material

Strings can be divided into two categories: natural gut and synthetic.

NATURAL GUT

In 1874 tennis rackets were all strung with natural gut – the outer skin of sheep intestine. Due to a shortage of sheep gut, both cow and pig gut have become the most prominent 'natural gut' strings on our shelves today.

Natural gut is actually very well suited for tennis and is generally considered to be the benchmark for all strings in terms of 'playability'. 'It is extremely powerful and it offers great feel,' says Roger Dalton, Head Stringer at the Wimbledon Tennis Championships. The main features are super elasticity, tension stability and liveliness, creating a 'crisp', 'clean' sensation of maximum control and 'feel' on contact. Natural gut strings are, however, very expensive and sensitive to moisture. Durability is also particularly low.

Although natural gut has been around since tennis started, many modern-day tournament pros continue to use it, especially in a hybrid set-up (*see page 109*) with a combination of other strings.

SYNTHETIC

Originally created to replicate the 'playability' of natural gut whilst minimizing the drawbacks, synthetic strings have been developed so extensively over recent years that their performance is almost directly in line with that of their natural counterpart. Although a slight disparity in performance and 'playability' will likely never cease to exist, synthetic strings are more reasonably priced, durable and weather resistant.

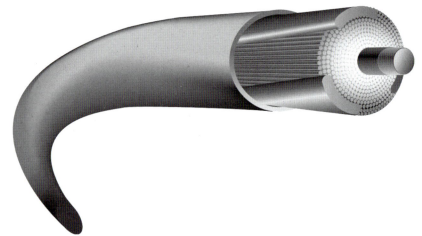

High-quality nylon string consists of a 'multifilament' structure, i.e. hundreds (or even thousands) of individual string filaments braided together and wrapped in a resistant cover

Synthetic strings are made primarily from three materials, either individually or in combination: nylon, polyester or Kevlar.

Nylon: Nylon is the most popular man-made material and it also happens to be the cheapest. There are a tremendous variety of nylon strings on the market today, all with an emphasis on certain traits (i.e. power, control etc.).

The performance of a nylon string will be largely determined by its construction, the spectrum ranging from cheap 'monofilaments' with a simple solid core and just a few outer wrappings to high quality sophisticated 'multifilaments' which consist of hundreds or thousands of individual string filaments (which can include other types of fibres) braided together and wrapped with a resistant cover. Generally speaking, the higher the number of resistant outer wraps, the higher the quality.

These leading 'multifilaments' are very receptive to the needs of the advanced player for they provide a very 'crisp' feeling on contact and hold tension well. In terms of 'playability,' they are widely perceived as being the closest to natural gut and are extremely popular due to their relative affordability. They are, however, more expensive and less durable than the solid-core variety because of their fibrous nature. For this reason, many players will combine a high-quality 'multifilament' with a cheaper, tougher nylon in a hybrid set up as described below (*see page 109*).

In comparison, although the simple solid-core nylon strings are durable and affordable, they lack any 'feel' and do not meet the needs of a modern-day competitive player. These strings tend to be found in beginner rackets and non-specialist tennis retailers.

Low-quality nylon string consists of a 'monofilament' structure, i.e. a simple solid core and an outer wrap

Somewhere in the middle of this seemingly endless array of nylon strings lies 'synthetic gut', one of the most cost-efficient strings on the market. 'Synthetic gut' offers all-round performance and high tension maintenance by surrounding a solid monofilament core with multiple layers of smaller filaments. Although slightly less durable than Kevlar and polyester, 'synthetic gut' offers reasonable 'feel' and 'playability' for a very inexpensive cost. American great Jim Courier was known to use Gosen synthetic gut over the course of his career.

Polyester/Co-polyester: According to Roger Dalton, Head Stringer at the Wimbledon Championships, 'Co-poly strings are extremely popular with professional players. If you go into a major tournament stringing room, co-poly strings will be found absolutely everywhere.'

The traditional polyester string consists of a single polyester fibre with a thin coating, i.e. a 'monofilament' construction. Although these strings have been around for many years, they have never quite gained popularity due to their low-tension stability, lack of elasticity and reputation for causing injuries.

This all changed at the turn of the century when Luxilon revolutionized the game by combining polyester strings with some powerful chemicals and element additives. The result was the next generation of polyester strings and the birth of the co-polyester string. These strings are softer than the traditional polyester, they feel more comfortable and, as a result, it is anticipated that almost 70 per cent of European professional players select a co-poly string in their rackets.

Co-poly strings have virtually defined the modern baseline game by allowing players to hit topspin drives, angled winners and 'kick' serves that were simply not possible in the days of wooden frames and nylon strings. Studies indicate that the average outgoing spin from a co-poly string is 25 per cent greater than other synthetic and natural strings. The only disadvantage is that they 'deaden' the string-bed with their low power, but for many professionals with complete swings, co-polys serve as the perfect complement to the modern-day highly-charged frames that make up the market.

The physics behind the unparalleled performance of co-polys dates back to 1971 and the invention of the 'Spaghetti string' by Werner Fischer, a German horticulturalist. The 'Spaghetti String' system was deliberately designed to reduce the friction and maximize movement between the strings. Fischer believed that this would give the ball an extra vertical kick and thus impart additional spin on the ball.

Fischer and his 'Spaghetti strings' generated so much spin that the stringing pattern was eventually banned by the ITF in 1978. But the modern

Synthetic gut strings offer a great all-round performance and are very cost-effective

Snapback: the elastic energy in the strings is transferred back to the ball in the direction parallel to the racket face

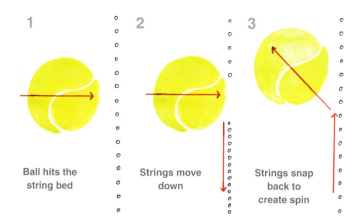

1 Ball hits the string bed

2 Strings move down

3 Strings snap back to create spin

game of tennis today has evolved to such an extent that the top players can now generate the same amount of spin without the need for Spaghetti strings – and the introduction of co-polys has been the driving force behind this development.

In their book, *Technical Tennis*, co-authors Rod Cross and Crawford Lindsey explain the physics behind the co-poly string – and it is exactly what Fischer had envisaged just thirty years earlier. The theory used to be that the more 'grip' between the ball and strings, the more spin would be generated. It would seem to make sense because it is this friction that creates the spin.

But in footage captured by Japanese engineer Yoshihiko Kawazoe in 2004, it was discovered that the slippery surface of co-polys allow the strings to slide more, maximizing the storage of elastic energy which is returned to the ball in the direction parallel to the racket face as the string snaps back into position. Co-polys generate more spin not because of more friction, but because of *less*.

Despite the obvious benefits of co-polys, young juniors are advised to stay away from a full polyester or co-poly string bed until they have first developed sufficient strength in their upper body to avoid suffering from wrist, arm and shoulder problems caused by the impact and stress created by these stiff strings.

Kevlar: This is the most durable string on the market. It holds tension very well, but the 'feel' and 'playability' is terrible. Kevlar strings feel very stiff, produce very little power and can be extremely uncomfortable, especially if strung at a high tension. In exceptional circumstances, Kevlar can be used in a hybrid set-up (*see page 109*) but is not recommended in a full string-bed because it can easily lead to arm injuries.

Textured/Shaped Strings

‘ I am a believer that pyramid-shaped strings offer the greatest ball "bite" by gripping onto the ball whilst allowing plenty of movement between the strings. ’

DUNCAN CALLAN, *Master Racket Technician*

In tune with the modern baseline game, the string market has become saturated with textured and shaped strings all designed to 'grip' the ball and maximize the spin that players are able to generate. While these strings can complement a player's spin game, they are not an excuse for failing to practise the proper technique. 'The swing will always be the primary factor in generating spin,' says Roger Dalton, Head Stringer at the Wimbledon Tennis Championships.

Textured strings are designed to maximize spin

TEXTURED STRINGS

Textured strings are constructed with the addition of an outer wrap which creates a raised band and gives texture to the strings. They were first launched onto the market with the Gamma 'Ruff' range and were quickly replicated in the form of Prince 'Topspin' and Luxilon 'Alu-Power Rough', the leading string of its type available over recent years.

The rough outer layer is supposed to enhance the rotations on the ball by 'gripping' it as the player swings through. However, using high-speed video analysis, it has been determined that the textured surface actually counteracts the spin by increasing the friction between the strings and minimizing any 'snapback'. While these high-end strings can be responsive, you should not purchase them only on the premise that they will increase the frequency of rotations on your outgoing balls.

But 'it is not an exact science,' says Roger Dalton. According to Dalton, this whole theory of 'snapback' is overestimated because the ball only stays on the strings for approximately four milliseconds, and so it has already left the string bed by the time the string does actually snap back into its original position. 'It depends on a variety of factors, including playing style and stroke speed,' he adds. He does, however, accept that the smoother the string, the greater the spin – all other things being equal.

'Most of the topspin players I have strung for say they get much more spin with the square-shaped Solinco Tour Bite string (where the very sharp edges cut into the ball) than with any strings that use snap-back technology,' says Colin Triplow, Master Racket Technician. 'The ball has left the strings before the snap back has been completed.'

Joe Heyott, professional stringer at the Australian Open Tennis Championships, also questions the efficacy of these textured strings: 'The rough strings have this texture pressed into the string, but I don't think they are as effective as shaped strings. It is as if you take a piece of paper and crumple it up – that paper is now springy. But when you take that paper and pull it, you then lose the texture. I think that these textured strings are more for the softness and the grab, but not for the added spin.' He does confirm that this is only a theory and that 'if they feel good to a player, they feel good. I can't tell them what they'll like and what they won't.'

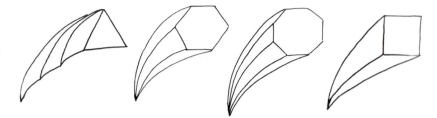

There are many different varieties of shaped strings, all of which are designed to promote spin potential

SHAPED STRINGS

'Shaped' strings are slightly different to textured strings, but they are also designed to maximize the amount of spin that can be generated by featuring an hexagonal, octagonal or pyramid-shaped profile. The angular shapes aid 'slip' between mains and crosses and cut into the ball on contact offering maximum spin potential.

These are some of the best strings on the market if you are an advanced player with a high string consumption and are looking for great 'playability', and there is also a feeling that they counter the tendency of the ball to slide across the strings when the swing is cutting across the trajectory of the ball.

You will need to replace shaped strings before they break because the sharp edges usually wear off after just a few hours of hitting.

Gauge

'Gauge' refers to the thickness of the string and has a great impact on both 'playability' and durability. Two systems of gauge labelling are used: the American system and the International system. Tennis string gauges range from 15 (thickest) to 19 (thinnest), with half-gauges identified with an L (15L, 16L, etc), which is short for 'light'. Most players do, however, find it easier to measure the diameter under tension in millimetres. Most tennis strings have a gauge between 1.10 mm and 1.34 mm.

The gauge of the string impacts its playability, feeling and durability

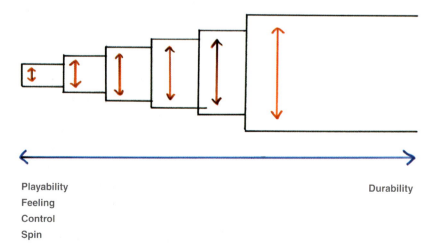

Playability
Feeling
Control
Spin

Durability

Selecting a gauge is always a case of compromise. A thicker string will give increased durability but reduced 'playability', while a thinner tennis string will snap more easily but is supposed to offer enhanced ball 'feeling' and control. Thinner strings also provide more spin potential by allowing the strings to embed into the ball and they are also considered to be more arm-friendly. Pete Sampras was known to use 1.20 mm gauge strings and even tested thinner squash strings in an attempt to increase his 'feel' on ball striking.

The general rule is to choose as thin a string as possible whilst maintaining a reasonable amount of durability. Rafael Nadal, for example, has been known to use a 1.35 mm Babolat 'Duralast' string on the basis that his heavy topspin game would cause any lower gauges to break after just a couple of games. Dominic Inglot, World Number 34 Doubles player, uses a 1.25 mm gauge string 'because although a thicker gauge will maintain its tension for longer and won't break as frequently, as a player you lose response and playability.' It is worth noting, however, that while thin strings are supposed to improve performance, some players do select a thicker string because they prefer the 'feeling' they offer.

You are advised to begin with a string in the middle of the range (i.e. 1.25 mm) and adjust as necessary on future restrings.

Hybrid Stringing

A hybrid set-up is where two different strings are combined in one string bed: one string is used for the mains and another string used for the crosses. Hybrid stringing ranges from simply using different gauges to using different strings altogether. By choosing a hybrid string bed, you can, in effect, fine-tune the 'playability', durability, responsiveness, and control offered by combining the best qualities of a string whilst minimizing its limitations.

Andy Murray's game excelled when the Scot switched to Luxilon Alu-Power mains (from Alu Power Rough) and Babolat VS natural gut cross just prior to the Wimbledon 2012 Championships. The components of a hybrid set-up differ greatly among the players. For example, Novak Djokovic and Roger Federer, respectively prefer Babolat VS natural gut and Wilson Natural Gut on the mains but both use Luxilon 'Alu-Power Rough' on the crosses. According to Colin Triplow, Master Racket Technician, this combination 'gives them greater topspin on their groundstrokes and more kick on their serves, but not the pinpoint and accuracy and control that Murray has.'

Besides these obvious performance benefits, hybrid stringing can also be a very economical compromise for players looking to minimize costs whilst maintaining performance. Players can enjoy the 'playability' benefits of natural guts and high-end nylons while increasing longevity and halving the string quantity by combining them with a cheaper, more durable string in the crosses. While the string bed will not feel exactly like a full set of natural gut, the overall performance remains sufficiently high to justify the concession.

Hybrid stringing allows you to fine-tune the 'playability', durability, responsiveness, and control of your racket

CHOOSING A HYBRID

'The main string is the most influential on the "feel" and control of the racket; this is the string that will define the ultimate playing characteristics of the string bed,' says Roger Dalton, Head Stringer at the Wimbledon Tennis Championships. Players seeking durability should install a durable string on the mains and those seeking 'playability' should select a natural gut or thin, high-end synthetic. The impact of the cross string will be far smaller than that of the mains.

In a uniformly strung racket, it is almost always the main string that breaks because they move a lot more than the cross strings. To counter this, it is common for players to install a polyester/Kevlar main string with a natural gut or premium synthetic cross string. Not only will this increase the longevity of the string bed, it will increase the 'playability' and reduce the stiffness of the mains string. Players can reverse this combination for a more comfortable, high-performance hybrid combination with reduced durability.

Some players will also tinker with the tension of the hybrid string bed. A higher tension in the main string will change the shape of the sweet-spot and reduce the vibrations on off-centre hits. It is also important to consider the type of string installed: stiff, hard polyesters and Kevlars must be strung at a lower tension than soft guts and nylons. In any case, any disparity in string tension between the mains and the crosses should not exceed 1.5 kg (approx. 3 lb).

To learn more about how professionals are choosing their hybrids, I spoke with Joe Heyott, a professional stringer working in the Australian Open stringing room.

'Hybrid tensions are a lot more popular than actual hybrid stringing amongst the professionals,' he says. 'The top players are still doing hybrids but we are seeing more dual tensions than actual hybrid stringing. When stringing a hybrid-tension racket, I would say it is about 60–40 in favour of a lower tension in the crosses. This changes the shape, but not the size of, the sweet spot.'

Choosing, Testing and Buying String

' Even the top players are steered by the advice of professional stringers – this is the best way. Quite often, players and coaches do not know a great deal and they will always be seeking advice from professional stringers as to ways to improve their performance. '
ROGER DALTON, *Head Stringer at the Wimbledon Tennis Championships*

The string market is extremely vast and there is a huge number of brands offering a great diversity of strings under their label. Fortunately, string technology has become so advanced that there are actually very few 'bad' strings on the market today, but you must choose your string carefully. It comes down to experimentation and you are encouraged to try many different types of strings and tensions before settling on a string bed with which you are satisfied. But how exactly are strings tested? How are they purchased?

With so many strings to choose from, an easy way to narrow down the options is to set a price range and, in doing so, you must remember that saving money in the shop will not necessarily save money further down the line. From a financial and performance standpoint, it is sometimes advisable to purchase a more expensive string in the knowledge that it will probably last longer and feel better on the court. While there are many small brands out there offering 'high-quality' string for low prices, there is certainly a positive correlation between quality and price.

'The most expensive brands spend a lot of money on marketing and it is debatable whether players are really getting value for money,' says Roger Dalton, Head Stringer at the Wimbledon Tennis Championships. 'But I do believe that they are better than the cheaper strings on the market which quite often break quickly and are inconsistent with both texture and gauge.' He adds, 'I advise players to look at it as an investment. If the string allows them to win the tournament then their winnings will make it all worthwhile!'

String Tension

6 Players should always select the lowest tension with which they feel they have control of the ball on contact. It is just not necessary to string at a high tension with modern strings because this will take away all of their properties. 9
ROGER DALTON, *Head Stringer at the Wimbledon Tennis Championships*

Measured in Imperial ('lb') or metric ('kg'), string tension is the pressure under which the strings are installed in the frame. The higher the measurement, the higher the tension, and all players should recognize how important string tension is in developing a solid, consistent, all-round game.

The basic rule is that you should string *tight* for control, and string *loose* for power. The caveat, however, is that this is only true for those advanced players who have a fully developed swing on their groundstrokes. Indeed, if you are an intermediate player, you will probably need a lower tension to allow forgiveness on off-centre shots.

The physics behind this is simple: the tighter string bed defects less and deforms the ball more, rebounding less energy than looser strings. Conversely, more energy is given back to the ball with a low tension, hence the increase in power. This effect, however, will only actually be marginal because the ball is not actually on the strings long enough for this trampoline-like effect to occur.

The confusion arises because the reduction in string tension increases the dwell time of the ball on the string bed. Because of this, the ball is released later in the swing motion, which causes the ball to land deeper in the court to give the illusion of more power. For the same reason, lower tensions are said to reduce control; the varying release time of the ball from the swing bed causes the ball to miss the intended target because it does not fit the player's swing speed and stroke style. For this reason, all and any modifications should be made incrementally in steps of 1 or 2 kg (approx. 2–4 lb).

Most frames have a recommended tension range printed inside the throat. You should begin in the bottom third of the range before tweaking until a point where the ideal tension is found. It is also important to remember that recommended string tension is a guideline only and you can move outside of the range where a need to do so presents itself. John McEnroe, for example, was known to string his rackets approximately 4.5 kg (approx. 10 lb) below the recommended tension range of his rackets.

TWEAKING THE STRING TENSION

After some measured experimentation, you should have a tension that offers you the perfect blend of power and control on the court. That said, the ability to adapt to surroundings is an important element of competitive tennis so you must learn to tweak your tension according to the circumstances at hand. To learn more about this, I spoke with Laura Robson and Filip Peliwo, the 2012 Boys' Wimbledon, French Open and US Open Champion.

'My string tension is never constant. I am constantly experimenting and adapting. I normally change it by a few pounds depending on the surface, temperature, stringer and machine. I also change it depending on how I am feeling at the time,' says Peliwo.

Robson's comments, interestingly, mirror those of Peliwo but she goes so far as to say that she would not normally choose her tension until the actual day of the match. 'My tension changes all the time,' she says. 'In Australia, at this tournament, I have already tried out four different tensions, but it will depend on the temperature on the day.' The top players can take up to ten rackets on court at a time, all strung at different tensions and can send rackets off to be strung in a match if they need a racket of a certain tension.

Let us now take a deeper look at what factors influence the tension.

Court Surfaces: Faster surfaces such as grass or indoor hard courts absorb less energy when the ball bounces, and most players will raise their tensions to maximize their control of the fast-moving incoming ball. The opposite applies to slower surfaces where players are forced to generate the power with their strokes. On clay, for example, many players will drop tension by approximately 1–2.5 kg (3–6 lb) to add power and depth to their shots.

Altitude: 'I went to Mexico City for a tournament at over 1,500 metres altitude and the balls were flying everywhere because I was using the rackets from my previous tournament week. I tightened it by 2 kg and it helped a lot,' says James Allemby, an ITF Futures player. The ball travels faster at higher altitudes due to the thinner air. These events will normally use special 'high-altitude' balls, but players are advised to raise tension by approximately 1–2.5 kg (3–6 lb) to maximize control.

Temperature: In the 2012 Wimbledon encounter between Andy Murray and Marcos Baghdatis, the Centre Court roof closed, causing the temperature to change. As a result, Murray sent all his rackets to the stringing room to be restrung before play restarted.

High temperatures cause the frame to flex, the strings to expand and the string tension to decrease. The balls also travel faster because the rubber becomes pliable. Most players will increase tension by a couple of pounds/kilogrammes in high temperatures, and lower tension similarly in low temperatures where the strings contract, the frame becomes stiffer and the balls travel more slowly.

Game style: Speaking very generally, aggressive 'baseliners' employ a lower tension (as far as it does not affect their control) to give them access to additional power and to hit with greater depth. Serve and volley players will use higher tensions for control with their intricate volleys around the net.

The balls: Different tournaments use different balls and this will directly influence the tension that players use. At professional level, event referees will publicize the 'Official Tournament Ball' weeks prior to the tournament. Dunlop balls, for example, travel considerably faster than most other balls and it is necessary to compensate with a slighter higher tension to retain control.

Most players will also change tensions over the course of a match as the balls become more worn. Due to its porous nature, the ball covering actually creates 'drag' and slows the ball down as it travels from one player to the other. As the material becomes worn, therefore, the 'fuzz' is depleted and the drag is reduced, causing the ball to travel through the air faster than a new ball. Balls at professional level are changed so frequently that this rarely becomes a factor.

Professional players will, however, switch to a higher tension on the change of balls to maximize control and will use a lower tension with older balls to maximize the power. This is because new balls are a lot more lively and energetic than older, used balls and so a racket with a higher tension will usually be used to compensate for the power. In reality, receivers will often switch frames when receiving serve before a ball change to give them a 'free' game to get used to the new racket.

Injuries: If you have a history of arm, wrist or shoulder injuries, you should always string at the lowest tension at which you can maintain control to maximize forgiveness on off-centre shots. It is also recommended that you stay away from Kevlar and Polyester strings.

Stringer, Technique and Stringing Machine: In *A Champion's Mind: Lessons from a Life in Tennis*, Pete Sampras admitted that he would get ' ... pretty neurotic about racket tuning. I would go to these events in my career and the stringing machines and the stringers were different guys, so I would have to get four or five rackets done before they got it right – if they got it right. I was always worried that poor or inconsistent stringing might cost me matches.'[1]

Different stringers, techniques and machines string at different tensions because during the stringing process, the tension of the strings can be 'lost' at different stages. Automatic machines, for example, are far more accurate than manual or drop-weight machines.

Because of this, Pete Sampras employed professional stringer, Nate Ferguson, to travel with him around the world to tournaments. Ferguson brought his own machine to ensure that Sampras' rackets were always strung by the same stringer on the same machine. Ferguson went on to form Priority One, a stringing service that travels to every major tournament, and has Federer, Djokovic and Murray among its customers.

There are not many players out there who can afford to hire a personal stringer, but you can minimize any discrepancies by considering the tension request based on the machine being used. You are also advised to always test a stringer's work before using a racket that he or she has strung in a competitive situation.

Racket Maintenance: Tension

All strings naturally lose their elasticity over time, and hitting with a 'dead' string bed will not only hinder your ability to generate power, but may also result in injury. Racket maintenance is a lot easier today than in the past. Gone are the days of clamping a big, heavy brace onto the frame to prevent it from warping, but the impact and speed of the tension loss can both be minimized with proper care of the racket.

Rackets should never be left in the car overnight because extreme temperatures can alienate the strings. Most racket bags have an in-built temperature maintenance system where rackets should be kept at all times when not in use.

Strings will eventually snap as they become worn over time, but many intermediate players simply do not hit the ball hard enough to actually cause a breakage. Nonetheless, it is important that the string bed is replaced on a semi-regular basis.

As a general rule, all intermediate players should replace the strings in their racket at least every month. Advanced competitive players should remove and replace their string beds far more frequently, prior to them breaking, and it is not uncommon for those with professional aspirations to install new strings just hours before they go on court in order to minimize tension loss.

The Bottom Line: What Works for You?

While all these guidelines exist, it is important that you find what works for you personally. Some players, including Richard Gasquet and Rafael Nadal, are known to stick with the same tension and set up in all different conditions, while many others are extremely specific about their requirements.

'As a professional stringer, I get some very unusual requests, including players wanting the top few strings strung at a lower tension than the rest of the string bed and others stringing at extremely high or low tensions,' says Roger Dalton, Head Stringer at the Wimbledon Tennis Championships, 'There really is a great variety on what the players want.'

You must always keep an open mind and continue experimenting to find a set-up that allows you to feel comfortable on that court. In this way, the above information must be viewed not as a set of rules per se, but as a detailed analysis allowing you to make informed decisions.

If you are competing on the ITF Circuits, you are advised to avoid anything particularly unique with your string bed set ups because when you are travelling to the corners of the earth, you will never find consistent stringers capable of offering you regularity in your racket set-ups.

Tennis Balls

' All balls are different. Head ATP balls, for example, are super fluffy and slow whereas US Open balls are heavy and fast. '
DOMINIC INGLOT, *World Number 34 Doubles player*

Tennis balls consist of a hollow rubber core (which may or may not be pressurized) covered by a textile material composed of wool, nylon and cotton. Surprisingly, they are actually quite heavily specified by the ITF (especially in contrast to the court surface), but within these clearly specified limits there is still some room to make different balls for different markets. As a result, not all tennis balls are the same. There are currently over 200 different ITF-recognized balls, all of which vary slightly in their appearance and playing characteristics.

The game has changed extensively over the past twenty years and the strings, the rackets and the onus of physical conditioning has led to players hitting the ball harder than could ever have been anticipated. In an attempt to keep up with the game, the ITF introduced three types of standard ball in 2002. Although the weight and rebound of the ball does not change across types, each type of ball is designed for specific use on set court types to speed up or slow down play.

Type 2 is the standard tennis ball designed for medium-paced courts. Type 1 balls are the same size as Type 2 balls but are manufactured with harder rubber for use on slower court surfaces. Type 1 balls, typically used on clay or slow hard courts, are too fast for indoor hard or grass courts. Type 3 balls are approximately 6 per cent larger in diameter than the standard Type 2 ball and so encounter greater drag when moving through the air. As a result, they move slower through the court and are designed for use on the faster court surfaces. Studies have also shown that Type 3 balls allow for greater amounts of spin to be generated.

The regulations for testing tennis balls to obtain official ITF approval can be found in Appendix 1 of the Rules of Tennis, and an official list of ITF-approved tennis balls can be found on the ITF website (www.itftennis.com).

Choosing a Tennis Ball

A tennis ball is a tennis ball, right? Wrong! Yellow tennis balls were first introduced into the rules of tennis in 1972 after research indicated that this colour was more visible to the spectator. They were later adopted by the US Open and All England Club in 1971 and 1986 respectively, and it is this colour that remains highly predominant today. But while all tennis balls may appear the same, there are a number of important variable factors which all have a significant influence on their quality, appearance and 'playability'.

The organizers' decision to switch the ball type at the 2011 French Open led to numerous complaints from the leading players in the game. The reason is simple: these players had spent the last six weeks using the traditional Dunlop balls, which were used at the other clay court lead-up tournaments in Rome, Madrid and Barcelona, only to be presented with a different ball type in Paris. Not surprisingly, the switch caused many to lose their touch and rhythm.

As Rafael Nadal said in his press conference, 'I only practised four or five days with this ball after one month and a half playing with another ball. The feeling is something [that is] very important in tennis. From the outside it is sometimes difficult to see. But from the inside for the players, it is something dangerous for the shoulders, for everything.'

Many players purchase a set of tennis balls without even considering the quality, play and type of ball they are buying. Tennis balls are all different, and you should always choose your balls wisely. This means always training with the ball that is used in the tournaments in which you are playing and also considering which balls are used on which surfaces. Where a ball is designed for a specific surface, this will normally be made very clear on the packaging.

Some tennis balls will also come with numbers on them, but this is no indication of the quality or nature of the ball. The reason is to give players a chance of identifying their balls when they get mixed up with balls from neighbouring courts.

Most major manufacturers produce three classes of tennis ball: professional, performance and championship. Professional level balls are the most expensive: these are the balls used in professional events and are the highest quality in terms of performance and durability. Championship level tennis balls are slightly cheaper and are used in training to reduce costs. Recreational level balls are low quality and are not recommended for competitive players.

Many manufacturers also offer 'Extra Duty', 'High Altitude' and pressureless varieties of their most popular ball models. Outdoor hard courts are the most wearing surface and so you are advised to purchase 'Extra Duty' balls if playing on this surface. Because these balls have thicker felt and a high nylon content, they stick to the racket strings, making them appear heavier than regular duty balls.

Pressureless balls are made with thick rubber walls with no internal pressure. They make very good training balls because they are very cheap to buy and are known to last for a long time. But they should not be used by competitive players because they do not provide the same feel or bounce as the regular, pressurized tennis balls mentioned above. They feel much lighter on the strings and establish a false perception of weight and movement.

Advanced players are advised to purchase the higher quality balls, such as the 'Head ATP', 'Wilson US Open', Tecnifibre or Babolat VS balls or Roland Garros balls (on clay) where possible, and should only use Slazenger balls on dry grass courts because they have very low durability and are particularly susceptible to moisture. You should stick to regular duty balls on clay or indoor hard courts because they do not pick up as much of the clay due to their scant fluff and tighter weave pattern. The same is true when playing on indoor hard: extra duty balls will tend to fluff up very quickly.

Dunlop balls are the heaviest balls on the market and their felt has a tendency to fluff up. They are used at the ATP Masters 1000 events in Monte Carlo, Madrid and Rome, but offer a completely different 'feel' to almost every other ball on the market. Other brands (Gamma, Penn, etc) are very rarely used as official tournament balls and should be avoided by the competitive player.

During a Match

Tennis players will regularly ask for three balls, choosing two and throwing the third away. While this may seem like a meaningless ritual, there is actually method behind the madness.

Players choose the ball in a match that best suits their aims for the point. For example, some players will choose the balls with the least amount of fluff on it so as to maximize speed through the court on the first serve. They may then choose a ball with more fluff for the second serve to maximize the spin and 'kick'. Similarly, baseline players may choose a fluffier ball against a powerful opponent in an attempt to minimize the power of their groundstrokes.

For others, it may well just be a ritual that helps them to get in the right mindset to play the point.

Stringing Machines

‘ My brother and I were breaking three or four rackets per day between us and it is not cheap – approximately $80 a day, $560 a week, $2,240 a month, $26,880 a year. In my first year on tour alone I spent over $10,000 getting my rackets strung. ’
RUBIN STATHAM, *ATP Tour player and New Zealand Davis Cup player*

With retailers and professional stringers charging anywhere between £20–30 to string a racket (excluding the actual cost of the strings themselves) racket stringing is by no means a negligible cost. You can drastically reduce this cost by purchasing a stringing machine and learning how to string your own rackets. This will also give you more control to be precise with your set-ups – and even allow you to earn money by stringing other people's rackets.

Stringing machines vary in price and quality but it is normally possible to make the financial outlay back in under a year. 'I always take my portable stringer to tournaments,' says James Allemby, ITF Futures player. 'It cost me a lot of money to begin with but it more than paid for itself within my first year on the tour,' he says.

Choosing a Tennis Stringing Machine

With so many stringing machines available, here are the key factors to consider:

TENSION SYSTEM

There are three recognized tension systems: (1) drop weight, (2) manual lock-out and (3) electronic.

1. Drop-weight machines are recognizable by their long, metal rod (the tension bar). The tension is controlled by moving the mounted weight up and down the rod; the further the weight is positioned up the bar, the higher the tension. Drop-weight machines are the cheapest on the market but are the least accurate because the desired tension is only achieved when the rod is exactly parallel to the ground.

As a competitive player, you are advised to avoid these machines because it is almost impossible to string at a consistent tension. It is hard to charge competitive rates to other players due to this flaw, and they are also very time-consuming.

2. Hand-crank manual lock-out machines operate with a crank and a reference spring. The stringer applies the tension, the lock-out stops the action, and a brake then holds the tension when this has been reached. These machines are slightly more accurate than the drop-weight machine, but the spring needs to be re-calibrated on a semi-regular basis as it loses elasticity.

Hand-crank machines are a great 'middle-of-the-road' option because they are slightly faster and more accurate than the drop-weight machine, but remain affordable. Interestingly, Monica Seles would insist on having her rackets strung on a lock-out machine, even when an electronic machine was available.

3. Electronic stringers are the most expensive but also the most accurate stringers on the market. They normally consist of an in-built LCD screen linked directly to a motor, which tensions the string on its own. Stringing with an electronic stringer is considerably easier and faster than with a manual machine.

CONSTANT PULL V. LOCKOUT

'Constant pull' machines pull the string to the desired tension and continue pulling at that tension. 'Lockout' machines, on the other hand, pull the string to the desired tension and then lock the string at that point without pulling. As a result, 'lockout' strings produce a tension between 5 per cent and 10 per cent lower than the average 'constant pull' machine. The majority of electric machines will be 'constant pull' while most manual (drop-weight/hand-crank) will be 'lockout'.

PORTABILITY

Stringing fees at tournaments can be expensive and tension inaccuracies can occur between stringers and the machines that they use. For this reason, many touring competitive players will take a portable stringer, which they can take to tournaments and string themselves. Electric machines are regarded as the least portable because they are extremely heavy and require electricity, which is not readily available at all venues – especially on the ITF Pro Circuits.

Players who simply need to move their machine from room to room (or even into the car) can use tabletop machines. While far from lightweight, there are many manual machines that can be used on a table, desk or solid surface. Other machines come fixed with a stand and so cannot be readily moved from one place to another.

Touring players who travel frequently will normally need a slightly more portable machine. Over recent years, a small number of specifically designed portable stringers have hit the market, the most lauded of which is the 'Pro Stringer'. The machine was created by Rubin

Due to its portability, the Pro Stringer allows players to string for themselves as they travel on tour

Statham, an ATP player himself, who observed his fellow players relying on different stringing machines at each tournament. This always resulted in variable racket tensions, hampering their performance on the court. To find the correct tension required repeated restringing, adding enormous financial costs throughout each playing year.

Though expensive, the machine is very accurate and is remarkably easy to use. Most importantly, the machine is completely portable, can be taken on flights and can fit in most hand-luggage. The machine is slightly less convenient to use than larger, sturdier machines and so should be saved for tournament-level players who spend many weeks on the road.

CLAMPING SYSTEM

The lower range portable or manual machines will have 'flying clamps' which are not attached to the machine. These clamps will normally result in great tension loss. If purchasing a manual machine, you are advised to select a higher-quality model with fixed clamps that swivel, such as the Prince NEOS 1500 or Gamma 6004.

MOUNTING SYSTEM

'Mounts' are the points that hold the racket in place and the number varies from 2 to 6, depending on the machine. Generally speaking, the more portable the machine, the fewer the mounting points. Machines with a higher number of mounting points are better for the racket because they minimize frame distortion, but each mount can block a hole and strings will often become tangled. Four-point mounting systems provide a great balance between convenience and racket-care.

Purchasing a Stringer and Learning How to String

The price of stringing machines range from £200 in the back of magazines to nearly £10,000 for the professional, tournament-level models. With all this in mind, how exactly should you choose which machine to buy?

The first thing to consider is the use of the machine. Is it strictly for personal use only or for other players too? How many rackets will be strung a week? Does it need to be portable? If so, how portable, i.e. do you spend weeks 'on the road' and fly to tournaments, or does it need to be taken in the car only now and then? If the machine is for personal use only, for example, it does not matter that the machine has a 'lockout' system because players will get used to the 5 per cent tension reduction. If you only need to string three rackets a week, the speed and ease of use is not really an important factor.

There is a positive correlation between price and quality, and you are strongly advised to purchase the best stringer that your budget will allow. When setting this budget, it is also important to acknowledge that you will be able to charge more with a high-quality stringer. Generally speaking, machines priced between £500–£1,000 will be of sufficient quality for high-level competitive players and more expensive machines are normally the tools of the trade for speciality racket shops and professional racket stringers. Unless buying a refurbished second-hand machine, you should be wary of purchasing anything priced below £300. If setting up a professional stringing business, you are advised to research the latest technologies thoroughly and select a professional-level machine.

On first glance, stringing a tennis racket appears very intricate and complicated, but it is actually very straightforward. There are many tried and tested methods to string, different knot patterns and positions, and some rackets and machines require methods unique to them. Most machines will come with either a free stringing lesson or a detailed manual describing the specific process for that machine. There are also many videos available online to guide you.

Tennis Shoes

Tennis is a sport: it requires fast, vigorous movements from short jumps, split-steps and little sprints. It is important that players have specialist tennis footwear because the standard running shoe does not provide the support and lateral stability required for the game. Wearing a running shoe for tennis can hinder performance and increase the chances of serious injury.

Running shoes are designed for forward motion and so have soft, flexible soles to absorb the impact. Tennis shoes are normally built slightly heavier but wider to offer optimal support and stability on the ankles during sudden stop-start movements. They are normally far more durable and designed with wider bases to accommodate for side-to-side motions as well as forward motions.

Selecting the right tennis shoe can be difficult and many players will base their decision primarily on the price or the brand. Factors to be considered include the weight, cushioning, flexibility, stability and traction. There are also biomechanical factors that can help enhance player performance.

Choosing a Tennis Shoe

Here are the important factors to consider when selecting a tennis shoe.

FOOT TYPE

The first thing to consider when selecting a tennis shoe is foot type. There are three different types of feet and you can determine yours by looking at your footsteps in sand or on a wet floor.

Pronated feet carry the weight of the body on the inside of the foot. If you have this type of foot, you will require extra padding on the medial (big toe) side to protect the inside of the foot and support the knees and ankles.

Supinated feet have high arches and carry weight on the outside of the foot. If you have this type of foot, you will have shoes that show wear on the outside of the heel and forefoot while the inner portions will be barely worn. If you have supinated feet, you will tend to have a wide forefoot and need shoes with extra padding around the ankle. You will also benefit from extra durable materials and added protection because this foot type normally leads to added wear of the soles.

Neutral feet are equally balanced and will not influence the selection of a tennis shoe.

SURFACE

You should match your tennis shoe to the surface upon which you are playing. As every court type calls for a different style of shoe, as a competitive player, you should have several pairs of shoes to choose from.

There are different types of tread patterns designed for different surfaces and it is not uncommon for shoes to incorporate small circles or 'pivot' points where torsional or rotational friction is reduced in order to make twisting easier, thus reducing torsional strain on the lower leg.

Clay Courts: 'Herringbone'-style Sole

Traditional clay court shoes are built with a flat, herringbone style soles designed to maximize the grip on forward sprints as well as stability on lateral slides (*see page 123*). Most clay court shoes have tightly positioned ridges to prevent them from getting clogged up. Because of the soft, forgiving surface, clay court shoes require less padding and so are normally lighter than their hard court counterparts to facilitate movement.

Clay court shoes can also be used on many synthetic grass courts.

Hard Courts: Herringbone/Dimpled Sole

You should select a high-quality, well-padded hard court shoe to prevent injury, reduce impact and ensure comfort on court. Hard court shoes must also be 'non-marking' to prevent discolouration and they most commonly adopt a mixture of herringbone and dimpled sole pattern to maximize traction and mobility. The upper shoe is normally made of synthetic leather and they are normally heavier due to the extra padding. Many hard court shoes come with added protection at the toe-end to maximize longevity.

Grass Courts: Dimpled Sole

Grass court tennis shoes have pimpled soles and can only be used on natural or artificial grass. The outer shoe is normally made of synthetic leather and they are designed with good lateral and ankle support to protect the feet on the slippery surface.

Carpet: Smooth Sole

Tennis shoes designed for indoor use on carpet have a smooth sole and cannot be used on any other surface.

QUALITY

The quality of a tennis shoe can be determined by considering:

Stiffness of the Sole: High-quality tennis shoes will have stiffer soles than lower quality shoes. This can be determined by twisting the sole left to right and front to back. High quality shoes will normally have a stiffener located in the middle of the sole.

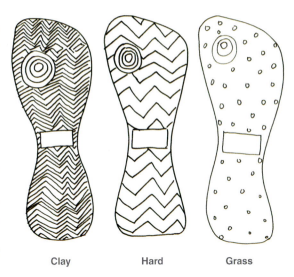

Clay   Hard   Grass

Shock Absorption: Tennis is a high impact sport and a high-quality tennis shoe will feel soft and springy when walked or jumped in.

Support: High-quality shoes will normally have plastic supports or firm fabric strips around the laces or down the side of the shoe to maximize ankle support.

The herringbone-style sole is used for both clay and hard-court shoes, whereas grass-court shoes have a dimpled sole for grip

The general consensus is that baseline players benefit from extra support to stabilize the ankle with the frequent lateral movements associated with this game style. Baseline players will also benefit from extra cushioning for comfort and a well-constructed lacing system to support the ankle and reduce unnecessary foot movement. Net players, on the other hand, tend to favour a lighter shoe with added protection towards the toe to counteract the added wear and tear.

MATERIAL

Manufacturers have created cushioning systems that are lighter and better at removing moisture away from the feet, but all materials used have their different advantages and disadvantages. All materials are effective for their purpose and so you should not get too hung up about these, but it is a factor worthy of consideration given that comfort really is paramount. Vinyl and leather are the most expensive materials on today's market, both providing high levels of support whist keeping the feet dry – but both can be uncomfortable because they do not allow the feet to breathe.

Clay court shoes are made out of canvas, which is light and breathable, allowing good ventilation but little support. Shoes made out of canvas are recommended for players looking for a strong, lightweight shoe to complement their agile, dynamic game style. It is not recommended for those with a history of ankle injuries.

Most tennis shoes today combine more than one material. The most common combination is a leather body with canvas or durable mesh built in to circulate the shoe and cool the feet. By keeping the feet cooler, comfort is increased and the chances of fatigue reduced.

You are advised to purchase a shoe manufactured with the appropriate material to complement your specific requirements, game style and preferences. Full-time players will normally switch between two identical shoes between sessions because this increases the longevity of the shoe by allowing the leather to recover.

WEIGHT

The weight and stiffness of a shoe will be key determinants in its comfort. Anything below 425 g (approx. 15 oz) is considered 'lightweight', and these are associated with rapid movement and agility. Players looking for durability and stability are advised to select a heavier shoe which will last longer and provide greater ankle support. Lighter shoes typically sacrifice both outsole durability and overall stability.

Buying Shoes

The easiest place to buy tennis shoes is online, but this is not recommended. They are the cheapest and normally have the most extensive selection to choose from, but buying without trying can result in an ill-fitting pair. Purchasing online is only advisable if you are buying another pair of a model you currently own.

Changing equipment and using different strings, rackets or even shoes will only work to hinder the process of developing a 'feeling' on court about any particular stroke. For this reason alone, it is important that you make informed decisions about the equipment you use, and are then consistent enough to allow you to focus on developing other important aspects of your game.

CHAPTER SIX

Improving Your Technical Game

always had a good forehand, I thought. It had spin, pace and was reasonably accurate. However, it was only by working with Chuck East, a close friend of mine and one of the most technically adept coaches I have ever come across, that it really grew into a *weapon*.

Over a two-week period on a court in the little French ski town of Les Contamines, Chuck, with the help of his son, Oliver, took my forehand and tweaked it into a real game-changer. He taught me about the importance of hitting with depth, finding a margin for error and creating space between myself and the ball to add power. It took another month or so for this input to really sink in, but Chuck gave me a great understanding of the small things that high-performance players do that is often not picked up by those competing at the lower levels. Although I never worked with Chuck on a formal basis, he is one person who perhaps shaped my game the most.

Many of the technical tips I am going to share with you here were taught to me by him.

The ability to serve and hit the ball inside the lines of the court on a semi-consistent basis is just the starting point to a strong tennis game. As the level improves, the margins become smaller and simply getting the ball back over the net and into the other side of the court is no longer good enough. In this chapter, I am going to discuss how to practise and consider some of the most important aspects of the advanced tennis game.

To develop these skills in practice, I will also mention a number of important on-court drills. It is, however, important to note that while this information can certainly teach the theory, including the techniques and tactics of the game, there are no shortcuts and the best way to learn is to get on a tennis court and practise. In this way, while this book will facilitate and should accompany your learning process, it cannot actually teach the game itself. Please also note that there are many more technical/tactical exercises contained in Chapters 4 and 7.

Before we dive into the theory, let's first consider how exactly we, as humans, learn and improve our skills on court.

The Stages of Learning to Develop a Tennis Stroke

You cannot instantly acquire a new stroke. Hitting a forehand cross court or a backhand down the line is actually the result of a long and gruelling learning process that normally begins on court at an early age. As with learning any new skill, the process must begin in its most simple form before progressing to reinforce the skill in more challenging situations. In tennis, this translates into five stages of training which lead to hitting the ball over the net from the baseline.

The first stage is developing your understanding of the technique and mechanics of any particular stroke, after which this motion is reinforced and repeated to begin building muscle memory. This can be done with 'dead-ball' feeds, by which a ball is simply dropped in front of you ready to be hit. Once this technique has been mastered, you can then begin the third stage: isolating the movement and practising the skill on balls coming in at a variety of different angles and speeds. This stage is normally completed with by a coach or practice partner 'feeding' balls to you from the other side of the net.

The fourth stage of the actual training process is sparring, and it is at this stage of the training process that this chapter is focused. Sparring uses two players hitting from the baseline, and is more challenging because the incoming balls will normally have spin and will come from different angles and heights. This stage is all about you getting comfortable executing the technique on a wide number of different balls similar to that of a competitive point situation.

The final stage is maintenance, in which the stroke must be practised to prevent degradation.

Similarly, you can do with through sparring (or 'hitting', as it is more commonly known).

The Tennis Learning Curve

The tennis learning curve is not lateral and the benefits of any change in technique will rarely reveal themselves until much further down the line. Indeed, any technical modifications can actually hinder your performance for the following weeks while your body attunes and adapts to the changes. In the 1990s, Noel Burch went a long way to explaining why this happens.

According to Burch, the stages to learning any new skill are (1) unconscious incompetence, (2) conscious incompetence, (3) conscious competence and (4) unconscious competence. Translating these to tennis:

1. Unconscious Incompetence: You do not recognize that there is any need for a change. For example, you do not think you need to extend your follow-through to generate greater depth on your groundstrokes.

2. Conscious Incompetence: Although you recognize that you need to extend your follow-through to get more depth, you cannot execute the action without your shots flying long or into the net. While you have identified the problem, you cannot correct it. Repetition of the mechanics hones your technique into an acceptable stroke.

3. Conscious Competence: You understand that you need to extend the follow-through and can now demonstrate the skill with a conscious effort as to the technique. The extension is not yet natural.

4. Unconscious Competence: You eventually begin to extend the follow-through and hit with more depth without even thinking about it. The extension becomes a habit and the learning process is then complete.

As you tweak and modify your game, it can be appealing to resort to old habits where new techniques are just not quite sinking in. It is, however, important to remember that any technical and tactical progression in tennis requires discipline, commitment and significant trust in the coach, and being aware of these stages can help you better accept that learning can be a slow and uncomfortable process.

How to Practise Effectively

Quality over Quantity

Clichéd though it may sound, it still bears true: the quality of a training session is more important than its length. While a tennis programme must incorporate all the necessary components, it is not always the case that more is better. To learn more about how to train, I spoke with Galo Blanco and Patrick Mouratoglou, two of the most highly respected coaches of the modern era.

'It is important to keep the intensity high at all times,' says Galo Blanco. 'An hour session with 100 per cent intensity is always better than a four-hour session at 80 per cent.'

Nonetheless, the actual length of a training session will vary from player to player. Jimmy Connors, for example, was rumoured to limit his training to just 1½ hours a day, while Rafael Nadal spends more time on the practice court than almost any other player.

According to Mouratoglou, the quality of a training session is a key determinant in success, and intensity is something that separates the best players in the world from the others.

'The best players in the world are more focused and more intense during practice than the others. If you have the chance to watch the top fifteen players in the world and compare it to all the others, the difference is quite astounding. It is this quality of training that takes them to the top,' says Mouratoglou.

Mouratoglou (*centre*) has become one of the most respected coaches of the modern era

The Importance of Variation

Research by Duane Knudson, author of *Fundamentals of Biomechanics*, has indicated that there are two aspects to high-quality stroke production: 'variable' and 'repeatable'. Taking the forehand as an example, Knudson explains that while the positions of the elbow and wrist remain consistent on each stroke, this 'repeatable' position is actually the result of a variety of different movement strategies in the lead-up to contact with the ball. In simple terms: the same angular position of the wrist and elbow ('repeatable') is achieved through inconsistent ('variable') patterns in the same joints.

For this reason, variety is an important aspect of tennis training. So you should aim to vary your drills (pace, spin, direction and height of ball or drill structure) to develop a wide variety of biomechanical timings associated with any given stroke and to achieve the almost infinite number of combinations of racket speed, and trajectory associated with a successful return. In this way, you are advised to play, train and compete with and against a variety of opponents with different game styles.

Hitting Partner

Almost all players, especially in the women's game, will be accompanied on the tour by a 'sparring partner' as well as their coach. Andy Murray, for example, used to travel with Dani Vallverdu, a friend from his days when training in Barcelona. The reason for this is simple: these highly-trained players have already passed the 'technique', 'repetition', and 'drilling' stages of tennis training and they want to find a rhythm to reinforce their strokes by hitting incoming balls which resemble those of a competitive match situation.

The same applies to most advanced players. The ideal scenario is to find a player of a slightly higher level, commonly known as 'up-hitting' because the weaker player will benefit from the consistency and technical ability of the stronger player's game. The leading tennis programmes will normally involve time with a coach to develop the technical fundamentals and working with a 'hitting partner' to practise and reinforce these techniques and tactics with a variety of different incoming balls.

Good Mistakes v. Bad Mistakes

You must distinguish between 'good mistakes' and 'bad mistakes'. To give an example, when you are trying to develop depth in your game, a 'good mistake' will be a shot that goes long, i.e. too deep, but a 'bad mistake' will be a shot that goes into the net. Mistakes are an important part of tennis development and you should not become overly frustrated when these occur.

The Importance of Being Able to Cope with the Modern Baseline Game

When Goran Ivanisevic fired down a record 213 aces on his way to the 2001 Wimbledon title, it was clear that something had to change. Concerns about the sport's capacity to handle the physical and technological developments had been growing stronger each year, but the manner of the Croat's 'bang-bang' victory proved to be a catalyst for widespread changes throughout the game. The answer was the gradual homogenization of court surfaces; the result was the death of the serve–volley and the birth of a baseline-dominated game.

It's a 'lost art', says Sampras in reference to the serve–volley game with which he ruled the world for many a year. 'No one is really doing it. Everyone is staying back and hitting the crap out of the ball', he adds. And how right he is. Roger Federer, an original serve–volleyer when he broke onto the tour, abandoned these tactics to become one of the most graceful baseline players of all time – a decision, no doubt, strongly influenced by the power and spin being generated by the top players making it almost impossible to answer with a volley.

Make no mistake: it is a huge loss to the sport. Watching the likes of Boris Becker, Peter Sampras and John McEnroe flying around the net was a wonderful sight for all to behold; a spectacular display of courage and aggression topped with a sprinkle of risk and adventure. By no means the most elegant game-style ever witnessed, but few could help but marvel at the sight of Pete Sampras storming in after that ferocious serve he possessed. Still today, it remains one of the most iconic sights in the history of the game.

The game today has become almost robotic; a game of two finely tuned specimens slugging it out from the back of the court until one guy is beaten to a pulp. But where is the imagination? Where is the creativity? The game we all loved has been reduced from an all-court game with a plethora of varying styles to one with just three primary strokes where vast chunks of the playing surface rest untouched. Would Novak Djokovic's crowning 2011 season really have been possible a decade ago before this surface uniformity?

The lost art it has become, but serve–volleying is still used as a change-up by the top players. Federer used this tactic to perfection is his victories against Nadal, both to surprise the Spaniard and give himself a breather after a gruelling point. But the serve–volley game remains nothing but that – a 'surprise' – and while many of the players today are all fine volleyers in their own right, none can even lay claim to being as adept in this department as their twentieth-century contemporaries.

But to what extent is this really true?

The last Grand Slam that Pete Sampras won was in 2002 and he won it with a serve-and-volley game. Were the rackets and strings really that different then? Of course, the modern courts are slower, and the players are running faster and hitting harder, but they are also running further behind the baseline, which opens up more angles to the volleyer. Sampras himself, one of the greatest ever serve–volleyers, questions why modern players 'just sit back and throw rocks'.

'People say it's harder to do it [serve and volleying],' he says. 'But I think technology would have helped me out. If I used the rackets that Rafa [Nadal] is using, it's easier to serve, it's easier to volley. I could serve harder, longer. It would have been easier. So it all evens out,' he says. 'But I think serve–volley tennis, it would have been just fine today. I just think you need to know how to do it'.

Let us also not forget that quite astounding performance by Sergiy Stakhovsky on the lawns of SW19 in 2013, a day when the watching world were given the rare treat as the Ukrainian tore a bewildered Roger Federer apart with a breathtaking showcase of near-perfect serve–volley tennis in all its glory. Perhaps, indeed, the serve–volley game has been extinguished too early; a spent force without actually being spent.

The truth remains that the game today has become one-dimensional and it is unfortunate that we will probably never know just how effective serve–volleying could be. But one thing is for certain: the modern game is played from the baseline and it is around this strategy that all players should base their training.

While players should look at their strengths and weaknesses to formulate a strategy that allows them to win, there is a certain game style that lends itself to the courts and equipment used in the modern age and players must mould their skills in a certain way if they are to succeed. 'In the past there was room for many different styles of tennis,' says Patrick Mouratoglou, 'but today the surfaces are very similar and all players must now conform to the same style.'

It is around this modern baseline style that the following practices are based.

Footwork

Agresividad empieza en las pierna. [1]

MARTIN CEJAS, *High-Performance Tennis Coach, Bariloche, Argentina*

In Australia watching Andy Murray battle the great Australian, Lleyton Hewitt, in an exhibition at Kooyong Lawn Tennis Club, I was accompanied court-side by a well-known tennis photographer. Typically intrigued, I began asking some questions about whether he had found the perfect shot, who was his favourite player to shoot and how he had entered into the industry. I found it all extremely interesting but there was one particular thing he said that stood out from it all. 'The top players are so much easier to photograph,' he said. 'They are always in position for the ball so I have a lot more time to get the shot.' The reason for this is footwork.

Good footwork means small steps, and the ability to change direction swiftly while remaining balanced and stable when performing sideways, forward and backwards sprints. Good footwork allows you to cover more court, recover quickly after shots and helps in preparation for the next shot. As a result, you are in position for the ball a lot earlier than your opponents who are not so highly developed in this aspect of the game.

Stripped down to its most basic level, tennis requires you to move to the ball and hit it back over the other side of the net. This can only be achieved if you can get the ball in the first place – which requires good footwork. In this way, poor tennis footwork will very quickly nullify any strong ground-stroke game, and properly trained tennis footwork will maximize performance by putting you in the best position from which you can hit your strongest shot. Although speed will inevitably help, you can still cover the court with accurate, precise footwork patterns.

Split-step

At Wimbledon a number of years ago, I was hooked on watching Maria Sharapova working on this single element of her game alone. While the practice courts at SW19 were littered with players practising their serves, volleys and smashes, Sharapova stood there without even hitting a ball, just trying to perfect the timing of her split-step.

The split-step is simply a small 'hop' and is one of the key factors that distinguishes an advanced player from an intermediate one. It is completed before every type of shot hit by the opponent: groundstroke, volley, serve and return. Next time you watch live tennis on television, forget the ball – watch one player, and you will see them split-step.

According to Isaac Newton's First Law of Motion, an object in motion tends to stay in motion and an object at rest tends to stay at rest. Applied to the game of tennis, this means that tennis players must avoid being 'at rest' by staying in motion at all times when the ball is in play. This is done via the split-step.

The split-step is key to good movement

The small 'hop' allows you to remain in motion in the air and regain balance before sprinting or moving to the next groundstroke. In short, the small hop prevents you from putting your weight on your heels between shots, i.e. becoming an object at rest. The split-step also allows you to neutralize the momentum in any direction of movement, loading up energy in the legs allowing you to push off more rapidly in a different direction. Without the split-step, you will be slow across the court and will be late arriving at the ball.

HOW AND WHEN TO SPLIT-STEP

To complete the split-step, you should 'hop' a couple of inches off the court. It is important that you land on the balls of your feet and load up energy in your legs, allowing you to rapidly explode in the direction of the ball. Landing the split-step on your heels will, in fact, work to slow your movement down.

At the higher echelons of the game, players will actually land on one foot before the other, allowing them to move in the direction of the ball with their hips open to facilitate preparation for the stroke. Developing the split-step is easily done through the following exercise, as recommended by Jez Green, former fitness coach to Andy Murray.

DRILL: *Split-Step*

Place two cones about 2 m (approx. 6 ft) apart either side of the centre line one metre inside the baseline. Place two other cones the same distance apart one metre (approx. 3 ft) behind the baseline. Each cone should be labelled A, B, C or D, respectively (*see the diagram on page 133*).

Stand on the centre mark, with your coach or practice partner calling out a letter (e.g. A). You must split-step *before* pushing off and driving forward in the direction of the corresponding cone. At the cone, you should then execute a 'shadow-shot' with the correct stance, go around the cone and then return to the centre line. Just before you return to the centre mark, your coach or practice partner must then shout another letter (e.g. D), at which point you must split-step and repeat on the corresponding cone.

To maintain an element of surprise, it is important that the letters are called out randomly and not in alphabetical order. Timing, as always, is important, and the drill must be executed at a high intensity with fast footwork at all times.

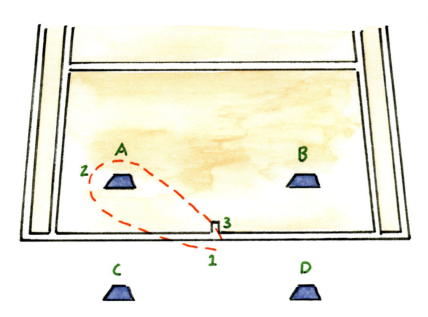

Split-step drill

You should look to do at least eight shots before resting and repeating. Focus – at all times – must be on proper execution of the split-step and at no point should you be flat footed. The aim of the drill is to develop fast footwork and a habit of split-stepping between each shot. This exercise will also work on forwards/backwards movements and the first-step driving towards the ball.

The timing of the split-step is of great importance, and developing this can be more challenging than learning the split-step itself. In a baseline-to-baseline rally, you want to start your 'hop' as your opponent begins their forward swing, allowing yourself to land and load up the energy in your legs at the exact moment your opponent makes contact with the ball. It is best practised in a baseline exchange in which your sole focus is timing the split-step and not the execution of the actual shot. With practice, you will naturally develop a habit of 'hopping' at the exact moment the opponent begins their swing forwards.

The timing of the split-step on the return of serve is detailed below.

Cross-Over Step

The second basic footwork pattern that is universal amongst the game's elite is the cross-over step. This rather overlooked pattern is actually quite simple: when you are pulled out wide on the forehand or backhand side, the first recovery step back to the centre of the baseline should be a cross-over step, i.e. the outside leg will come across the front of the inside leg. This allows you to cover a lot of ground with one swift movement. As 2003 Australian Open finalist, Rainer Schuettler, remarked: 'Ten years ago when you ran to the corner to hit a forehand, you did a side step back to change direction and recover your position. Roger [Federer] doesn't do this. Roger normally makes a cross-over step. As a result, he is two steps faster going back to the middle.'

The basics of the cross-over step are best practised with the following drill:

DRILL: *The Cross-Over Step*
Set up two cones approximately 2 m (approx. 6 ft) apart. Stand at one cone, then move from one cone to the other, starting each change of direction with a cross-over step before shuffling as necessary.

Once you have developed the necessary co-ordination, you can then move to the baseline to practise the cross-over step in a tennis-specific scenario. This will normally be achieved by having your coach or practice partner basket-feed balls to you from across the net before incorporating the skill into a baseline-to-baseline exchange whereby you must focus on moving back to the middle with a cross-over step instead of focusing on executing the stroke itself.

Adjustment Steps

Ever wondered why players' shoes squeak just before they hit the ball on a hard acrylic court? After moving into position for the ball, highly trained competitors will execute a number of very small precise adjustment steps to ensure that they are in the right position for the ball. Adjustment steps are commonly overlooked by the less advanced players. You can practise this skill using the split-step drill (page 132–3) by ensuring that you execute these small adjustment steps *before* completing the shadow-shot.

Applying Footwork Drills

Tennis footwork skills are quite easy to develop but they must be trained logically. Many players also wonder how these footwork drills are going to be implemented in a match-play situation. How does jumping over a rope *really* benefit your movement?

A player's ability to transfer skills from a different learning environment has been an area of detailed study for many years now, and while the benefits of working on technique and physical strength will be seen by increased accuracy and control on shots, the rewards for tennis footwork exercises tend to be far more subtle.

The answer lies in the 1975 publication of *The Schema Theory* by Dr Richard Schmidt. According to Schmidt, with each bodily movement the human brain fathers three things: starting point, details of the action and how it felt to complete.

Using this information, the brain can then construct a 'recall schema' and 'recognition schema', which work in unison to develop a wide programme of movements that can be varied to the infinite number of movement patterns associated with the game of tennis according to the precise requirement of the situation.

In this way, once you have worked on the foundational footwork patterns (i.e. basic movement out wide for the forehand cross-court) with the help of your coach, you do not actually need to learn a single motor response for each of the infinite number of patterns required by the game. Instead, your brain will then be able to adapt these foundational patterns to any additional pattern as required. It is important to note that these foundational patterns must first be practised on court with a coach, and are normally developed at an early age. Without these patterns, many of the footwork training patterns will prove ineffective.

Nonetheless, once learned, the focus of the footwork drills should be on developing speed, strength, coordination, explosiveness, and endurance in these patterns. But good footwork drills should also imitate the movements on the court: short sprints and rapid changes of direction. In other words, all footwork drills must be directly applicable to the movement required on court, and if the drill does not actually mirror the movement then the transferability of that movement may never actually be seen.

Skipping

'Besides a tennis racket, I can think of few things that are more important to a tennis player than a skipping rope,' says Terry Longmore, former Director of Fitness at Dukes Meadows Tennis Academy. Not only does skipping improve balance, coordination, speed, power, and overall conditioning, skipping also trains the muscles in the back of the leg to allow the player to stay on their toes when on court. Ancillary benefits include strengthening of the muscles in the hip which assist in the stabilization of the pelvic muscles, both necessary during the execution of any stroke.

Skipping for the first time can be both difficult and frustrating. You must be patient and first find a rhythm before attempting to increase the speed. While skipping

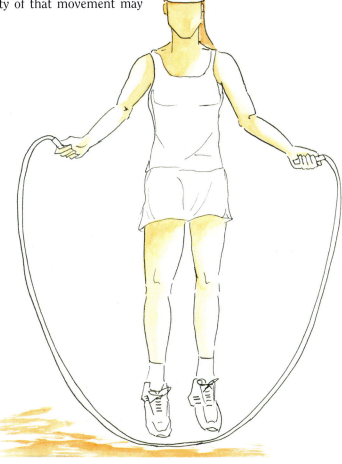

Skipping is a great way to develop balance, co-ordination, speed and power in your lower body

is an excellent conditioning routine, you must avoid overdoing it when starting out. It is advisable to begin with twenty-second short bursts at an average tempo before working this up to two or three minutes at a higher tempo. With this achieved, you can then introduce more advanced jumps to further develop foot-speed, coordination and balance. The routines can include any or all of the following:

- Jumping on both legs
- Jumping on one leg
- Alternating legs between each jump
- Crossing arms in the jump
- Double/triple jump (turning the rope twice/three times under feet during one jump)
- Travelling sideways, forwards or backwards while jumping
- Skipping backwards

SKIPPING TRAINING ROUTINES

The most common training routine for skipping is to complete timed rounds of high-intensity skipping followed by a period of rest and recovery. This style of rope work is designed to mimic the physical demands of an actual tennis match – intense periods of high activity (points) followed by the twenty-five-second rest between points. Begin with thirty seconds of intense skipping followed by a twenty-five-second rest. This can be adapted to fit your fitness levels and requirements (high performance players should try to complete eight sets).

Roger Federer is renowned for using a jump routine as part of a core stability and balance circuit training routine. Mixing the jump rope in with several bodyweight exercises is a great way to create a brief yet intense conditioning routine and represents just another way of incorporating a jump rope into any tennis training programme. An example routine could be 100 skips followed by 10 burpees, 10 push-ups and 10 body-weight squats. The circuit should be repeated ten times with clear emphasis on speed.

You can specifically work on the speed of your footwork by counting the number of jumps you can complete in a given timeframe. As a reference point, 60–70 rotations per minute is a strong starting pace for a competitive player. Advanced to professional players will normally achieve around ninety jumps per minute. Anything above this is a sign of extremely advanced foot speed.

'In the Saddle'

'In the saddle' is designed for more advanced players and will require a very astute volleyer if it is to be executed effectively.

DRILL: *In the Saddle*

Position yourself in the middle of one baseline with your practice partner on the other side by the net on the inside tramline. To begin the drill, you must feed a ball into your practice partner, who will then volley the ball back into the court.

The goal of your practice partner (A) is straightforward: to move you around the court with short, acute volleys. Your goal, on the other hand, is to simply hit groundstrokes to return the ball to your practice partner. To do so, you will require great skill, and this drill will assist in developing your footwork to be in the correct position to execute the groundstroke. The exercise is known as 'in the saddle' because you must learn to stay on the balls of your feet every time A hits a volley. In this way, you look like you are 'in the saddle'.

This drill is also great for practising the split-step.

Adding Power: The Kinetic Chain

Generating power in a tennis strokes requires a number of body segments to be coordinated in such a way that the racket-head speed is maximized on contact with the ball. Commonly referred to as the 'Kinetic Chain', linked muscle groups perform rigid movements and act as a system of chain links to maximize the force created. The energy of force generated by one link (part of the body) is transferred successfully to the next link, and any break in this chain will lead to reduced power or increased stress on the joints. For example, the speed of the outgoing ball decreases by approximately 60 per cent when the athlete does not move from the waist down.

Correcting this kinetic chain is the easiest way to add power to your strokes. The more efficient the chain and the fewer breaks, the more power that can be generated with the minimum physical exertion. The normal kinetic chain for most tennis shots starts at the ground and moves up through the legs, torso, shoulder and arm to the racket, and the easiest way to create and develop the chain is

The kinetic chain

with a qualified coach who can break down each element of the stroke to determine where energy is being lost. The most common errors are not loading up on the back leg and failure to rotate the shoulders.

The Importance of Topspin

Topspin has gradually become more and more prominent in the modern men's game, and it is slowly making its way into the women's. But what is topspin and what are its advantages?

A topspin shot is hit by sliding the racket up the back of the ball as it is struck. This friction causes the ball, and a layer of air around the ball, to spin forwards. Because the layer draws the air down, more air gets pulled under the ball than goes above it, and this causes a higher velocity under the ball and a lower velocity on top of the ball. Using Bernoulli's principle, the resulting pressure under the ball is lower than the pressure above the ball, which causes a net force in the downward direction. This brings the ball back down into the court even when hit hard.

To understand the benefits of topspin, it is first necessary to consider the alternative option: the 'flat' shot. A 'flat' shot is one without spin (topspin or 'slice') and, as a result, there is nothing to bring the ball back down into the court except gravity itself. The margin for error is very small because the ball must travel low over the net if it is to land in the court. The court surfaces have also become slower over the years, which means that a ball without spin slows down more on contact, resulting in a far less potent and less consistent shot.

Hitting the ball with topspin creates an 'arc-like' trajectory: the ball rises on contact with the strings before the spin causes the ball to accelerate downwards into court. On contact with the court surface the ball then 'kicks' off. The bounce is also higher because the incoming angle to the court is more acute than on a flat shot. You can hit with a higher net clearance, giving yourself more margin for error in the knowledge that the topspin works to 'pull' the ball back down into court.

Topspin

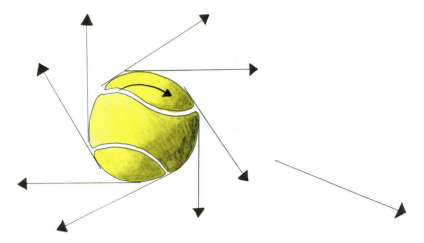

The arc-like trajectory of the topspin stroke also allows you to return the ball with a greater range of angles. The 'dip' generated as the topspin 'pulls' the ball downwards into the court in effect allows you to bend your shots into play because you can get the ball up and down over the net faster than a regular flat shot. This allows you to hit short little angles that would just not be possible without topspin (*red*).

Hitting with topspin does, however, have its dangers. From a purely mechanical standpoint, it is a highly inefficient way to strike the ball because a large proportion of the input energy is 'wasted' as the player brushes 'up' the ball and not directly 'through' it. The great danger for topspin players is that they reduce their racket-head speed as they lose confidence or become fatigued. Any reduction in racket-head speed will lead to a corresponding reduction in ball-rotations, causing the ball to sail long because there is only gravity to bring the ball back down into court. Therefore, as counter-intuitive as it may feel, you must maintain your racket-head speed at all times, even when you are low on confidence.

Topspin (*red*) allows you to hit with a greater variety of angles than a 'flat' shot (*blue*)

The Importance of Depth

'The biggest difference between the top players and the average players is that top players hit deeper,' says legendary coach Nick Bollettieri. Ever wondered how Nadal's performance hinges on whether his heavy topspin forehand penetrates with depth or lands short in the court? It is the same for all the top players: they all keep themselves on the offensive by hitting with depth.

There are too many intermediate players who are content with a groundstroke that travels an inch over the net and lands in the middle of the court, but this type of play is actually the hallmark of a poorly educated player and will be punished by opponents towards the upper echelons of the game. Here is why.

The completion of the kinetic chain (see pages 137–8) requires your opponent to load up and put their body weight through the shot. This is

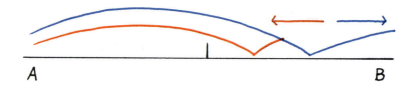

A deep shot pushes your opponent back (*blue*) but a short ball allows them to move forward (*red*)

only possible where your incoming ball allows them to move forward into it because it is very difficult to move forward into a deep, incoming penetrative groundstroke (*blue*) which pushes them back. This prevents them from attacking your shot and ultimately neutralizes their efforts.

On the other hand, a short ball (*red*) that lands in the middle of the court allows your opponent to move forward and complete the kinetic chain, normally resulting in a powerful and penetrative return. While making it much tougher for your opponent to attack, keeping the ball deep will also elicit more errors and weak returns.

At the higher levels of the game the word 'error' becomes more refined. The strict meaning of 'error' is a wayward shot that does not land within the court, but well-trained players will very rarely miss the court, and so hitting the ball into the mid-court constitutes an error at their level. The area into which players can hit the ball effectively becomes smaller as the level improves; a shot that lands in the service box is as much of an error as a shot that sails long.

In a baseline exchange, the ultimate aim is to hit a ball that:

1 Passes approximately two racket lengths above the net
2 Bounces close to the baseline
3 Continues rising as it passes over the baseline after the bounce

To understand why these three characteristics are so fundamental in the efficacy of a topspin shot, it is necessary for us to step into the shoes of your opponent.

The most comfortable place to make contact with the ball is somewhere between waist and shoulder height. It becomes difficult to complete the kinetic chain and create power above this area and anything lower requires excessive knee bend. Some players will naturally feel more comfortable hitting the ball at different heights than others and this will partly depend on style of play and grip. European clay courters employing a western grip, for example, normally find it easier to hit a ball above shoulder height than a grass courter with a more conventional eastern grip.

Most players also want to make contact with the ball at the peak of the trajectory after the bounce, not when it is dropping after the peak or when it is rising up to the peak. Ideally, this peak will be between waist and shoulder height, but when the ball is rising as it passes the baseline after the bounce, an opponent only has two options:

1 Move backwards behind the baseline to wait for the ball to reach its peak
2 Step into the court and take the ball when it is rising immediately after the bounce.

While effective, with Option (1) your opponent is giving up both court space and time. Their stroke is likely to lack any penetration, power and velocity. Option (2) is more difficult. The advantage for your opponent is that they are not giving up time or space, but this technique is very difficult to execute, especially off a high-speed groundstroke. Only highly skilled players who are sufficiently accurate with their timing can achieve this with regularity because any slight misjudgement will lead to a mistake.

This principle goes a long way to explaining Rafael Nadal's continued success over Roger Federer. Nadal has destroyed his Swiss rival on numerous occasions by targeting his backhand with a heavy topspin forehand. Federer is forced to make contact with the ball well above his head height because taking the ball on the rise is especially difficult with his one-handed backhand. On the other hand, Novak Djokovic has enjoyed great success over the Spaniard because he has the incredible ability to step into the court and take Nadal's rising forehand before the ball has reached the peak, by which time it would be too late.

Developing Depth

You must also recognize the bigger picture, for hitting with depth is not the be-all and end-all of a tennis game. The ultimate goal is learning to manipulate the depth of the ball, and this involves hitting short, sharp angles as well as long, deep, penetrative groundstrokes.

Here are some pointers to accelerate your development when looking to develop depth in your groundstroke game.

HEIGHT OVER THE NET

Topspin players should aim approximately 2 m (6 ft) over the net cord. This will help improve depth and the topspin should bring the ball back down into the court. It is extremely difficult to hit consistently with depth when the ball is clearing the net by a couple of centimetres/inches each time.

A celebrated Australian coach once said to me, 'The topspin ball should always be rising when passing the net.' To explain the reasoning for this, it is necessary to consider two scenarios:

Ball rising when passing the net: If the ball is rising when it passes the net cord, there is greater net clearance and the ball will land deep in the court as a result.

Ball dropping when passing the net: A ball that is dropping as it passes the net cord will land short in the court. As a result, the ball will reach your opponent

You can work on developing depth by imagining a 'goal' positioned above the net

at waist or shoulder height, allowing them to step into the ball and attack.

The easiest way to develop this height over the net is by imagining a 'goal' situated approximately 2 m above the net. It is important to continue hitting with spin to ensure that the ball is brought back down into the court.

CREATING SPACE: THE FOREHAND CONTACT POINT

In physics, the moment of a force can be worked out using the following formula:

$$\text{moment} = \text{force applied} \times \text{perpendicular distance from the pivot}$$

As with all great forehands, Novak Djokovic keeps his arm straight on contact

Force applied being equal, the moment of the force applied to the ball will be greater if the perpendicular distance from the pivot (shoulder) is greater. In other words, the force applied to the ball will be greater if the arm is straighter on contact and the less effort the player must put in to create the power. It is simple physics.

An ancillary advantage to this adaptation is that the contact will naturally be out in front of the player, thus ensuring that the follow-through is extended right through the ball. As a result, depth will develop naturally.

Your role as a player then becomes finding the correct position relative to the ball to allow yourself to make contact with your arm straight, slightly bent at the elbow. It will normally take many hours on the practice court to make these modifications to the foot-work and swing but the benefits can be extraordinary and many will find that the ball actually sails long to begin with.

Like Djokovic, Del Potro keeps his arm straight on contact for maximum power and more depth

Developing Your Groundstrokes

As world-renowned tennis coach Peter Burwash says, 'Tennis is a 'game of emergencies.'[2] It is unrealistic to expect the players to be balanced and in position for each shot of a tennis match. Just as players must learn to hit with consistent depth when they are in position for the ball, they must also learn to hit with depth when their feet are not set and the ball is not in the perfect strike zone.

A very good way to develop this advanced-level skill is the following drill.

DRILL: *Hitting to Chest*
You hit from the baseline and your practice partner volleys at the net (*see diagram on page 144*). You must aim to hit the ball to the volleyer's chest (*green*) – anything lower signifies a short ball, whereas anything higher will probably lack penetration and may fly long.

This drill is especially difficult because the ball is only travelling half the distance of the court and so you only have half the time to recover to hit the next shot. Very rarely, therefore, will you have the time to completely load up and set yourself for a stroke and so not only will this drill encourage fast footwork and recovery steps, you will also learn to hit deep ground-strokes when you are not quite in position for the shot.

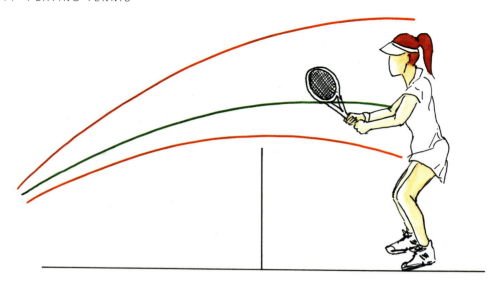

Hitting to the chest

The key to this exercise is regularity. You are working *with* – not against – your practice partner. Your partner should begin by taking some of the pace off the incoming ball, allowing you enough time to work up a sweat before raising the tempo progressively. You must remember that the harder you hit, the faster the ball will return. A fun way to incorporate competition into this drill is to start the point after a twenty-five shot rally. This ensures that you can develop regularity in your ball-striking whilst making it both fun and interesting.

Targets

The simplest way to develop accuracy and consistency with tennis strokes is with targets. Targets can be anything from cones and buckets to court sweepers; it really is not important. Targets are there to give you a visual representation of the zone that you are trying to hit and they also help keep you focused on the task at hand. Here's a great drill I discovered in Germany.

DRILL: *The Broadsheet Challenge 1*

You and a practice partner each have a broadsheet newspaper. You both open up your respective newspapers and place them somewhere on the opposite side of the court to form the target. Rallying from the baseline, you both try to hit your partner's newspaper. If you are successful, he or she must fold that paper in half, making it half the size and thus correspondingly harder to hit. The rallying must continue.

You both continue trying to hit one another's newspaper until one of the papers becomes too small to fold. At this point the winner is congratulated before you both move the paper to another target area to start again.

> **DRILL:** *The Cone Challenge*
> This is a similar exercise to the one above, but executed with cones instead of newspapers. In this case, you and your partner will simply move the 'hit' cone to a different position on the court, forcing the successful player to a different position on the court while their opponent continues to target the original cone.

You must work up the pace of your strokes gradually and work together with your practice partner. Remember, points are awarded for accuracy – not speed – and so you should avoid trying to 'overplay'.

Tempo: Controlled Aggression

The accuracy and power of the modern game is greater than ever before. At times, the groundstrokes of the top players can appear laser-like, their technique almost robotic and execution supreme. While there are many players out there who can hit a given target on a tennis court, the hallmark of quality is the ability to do so at a high tempo whilst maintaining consistency.

If two intermediate players were asked to hit a forty-shot rally, almost inevitably they would retreat behind the baseline, slow down their racket-head speed and reduce the tempo of the rally. Advanced players are able to hit with 'controlled aggression', in which they hit highly penetrative groundstrokes at a high tempo whilst remaining in complete control of the shot. The point at which players loses control of their groundstrokes will be largely dependent on their standard. This drill is excellent for developing this skill.

> **DRILL:** *Tempo*
> Rally down the line with your practice partner in a half court and count how many shots you can hit together in a sixty-second period. Stepping too far behind the baseline and reducing racket-head speed will result in a low score, as will trying to hit too hard and missing. Therefore, you are encouraged to find the maximum speed and intensity at which you remain in control of your shots.

This drill should be a regular feature of high-level tennis training and you should keep a track of your scores as you develop over time. As a reference point, professional players will achieve approximately forty-five shots in a minute at full pace (but anything above thirty is respectable).

To increase your scores, you should try hitting harder, taking the ball earlier and 'flattening' out your strokes.

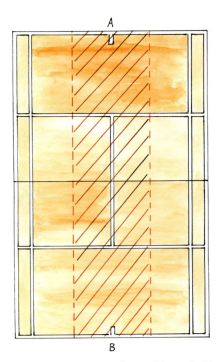

Hitting down the middle

Accuracy: Hitting Down the Middle

It is easy to overcomplicate tennis development with drills and exercises that are hard to understand, never mind execute. A great way to practise consistency, footwork and accuracy is to practise hitting down the centre of the court – something that sounds far simpler than it actually is. You should draw two lines about 2 m (approx. 6 ft) apart from baseline to baseline and simply rally with your partner within these boundaries (*see the diagram on the left*).

By hitting within a defined area, you are forced to create the space for the correct contact point because the ball is coming directly into your body. The margins are small and contacting the ball too early or too late will normally result in the ball sailing wide or long. You will need highly accurate strokes and great footwork if you are to execute this drill at a high tempo. Hitting down the middle into a small channel is probably the easiest way to develop this laser-like precision.

Counteracting the Topspin Ball: Stepping into the Court

Topspin is a powerful weapon at all levels of the game. That said, you must also be able to 'flatten' the ball to put pressure on your opponent. More importantly, tennis requires flexibility and you must be able to adapt your game accordingly if you are to overcome opponents with different game styles, and this may involve adopting a slightly 'flatter' groundstroke in the match.

This drill is normally executed on a half court with players who have a high standard of tennis and a decent technical understanding of the 'flat' shot, i.e. the swing starts 'high' and finishes low. If not, you should work with a coach to develop this technique before attempting this drill.

DRILL: *Stepping into the Court*
Draw a line running parallel to the baseline and approximately 1 m (approx. 3 ft) inside the court. Balls that land before this line are considered 'short'. Rally up and down the line with your practice partner and whenever the ball lands 'short', you must step forward into the court and take the ball early while it is rising, i.e. hit a flat, aggressive shot (*see the diagram on page 147*).

This drill requires a certain amount of anticipation because you will be required to contact the ball before the ball has reached the peak of its trajec-

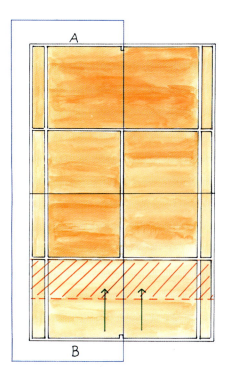

Stepping into the short ball

tory following the bounce. To do this, you will often need to begin your movements into the court before the ball has actually bounced.

Consistency

After a wonderful junior career, including lifting three of the four junior Grand Slam events in 2013, Filip Peliwo's next step was to make his mark on the senior professional tour. Besides the incredible mental strength and intensity of the top players, Peliwo noted that the hardest adjustment has been consistency. 'I have to always keep my average level high in order to succeed. I can no longer afford to make silly errors or give free points away,' he says.

Consistency is important at all levels of the game, but what often distinguishes the winner from the loser in a match is the number of unforced errors. Giving away cheap points is a sure-fire way to lose a match. Coaches will often teach you to either defend or attack – it is either black or white, with each shot you are either attacking or defending. This, however, is unrealistic.

While you can defend and you can attack, a high number of shots in the ball will be neutral, i.e. you are neither attacking or defending. The goal with these 'rally' shots is to probe your opponent, applying pressure but not trying to hit a winner, and looking to create the opportunity to attack. These shots have to be deep, penetrative but low risk, and to learn this skill you must be patient. All these attributes are required to succeed in this exercise. This drill is particularly applicable to clay-court training where the slow surface does not lend itself to high-risk strategies.

From the baseline, both you and your practice partner begin with five 'lives' and hit into a full, open court. The only rule is that no 'winners' are allowed. If either of you hits a 'winner', i.e. a shot where the other player does not touch it and cannot reasonably be expected to reach it, you must restart the point. It is important that you both attempt to get to the ball, avoiding the temptation to let a ball fly past for an illegitimate 'winner'.

The scoring system is also slightly different. When one of you 'wins' a point through a forced or unforced error by the other, the 'winner' receives one of the opponent's 'lives' to go 6–3, 7–3, 8–2, 10–0. The winner is the first to reach 10-0.

The idea behind the drill is quite simple: you must learn to construct the point by moving your opponent around the court and forcing an error. Hitting winners will inevitably win the point, but you are unlikely to win the match if you adopt such high-risk strategies that require you to hit 'winner' after 'winner'. This drill, therefore, encourages you to hit with controlled aggression, moving the ball around with depth and accuracy, probing and testing your opponent until you draw a forced error and, ultimately, in the point. The scoring system strongly discourages unforced errors by penalization.

An ancillary benefit of this drill is that it teaches you to adapt your tactics to the scoreline. For example, if you are losing 8–2 in this drill, you must learn to adapt your game accordingly to minimize the chances of making a further error. Conversely, if you are leading 8–2, you can afford to take some more risks and be more aggressive. This skill is particularly important in high level tennis and can be seen where the top players play faultless tennis on the big points or for the duration of the tie-breaker, for example. For this very reason, this drill should almost become never ending when executed by advanced players of similar standards because both should be able to adapt their games to the scoreline.

Achieving Movement and Accuracy

Success at any advanced level requires both excellent movement and strong, accurate groundstrokes. To practise both these skills together, you can execute the 2-on-1 drill as used by Harry Hopman, one of the most highly respected coaches in history, on players including John Newcombe, Tony Roche and Roy Emerson in a time long before tennis academies existed.

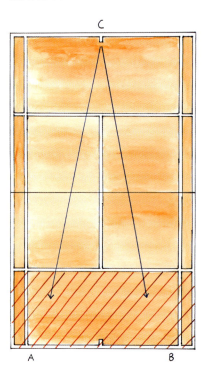

The 2-on-1 drill

DRILL: *The 2-on-1: Basic*
Two players (A and B) stand in the corners on the baseline on the side of the court while you (C) – the subject of the exercise – stand on the opposite side covering the whole court. A and B are there simply to return the ball and give you as many balls as they can while you must focus on moving towards the ball and using a controlled, accurate groundstroke to hit the ball at their target area.

The benefit of the exercise is that exchanges are more intense because you will have to hit more balls and cover more court than against just a single player. It is important that this intensity is maintained at all times and each player should carry balls in their pockets to feed into play as soon as a ball goes astray.

The 2-on-1 drill can also be used to practise both defence and offence – see the drills below.

DRILL: *The 2-on-1: Offence*
Instruct A and B to hit neutral, controlled balls back to you (C), moving you around without applying too much pressure, thus allowing you to attack.

Hitting with too much power will only prevent you from attacking. Conversely, the drill will become ineffective should A and B begin 'pushing' the ball over the net with little force. So, there is a balance to be struck and A and B must move the ball around the court with pace and consistency, but also allow you to retain the initiative in the rally.

Your goal is to hit the ball with consistent depth to A and B in the corners. You must try to be as aggressive as possible but not to the extent that you lose control of the ball. In this way, it is the ability to change the direction of the balls and hit targets rather than the actual speed of the shot that is being practised.

As accuracy and control develop, you can then begin to hit with more power. At all times, you must try to put A and B under pressure, hitting with regular depth, using angles and maintaining a very high intensity in your movement and groundstrokes.

This drill should also be attempted with both A and B volleying at the net to put you under more pressure and force you to hit with aggression when not fully in position for the ball.

To practise your defence and the ability to neutralize an opponent's attack, try the following drill:

DRILL: *The 2-on-1: Defence*
Instruct A and B to hit with more aggression and move the ball around the court using angles.

This drill is particularly applicable to clay court players where the ability to hit consistently and defend is perhaps tested most vigorously. Your single goal here is to get the ball back in play, neutralizing the attack and forcing A and B to play at least one more ball. It is important to note that A and B must once again strike a balance for this exercise to be effective. While they must apply pressure by moving you around, they are not looking to win the point by putting the ball away.

The following adaptation of the 2-on-1 exercise allows you to drill one particular stroke with great intensity.

DRILL: *The 2-on-1: Intense Stroke Development (Forehand)*

A and B play against you as before (*see 2-on-1: Defence, page 149*), but here you only have to cover half the court depending on the shot you need to practise. So, if you are a right-hander and want to practise your forehand (*see diagram on the right*), A and B must hit only to the forehand side of the court you are covering.

You must recover to the centre of the baseline after each shot and should focus most of your attention on hitting cross court to ensure you are hitting over the lower part of the net and giving yourself more space into which you can hit.

The 2-on-1 drill tweaked to focus on your forehand groundstroke

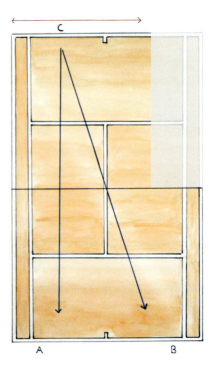

This adaptation can be used to great effect to develop your inside-out/inside-in forehand. (*see diagram below on the left*)

DRILL: *The 2-on-1: Intense Stroke Development (Inside-out Forehand)*

Place a line of cones from the baseline to the net down the middle of the court. A and B must strike the ball with consistency and depth to your backhand side, but give you enough time to run around the backhand to hit the forehand. Alternatively, you are permitted to hit backhands but must work the opportunity to run around your backhand to attack with your inside-out/inside-in forehand.

To increase the difficulty of this drill, you can open up more space by moving the cones across the court to the forehand side (approx. ¾ of the court width).

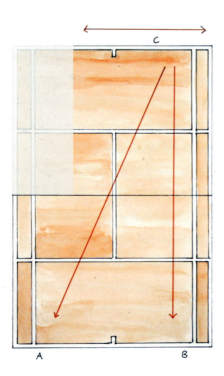

The 2-on-1 drill tweaked to focus on your inside-out forehand

This drill will allow you to practise the inside-out/inside-in forehand and the rapid footwork required to get around the ball and open up the space. It is imperative that you recover to the middle of the baseline after each shot.

Practising the Serve Effectively

A positive it most certainly is, but an accurate groundstroke game will not win matches on its own. The serve is the only shot where you have complete control of placement of the ball and taking the time to improve this stroke will have a greater impact on your game than spending the same amount of time on any other area of technique.

For many, the serve is the foundation for tennis success. Pete Sampras, Serena Williams and Roger Federer – three of the greatest players ever to grace a tennis court – undeniably have three of the most consistent and accurate serves ever seen and it is no coincidence that all three have ruled tennis' elite for many a year. But what constitutes a strong serve?

Speed? Power? Certainly. It is unfortunate really, because the sublime shot-making and ballet-like movement of Roger Federer has actually drawn attention away from his service delivery. With an average first serve speed of 201 km/h (approx. 125 mph), the Swiss may not have the speed of Roddick's, or the topspin of Sampras', but he still wins approximately 70 per cent of his first serve points. Why, you ask?

The answer is simple: accuracy and disguise.

Federer shows that bigger is not always better. The Swiss is deadly accurate at hitting all different targets off exactly the same ball toss, and the same applies in the women's game. Serena Williams has taken women's tennis to a new level with her powerful, elegant serving. Her motion is exactly the same regardless of what side of the box she is hitting and, as Martina Hingis said after one their duels at Flushing Meadows, it is 'impossible to read'.

While you need a certain amount of speed and power on delivery, there is a point where the influence of these aspects will begin to plateau. At this point, accuracy and disguise on the motion become imperative. In this way, hitting a 225 km/h (approx. 140 mph) rocket down the centre is actually less effective than a 193 km/h (approx. 120 mph) serve carefully placed in the corner of the service box.

Although it can be less fun than sparring, practising the serve is fundamental to success at any level

Second Serve

As Pete Sampras once claimed, a player is only as strong as their second serve. Looking at the statistics on the ATP Tour, there is a very strong correlation between the percentage of second serve points and the world rankings. Many of the game's greats, including Roger Federer, Rafael Nadal, Novak Djokovic, Pete Sampras and Jim Courier, all feature towards the top end of rankings of percentage of points won on second serve. Indeed, seven of the top ten on this list made it to World Number One and only three of the top twenty have failed to break into the top ten: Wayne Arthurs, Kohlschreiber and Wally Masur. 'Pistol' Pete, it would seem, was right.

But questions still remain as to what exactly you should do with the second serve. For many years, coaches have been encouraging their players to just get their second serve 'in' the court. It does make sense: you cannot win a point if you do not put the ball in play. However, there is a growing body of evidence, especially on the men's side, that advanced players would actually benefit from hitting two first serves – even factoring in for the rise in double faults.

Figures indicate that the average professional player will make approximately 65 per cent of their first serves and over 90 per cent of their second serves. Of these points, the player will win approximately 65 per cent of the first serve points, while their second-serve percentage will sit at around 50 per cent. From a purely statistical standpoint, therefore, hitting two first serves would appear to bear more reward.

This is not to say that you should hit two first serves. We cannot place too much onus on these statistics for they fail to account for other key considerations including confidence, the opponent, the surface and, most importantly, the psychological impact of hitting a double fault.

For this reason, as explained by renowned coach and former ATP player, Galo Blanco, you are advised to simply make a tiny adjustment for your second serve to hit with greater spin, marginally less speed and more safety. To do this, it is important that you maintain the racket-head speed but brush the ball to generate more spin. This will add control and bring the ball back into the court. At all times, the motion must remain the same as the first serve. It is, however, important to get the right balance between control and aggression and this will be specific to you as a player.

Practising the Serve

The secret to a good service is practice. All you need is a basket of balls, a tennis court and some targets. The drill does not even need a partner. That said, you should aim to train 'smart'. This means practising serving at the beginning of each training session, after the body is warmed up but before the body is fatigued from running around after that yellow ball for two hours. The serve is best practised when fresh and focused, not when tired and exhausted.

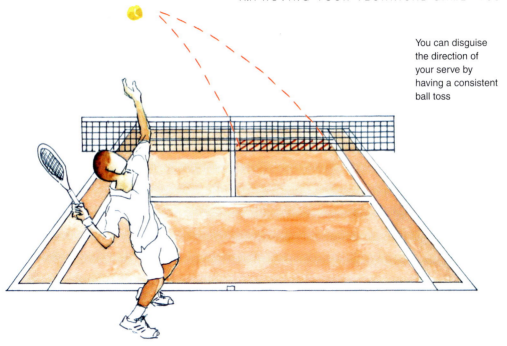

You can disguise the direction of your serve by having a consistent ball toss

The ball toss is fundamental to a quality service delivery. The contact point for all serves, except the 'kick', should be out in front of you to your forehand side. Practising the ball toss does not require a tennis court or even a racket. With your non-racket-holding hand, toss the ball up in the air and see where it bounces.

If you imagine yourself standing in the middle of a giant clock face, you are trying to get the ball to land at between 1 o'clock and 2 o'clock about a foot in front of your leading leg, or just inside the baseline. Open the palm of your hand on release and pivot at the shoulder, not the elbow. It really is a placement rather than a 'toss', as such. Only with a consistent, well-placed ball-toss should you begin hitting the serve.

The best servers in the world can all hit different targets with exactly the same motion. The only differences in their service motions will occur high up the kinetic chain, namely at the racket face angle as determined by the forearm pronation and internal shoulder rotation. This is best described using a clock-face analogy.

Imagining the ball up in the air, to hit a flat serve you must contact the ball where the hands attach to the clock face, i.e. in the middle of the face (*top*). To hit a slice serve, the angle of the racket face will be changed slightly to make contact at 3 o'clock on the face (*middle*). This will impart spin on the ball with a brushing motion.

In this way, your ball toss and stance must remain constant if disguise is to be maintained. It is important, therefore, that you have a consistent, regular ball toss off which you are able to hit a variety of different serves and targets. Pete Sampras was famous for practising his serve with his coach calling out the target after the ball toss had been released to ensure that his player was not changing the toss.

Tom Berdych's well-drilled ball toss allows him to deliver the ball with both power and accuracy

Flat

Slice

The direction of your serve is controlled by where you make contact with the ball

Topspin / 'Kick'

The 'kick' serve is an exception to this rule because it requires the ball to be tossed above the back shoulder, landing on the server's head. Arching the back, you will then brush up the back of the ball from 7 o'clock to 2 o'clock, thus generating topspin on the ball (*bottom*).

You must learn 'smart' and this can be done by correcting yourself after each misplaced toss. Any ball toss that sways too far to the left should be followed by a ball toss further to the right. Any ball toss too far behind you should be followed by a ball toss further out in front. By self-correcting, the body and mind will learn to calibrate the position of the placement. To practise this, you must learn *why* your ball toss is going where it is.

The forward and backwards position of the ball is controlled by the timing of the release. Releasing the ball later in the motion will push the ball further back, and releasing earlier will fire the ball forward. The sideways motion is slightly trickier and must be learned by straightening out the movement of your arm up to the point of release. You should also practise an abbreviated ball toss designed for windy conditions.

The tennis serve is probably the most complex stroke in the game. To hit with accuracy, power and control requires a very precise synchronization of limb and joint movements to summate and get the transfer forced from the ground up through the kinetic chain and out into the ball.

While it is not possible to write an exhaustive guide to correct all problems of the tennis serve, here are some tips that can help remedy some common mistakes.

The easiest way to counteract a 'long' serve is to make contact with the ball further out in front of the body. This can be done by adjusting the ball toss to land slightly further inside the court. You can also add some slice or 'kick'. This can normally be compounded with a little bit of wrist-snap on contact to further bring the ball down into the court. The ball will go in the net if the contact point is too far in front of you. To counteract this, toss the ball slightly closer to the baseline.

Serving under pressure can be a major obstacle for even technically advanced players. It is, however, possible to practise the ability to maintain a fluid, consistent serving motion when under pressure through a series of training drills. Jimmy Connors, for example, was known to regularly play sets where the server always starts at 30–40, the goal being to build confidence and hone the ability to hit the biggest serves when most needed. Other great drills include playing best-of-five-set matches from four-all to train the mind to focus from the first game of the set, and simply counting how many times the server can hit a specific target out of a set number of balls. This immediately applies pressure because each serve is recorded.

The Return of Serve

'What you've done this year will probably never be repeated,' said an ever gracious Rafael Nadal as he addressed the crowd on a blustery Arthur Ashe Court in New York. He was, of course, talking to Novak Djokovic, the man who had just defeated him for a sixth consecutive time, this time in the 2011 US Open Final to lift his third Grand Slam title of the year. And Nadal was right: it was a breathtaking season; one in which Djokovic made history and raised the bar of world tennis to unprecedented new heights. Going forty-three matches without a loss and finishing the season with a 70–6 overall record, at times Djokovic appeared almost unbeatable.

We can all watch in awe at his forehand. We can smile at his movement, and we can gaze in wonder as he dips a backhand passing shot inside the service line with all the precision of a mathematician, but a key ingredient in the Serb's success is his return of serve.

Statistics point out the Djokovic regularly wins more than 60 per cent of points returned on second serve and nearly 40 per cent of first serve returns. For many years, the return was used to neutralize the server's advantage and put the receiver in the rally on equal terms, but the slowing down of the court surfaces and the development of better equipment has seen the return being used as a weapon by the stronger players in the modern game as they are now able to attack the serve and start the rally on the front foot themselves.

In 2012 Nadal returned to the top of the men's game, turning the tables on his Serbian rival. The Spaniard's return of serve is greatly underrated. He is not flashy but he is intelligent with his variation and he reads patterns better than anyone else on the tour. A great factor behind Nadal's success was that he simply returned a higher percentage of serves to draw a line under his seven-match losing streak to Djokovic. Just as important as the serve may be, the return of serve is equally influential.

All greatest returners have an incredible ability to take the return when it is rising. They step into the court and are sometimes inside the baseline when making contact with the ball. These players will normally begin about three or four feet behind the baseline and move in to the court with a split-step as the server completes their motion.

Other players actually move backwards on the return of serve. Rafael Nadal is a great pioneer of this tactic on his beloved clay, and Roger Federer began to use it on the hard courts. Instead of moving into the court to use a compact motion, the returner moves backwards to take a bigger swing. This is normally used on second serves to buy the returner enough time to attack the serve with their favourite groundstroke.

Another common belief is that the player should split-step as the server makes contact with the ball. Research actually indicates that the best returners are normally in the air at the point of the server's contact; the split-step is actually executed just before the server makes contact with the ball. The player should be landing from the split-step just as the ball is crossing the net, allowing them to explode in the direction of the ball.

Interestingly, studies also indicate that the best players are actually looking at the body of the returner instead of the ball itself when returning serve. In other words, they are reading the serve by looking at the body position of the server, moving almost before the server has executed the stroke. Anticipation becomes key at advanced levels because the returner only has approximately 0.3 seconds to react to return a 209 km/h (130 mph) serve.

RETURNING A 'KICK' SERVE

Drills to develop the return of the serve are detailed in Chapter 7, but if you are competing at the higher levels, you must also develop a 'kick' serve return. Very much a hallmark of the advanced tennis game, the 'kick' comes in slowly but jumps high in the opposite direction to a slice serve on impact with the ground. Identifying, or 'reading,' a 'kick' serve is actually very easy because the ball is tossed above the server's head and the trajectory of the ball is higher over the net. Generally speaking, returners have three options:

- Hit the ball at its peak after the bounce. A good 'kick' can bounce 6 ft high and so the returner will be swinging out of the comfort zone and will have been dragged off court.
- Wait for the ball to come down after the bounce, at which point the player will normally be behind the baseline or out of the tramlines; the returner is sacrificing time and space on the court.
- Step into the ball and take the ball before it has 'kicked' to the peak. This prevents the ball from reaching an uncomfortable height and stops the returner from being dragged off court. By taking the ball on the rise, the returner can also be more aggressive and will often catch the server off guard. This is the best method of returning a kick serve, but it will require an advanced player to anticipate the 'kick' so as to allow them to move up the court and take the ball on the rise.

The Shot After the Serve: Setting Up the Point

‘ I serve where I can serve. I serve [to a] position [where] I will have
better chance to start better the point. ’
RAFAEL NADAL, *speaking in a press conference at the Australian Open*
(24 January 2014)

Rafael Nadal's precise lefty serve and heavy forehand provided the platform
for his rise to the very pinnacle of his beloved game, but he does not have
a very powerful serve. And neither does Roger Federer. The list can go on.
David Ferrer, former World Number 3, has a below-par service but an
incredibly precise forehand. All of these players – and there are more –
possess incredibly strong forehand groundstrokes but slow services relative
to many other, less successful players on the ATP Tour. How, then, do all
three sit comfortably within the world's top ten?

In their 2013 meeting in London at the end-of-season Masters, Rafael
Nadal made Roger Federer hit an incredible 87 per cent backhands from
his first serve and 76 per cent on his second serve. Federer knew what was
coming but he could do nothing about it. The benefit to the Spaniard is
twofold: not only is he targeting the weaker shot (the backhand) of the
Swiss, but he is also setting himself up for a forehand as his first shot after
the serve. Indeed, 71 per cent of Nadal's shots after the serve were forehands
and he won 70 per cent of those points. Nadal's forehand is the most potent
the game has known and he brings it into play
by serving intelligently.

The shot after the serve is one of the most
widely overlooked shots in the game. Not even
the best servers in the world can hit endless
consecutive aces in a match and so you must
be able to use the serve as a set-up to allow
you to dominate the point with your groundstrokes. Mistakes in tennis come by applying
pressure, and controlled aggression on the
shot after the serve immediately puts the
server in a dominant position. As a server, you
must learn to serve intelligently to set up your
strongest groundstroke after the serve; if
returning, you must prevent the server from
doing so.

For many years, Nadal's success over
Federer was based on a simple game-plan:
target the backhand (*green*). Following his
semi-final victory over the Swiss at the 2014
Australian Open, Nadal was asked why he
served almost exclusively to the backhand, to

Djokovic puts
Nadal on the back
foot by returning
the ball to Nadal's
backhand (*red*)
instead of his
forehand (*blue*)

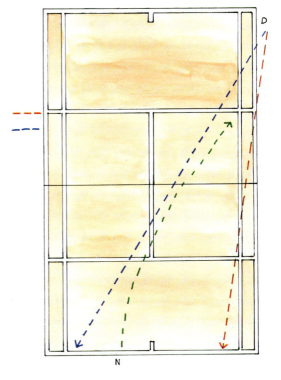

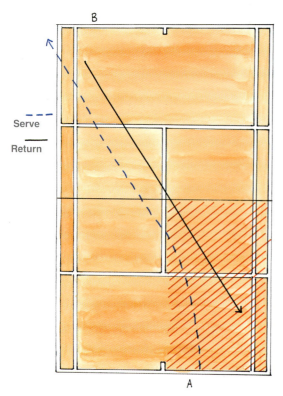

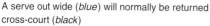

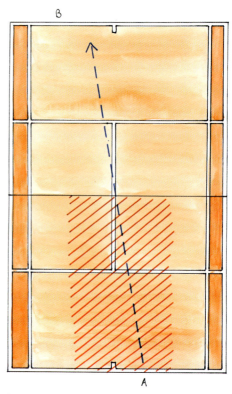

A serve out wide (*blue*) will normally be returned cross-court (*black*)

A serve down the middle (*blue*) will normally be returned down the middle (*red*)

which he replied: 'Today I felt that serving against his backhand I had the chance to start the point with a little bit of an advantage.' Federer, with his preference for the one-hander, always struggled to combat the Nadal serve and so was consistently returning the ball cross court into the Nadal forehand (*blue*) and thus starting points on the back foot.

For Djokovic, however, it could not be more different. Nadal has always struggled against the Serb, and one of the primary reasons behind this is Djokovic's ability to counter Nadal's one–two combination that had been so potent against Federer. The 'Djoker's' double-handed return was strong enough to return Nadal's out-wide lefty serve on the advantage side down the line (*red*), thus preventing Nadal from dominating with his forehand. Djokovic used his return down the line to put Nadal on the back foot from the beginning of the point (*see diagram on page 157*).

Developing this skill and learning to attack with the shot after the serve is inextricably linked to intelligent serving. Different serves will initiate different replies; a serve outside (*see above diagram, top left*) will normally generate a cross-court return and a serve down the middle will normally generate a return down the middle because there are few other angles open (*see above diagram, top right*). David Ferrer and Nadal will even take a step to their backhand sides to open up their forehand side. A risky strategy it may appear, but it's a risk they are willing to take.

Practising the Shot after the Serve

To execute this shot effectively, you will need a good recovery step after the completion of the serve motion. The best servers will jump and land inside the baseline following the serve and the recovery step allows them to return to their position behind the baseline. This footwork pattern can be developed by your coach dropping a ball in front of you immediately after the service motion has been completed. For this to work, you will need to recover behind the baseline in order to attack the dropped ball. The idea is to develop a habit of completing this footwork pattern that can then be applied to a point situation when the ball is returned from the other side of the court.

Once this pattern has been developed, there are two great drills to develop the skill of attacking the shot after the serve. It must be remembered that the serve is the foundation for setting up a strong shot after the serve and so there is little point practising the drills below unless you already possess a consistent service motion. Both drills will also work on your serve and your return of serve.

> **DRILL:** *Conditioned Point Play*
> You serve the ball to your practice partner. You must then finish the point within three shots after the serve, or you forfeit the point.

This drill forces you to be aggressive and serve intelligently with a view to setting up a short ball to attack. It is only natural that mistakes will be made so you must be patient. Improvements will come.

> **DRILL:** *Half-Court Point Play*
> You serve the ball to your practice partner, who must return to ball cross court to you. The point is then played out cross-court and you are only allowed to hit forehands. You benefit by knowing where the return will land, and your partner practises the return of serve. Switch side after each point.

It is often said that tennis is a game of inches, and at the higher levels, it is. As you develop, it will quickly become apparent that simply hitting the ball over the net and into the court no longer suffices. In addition to hitting the ball over the net and into the court, you must learn to hit with consistent precision in *all* areas of your game, and this can be only achieved by training intelligently. The above drills represent the first step along this long and arduous pathway.

CHAPTER SEVEN

Fitness Training for Tennis

> ❝ I have lost many matches where I have had to over-risk because I was not there physically. ❞
> ALEXANDR DOLGOPOLOV, ATP *World Number 53*

I used to run a lot as a kid. As a fifteen-year-old, I remember running around the school fields at lunch to try to get fit for tennis. My understanding was that this was enough; I rarely went to the gym and I never worked with a fitness professional. This all changed when I went to Spain and was given my own personal training programme. Before and after tennis each day, I would head down to the park to complete my fitness work. I also began Pilates and yoga work both to relax and increase my flexibility. I could feel the difference after just four weeks. I felt lighter on the court. I was faster moving to my shots. I could play for longer and hit the ball harder. My shoulder injuries were no more, and my results began to improve. It quickly became apparent that the game of tennis requires a very specific type of fitness – one that favours squats, jumps and sprints instead of running, running and more running.

To learn more about the best physical conditioning for tennis, I spoke with Jez Green, former fitness trainer to Andy Murray, and Terry Longmore, former Director of Fitness at Dukes Meadows Tennis Academy, London.

Being Fit to Play with the Best

The importance of physical conditioning in success can be seen right at the top of the modern game. According to Alexandr Dolgopolov, the World Number 53, physical fitness is what separates the top players from the rest. 'They [the top players] are clearly very technically talented but they can also hit harder, run faster, run longer than the others,' he says. 'They are just too solid for everyone else and they outrun them.'

Inducted into the Australian Tennis Hall of Fame in 1996 after steering his country to an astonishing fifteen Davis Cup titles, Harry Hopman's coaching methods became notorious after his nurturing of such prestigious talents as Frank Sedgman, Tony Roche, Ken Rosewall, John Newcombe, and Rod Laver. He was known as 'The Wizard' – and the wizard he was.

A fundamental ingredient in Hopman's success was his work ethic. Demanding complete commitment and dedication from his players at all times, Hopman recognized the importance of physical fitness in on-court success. 'He was a man who looked after everything,' says Lewis Hoad, Hopman's contemporary, in an interview with *L'Equipe*. 'For example, on my first trip around the world in his team in 1951, I had to work on my fitness more than others. So he regularly took me for extra jogging at night-fall while other players were at the hotel.'

Hopman was ahead of his time: he recognized the importance of physical conditioning well before the game did. This was a time when strength training for tennis was not standard even among the most professional of players, and it was not until the late 1980s, and the great Ivan Lendl, that physical conditioning was finally recognized as an established element of performance tennis. Indeed, John McEnroe, the player who gave way to Lendl's dominance, avoided the gym almost completely and played doubles instead of working on his fitness.

Similar to Hopman, Lendl was known for his tireless work ethic and focus on physical fitness. In order to reach the top of the game, Lendl believed he had to work harder than anyone else. He went on 10-mile runs after matches and took regular blood tests to ensure that he was eating correctly. He once celebrated his seventy-seventh professional tournament victory with a 37-mile bike ride around Greenwich, Connecticut. Labelled the 'father of modern tennis', Lendl's obsessional approach to physical fitness marked the start of the modern era.

Lendl's contemporaries quickly followed. On the women's side, Martina Navratilova became the first to incorporate a weight-training programme into her regime. Just a couple of years later, a nineteen-year-old Andre Agassi walked into a gym at the University of Nevada, and began work with Gil Reyes – an important step on the path to becoming one of the game's finest ever players. Fast forward to today and every young athlete now has a strength-training coach and a conditioning routine.

In the last twenty years, tennis has changed. Gone are the days of deft touches and precision serves. Developments in sports science alongside advances in technology and evolution of techniques have led to a more physical game; a game where brute force and physical endurance have become key factors in determining who wins and who loses.

The importance of physical conditioning rests upon the sheer physicality of the game itself. On top of the power and strength required to hit the ball, matches can last anywhere from thirty minutes to five hours and players must be able to maintain these high standards throughout the entire duration. Regardless of their technical ability, players must be able to maintain the intensity, the footwork and the power at all times while on the court.

Physical conditioning is also closely linked to mental strength. As Dolgopolov points out, 'It's easy to be mentally strong when you know you're properly physically conditioned. Lots of players will break mentally because

Rafael Nadal's physical conditioning programme is tailored specifically for his needs to both prevent injury and maximize his performance

they know that they can't last the whole match,' he says. 'If you're ready physically, then mentally it's much easier,' Richard Gasquet told me.

Forming a Fitness Plan

> ❝ If I was training Novak [Djokovic] or Rafa [Nadal], I would not train them in the same way I have trained Andy. ❞
> JEZ GREEN, *former Fitness Trainer to Andy Murray*

Andy Murray first broke onto the international tennis scene in 2005 with a defeat to David Nalbandian on the lawns of SW19. Cramping up over the course of the five-set thriller, the Scot showed he had the game to become a champion but that he lacked the physical fitness. With the help of Jez Green, a former pro kickboxer, Murray has gone on to become one of the most physically well-rounded players in the game.

Well documented, his fitness plan includes weights, running and sprinting in a regime that would make the average man cry. 'Andy was so quick, he just needed strength; he realized he had to last longer and be stronger, and so we formulated a programme around that,' says Green.

Andy Murray's strength and conditioning programme allows him to hit harder and outlast many of his opponents

Unloved by the wider world at the age of eighteen, Novak Djokovic was considered fortunate to have faced Jo-Wilfried Tsonga, rather than Federer or Nadal, in his first Grand Slam final in Melbourne. Indeed, it was not until 2011 that the world began to recognize the Serb for the prolific talent that he is. Besides fine-tuning his transition from the baseline to the net and adopting a gluten-free diet, the major change came in the form of Gebhard Phil-Gritsch, former strength and conditioning coach of Thomas Muster.

Under the Austrian's supervision, Djokovic has gone on to become one of the most resilient performers the game has seen, beautifully showcased by his 2012 Australian Open victory where he ousted Nadal in a 5 hr 53 min final – just forty-eight hours after his breathtaking semi-final triumph over Murray in a highly physical five-set thriller. Unlike Murray, Djokovic spends less time with weights, and works primarily on court with core stability drills alongside high-intensity movement exercises designed to boost his speed, endurance and agility.

Jez Green (*far left*) has moulded Murray into one of the world's fittest tennis players

Rafael Nadal naturally has a very muscular body type and so he does not need to overdo his time in the gym. The Spaniard's programme is largely dictated by his troublesome knees; he works with his fitness team, Rafael Maymo and Joan Forcades, to maximize performance and prevent injuries by taking pressure off the lower body. Exercises include

Novak Djokovic's incredible fitness levels saw him overcome Rafael Nadal in a stunning 5 hr 53 min. final victory at the 2012 Australian Open

improving cardio-fitness by running in waist-high waters and using a balance board or Bosu ball to develop all-round stability. Nadal also works extensively on shoulder stability exercises with resistance bands to minimize the chances of injury in light of his extremely physical playing style and 'lasoo-like' forehand.

The point is that all tennis fitness regimes are unique to the individual needs of the player. While all players will incorporate flexibility, strength, endurance, and agility training into their individual programmes, each will focus on these aspects in varying amounts.

'The plan is based around the player's game style, body and the style of their trainer,' says Green. 'You build a professional player; you don't guess,' he adds. 'Developing players will need expert advice on physical training as early as sixteen years old.'

Tennis Conditioning in Performance Maximization

Training to develop the unique blend of endurance, strength and flexibility required for high-performance tennis simultaneously is no easy task. There are two elements to fitness training for performance maximization: flexibility and weight training.

A word of warning: you are strongly advised to consult a qualified fitness professional before starting a new physical conditioning routine.

Assuming that you have been given the all-clear, the following exercises can be used to enhance your performance on the court.

Flexibility

Novak Djokovic has many qualities that have allowed him to reach the very pinnacle of the game: he possesses almost flawless technique, astounding mental strength and the tactical acumen of a great champion, but it is his remarkably elastic frame that became one of the defining characteristics in what was a golden era of men's tennis. The Serb has an incredible ability to stretch himself to the corners to reach balls that would have been perceived as 'unreturnable' before his meteoric rise to superstardom.

While genetics are inevitably a factor (his father, Srdjan, was a competitive skier), the Serb's elasticity is far from coincidental. Instead, it is a result of a very specific training routine masterminded by Jelena Gencic, the coach with whom the Serb worked from the age of six until his early teens when he left to attend Niki Pilić's tennis academy in Germany. Gencic recognized just how important endurance was going to be in the modern game and imparted to Djokovic a number of key virtues about taking care of his muscles.

'You know Novak was not a strong boy. You know how he is now elastic and flexible. Do you know why?' Gencic once asked in a 2010 interview in

Belgrade. 'It is because I didn't want to work too hard with him. [Pointing to her racket] This is the heaviest thing he has to handle. We only worked on his legs, his fitness on the court, not in the weight room. We stretched and did special movements for tennis, to be flexible, to be agile and to be fast and with the legs.'

Today, flexibility remains the cornerstone of the Serb's physical training routine, stretching whenever the opportunity allows. It plays a key role in Djokovic's on-court performance, allowing him to recover faster between matches and minimizing the chances of injury – is it really any coincidence that Djokovic has not been absent from a Grand Slam event since 2005? So proud he is of his bendiness that the Serb is rumoured to keep a treasured photo of himself at his Monte Carlo apartment – he just so happens to be striking a backhand return with his left leg above his head.

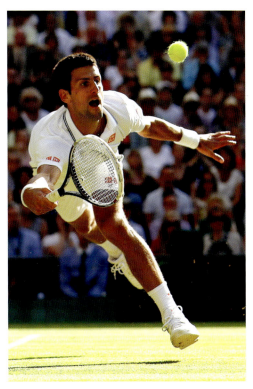

Defined as the range of motion of the joints and the degree to which muscles, tendons and connective tissue around the joints can elongate and bend, flexibility is an incredibly important part of a player's physical development and is incorporated into all training routines of the top players.

Novak Djokovic's well-documented flexibility routine allows him to reach shots that other players simply cannot

Flexibility does, however, remain one of the most overlooked elements of fitness. Most players don't like stretching because it doesn't feel good and the benefits do not immediately present themselves. There is also very little guidance of how, why and when to stretch.

There are two types of stretching: static and dynamic. Static stretching, the most commonly used, is the safest way to encourage elongation of the skeletal muscle. It involves the isolation of the muscle followed by a slow, steady movement through the complete range of motion and by a period during which the muscle is held in this extended position.

Dynamic stretching, by comparison, is the use of specific body movements to mimic a movement in an exaggerated but controlled fashion to promote range of motion at the joints. At no point is the muscle held in the extended position. Examples include running with high-knees and lunges.

For long periods, sports scientists and medicine professionals recommended static stretching before and after any type of vigorous exercise because the slow movements and periods of holding provided optimum lengthening of the muscle tissues. Research has now actually identified temporary decreases in muscle performance immediately after static stretching. As a result, dynamic stretching is recommended prior to exercise. Static stretching within forty minutes of play will cause a decrease in muscular strength and power.

Static stretching is most commonly used and recommended after the workout to accelerate recovery and decrease soreness. Certain areas of a tennis player's body become characteristically tight from tennis play and, by encouraging the muscle fibres to accept the stretch through static stretching, players can increase the length of the muscle and improve the range of movement. Static stretching should last at least twenty-five minutes and can also help players mentally 'switch off' and relax.

A detailed stretching routine can be found below in relation to 'cool-down' (see pages 189–94).

YOGA/PILATES

It is claimed by Olga Allon, the yoga trainer who introduced Andy Murray to *bikram yoga*, that the demanding routine has played a significant role in the Scot's evolution into a mental and physical specimen capable of ending Britain's seventy-seven-year wait for a Wimbledon Men's Champion. The demanding discipline was introduced into Murray's regime by Jez Green as a way of maximizing balance and complementing his daily flexibility and stretching routine. It is also supposed to rejuvenate the muscles and challenge the Scot mentally over the course of the session. 'Andy has been doing yoga throughout his career and the goal is to increase his range of movement,' says Green.

Similarly, Pilates, a discipline that promotes control, precision and focus, is becoming more and more popular with competitive tennis players as a way of reducing the number of injuries and improving movement, power and balance. In modern tennis, it is simply not possible to return a ball from the perfect position every time and players need a strong core and suppleness in their joints. Pilates is a great way to develop these muscles and increase flexibility in the lower back and hips.

Weight Training: Strength and Balance

The modern baseline game involves a lot of corner-to-corner movement and the longer matches force players to put their bodies under more strain than ever before. Players today must adapt by making their muscles capable of maintaining performance over a longer period of time.

Weight training for tennis is designed to strengthen the upper and lower body to develop power and endurance in the muscles used when moving or executing a stroke. The recognized benefits include increased power and control on strokes, combined with improved muscular endurance helping to maintain a high level of performance for longer. As a strong player, you can generate more racket-head speed and can therefore hit the ball harder. Well-conditioned muscles and joints also facilitate the development of proper stroke mechanics, allowing you to hit with more control.

The method is quite simple: you must isolate the targeted muscle and use it to lift the weight. Lifting the weight develops strength and endurance by forcing the muscle to contract, while lowering, or releasing, the weight promotes muscle control. You should exhale in one count when lifting, and exhale on two counts when lowering or releasing the weight. You are advised to use a variety of free weights and cable machines to prevent your muscles adapting to the exercise.

Strength training for tennis is not body-building; you are simply conditioning the muscles and joints properly for the unique demands that the sport of tennis places upon your body. 'Tennis players should focus on light weights and more repetitions,' says Terry Longmore, former Director of Fitness at Dukes Meadow Tennis Academy. 'They are not aiming to put on bulk muscle.'

The weight lifted should be approximately 60 per cent of your maximum lifting capacity and each exercise should be done in three sets of approximately fifteen repetitions. Completing lower repetitions of higher weights will lead to excess weight and a reduction in endurance.

The Exercises

Variety, in body conditioning, is extremely important and you are advised to consult a doctor and a fitness professional to develop a programme with a wide range of exercises to ensure that positive progression is maintained at all times. With this in mind, the following are only the most basic strength exercises, which are suitable if you are looking to condition your upper and lower bodies for tennis.

As with any new strenuous activity, check with your doctor or a qualified fitness professional before attempting these exercises.

Lower body

> Strong legs obey, weak legs command.
> GIL REYES, *the man who helped to shape Andre Agassi*

Lower body strength is vitally important for tennis. While poorly conditioned players will be forced to take risks in an attempt to shorten the point as they become exhausted, stronger players are able to maintain their intensities throughout the course of a match. In many cases, this will allow the fitter player to overcome their opponent even if they are not technically or tactically as advanced.

Aside from helping in the development of movement and balance, the lower body is also the starting block of the kinetic chain – a key component in generating power on all strokes. For this reason, properly conditioned players will also be able to hit harder for longer. According to Jez Green, tennis is almost 75 per cent focused on the leg muscles.

Dead-lift exercise

A lower body session in the gym should involve at least the following exercises:

EXERCISE: *Dead-lift – Hamstrings and Lower Back*

Stand with your feet shoulder-width apart while you hold a barbell or two dumb-bells with a double overhand grip. Without lifting, stick out your chest and bottom to hold the weights on the floor. Position your thighs parallel to the floor and your knees directly over your feet.

Now raise the bar by first straightening your legs, then your torso and legs simultaneously when the bar reaches your knees. The lift is completed cleanly when you are standing up straight with the weights in your hand.

EXERCISE: *Squats (with or without weights) – Hips, buttocks and quads*

Stand with your feet just over shoulder-width apart, keeping your back straight. Bend at the knees and hips until in a 90-degree seated position, with your buttocks close to the ground. This can be done with or without weights in hand, and you should focus on breathing in as you get down and breathing out as you return to the starting position. Your knees should not come over the end of your toes.

For added variety/difficulty, this exercise can also be executed on one leg to further focus on balance and stability.

You can exercise the squat anywhere without the need for any equipment. The squat focuses on your leg muscles, including the quadriceps, hamstrings and calves, but also works to promote muscle-building in the whole body.

Squats

EXERCISE: *Static Lunges (with or without Dumb-bells) – Hips, Glutes and Thighs*

From the standing position, step forward with one leg, bending your knees to lower your hips to the floor until both knees are bent at approximately a 90-degree angle. Your front knee should be positioned directly above the ankle. Neither knee should touch the floor and weight should be distributed evenly across the foot – including the heels.

Hold for 30 seconds, then return to standing position. Repeat.

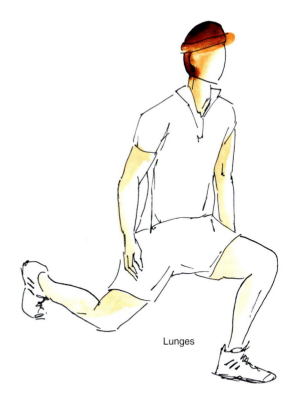

Lunges

Lunges must be executed correctly to avoid putting unnecessary strain on your joints. During a lunge you *must* keep your upper body straight, your shoulders back and your head straight. Your core should be engaged. This can be done with or without weights in hand.

The following exercise will help your calf muscles.

EXERCISE: *Calf Raise (with or without Dumb-bells)*

Hold a weight and stand on the spot. Now move up onto your toes and back down to your heels ten times. Rest, then repeat.

To develop this further, try jumping without bending your knees, i.e. use your calf muscles only.

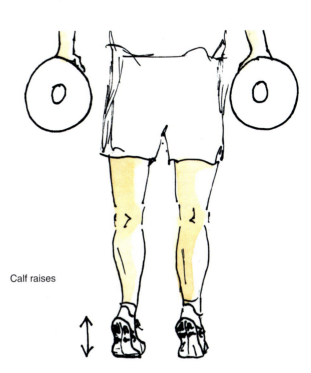

Calf raises

Upper Body

EXERCISE: *Chest Press 1*

Lie on your back on a weights bench (flat or inclined) with a dumb-bell in each hand. Hold your arms out to the side and perpendicular to your body, with your forearms perpendicular to the floor. Slowly push the weights upwards until your elbows are almost straight before lowering slowly until your elbows are level with your body. Repeat.

Chest Press 1

The aim is to develop explosive strength for the groundstrokes, so here is an exercise to help your shoulders.

EXERCISE: *Dumb-bell Shoulder Press*

Stand with your feet shoulder-width apart with a dumb-bell in each hand. Bending at the elbows, raise your upper arms to shoulder height with the palms of your hands facing forward. Then push up until the ends of the dumb-bells touch directly overhead before lowering the dumb-bells back to ear level.

Dumb-bell shoulder press

This is a good exercise to strengthen your wrists and forearms:

EXERCISE: *Wrist/Forearm*
Sit on a bench, holding a light dumb-bell in each hand. Your palms should be facing up and your elbows should be fixed to your side. Your wrists should be flexed up and down before you turn your palms upside down and repeat.

For variety, repeat the same exercise with your palms facing left/right respectively.

You should also work on developing strength in your upper arm by using tricep extensions and bicep curls.

Developing the Core

Comprising the abdominals, lower back and the side-muscles responsible for the extension/rotation of the torso, the 'core' is at the centre of every movement that you make. Not only does the core connect the top of your body with the lower half, it also provides strength, stability and balance to allow you to hit with more control and power in a greater range of positions.

Although many players will often neglect the core muscles in favour of their so-called 'mirror muscles', advanced players will come to recognize that the core plays a fundamental role of all tennis movements, and they will work hard to properly condition this part of their body.

Almost all core stability exercises can be executed using just your own body weight. There are many core stability/stability exercises for you to choose from, but the following are the easiest to carry out and require no specialist equipment.

A word of warning: the more advanced exercises involving medicine balls can be dangerous and are best executed only after consultation with a qualified fitness professional.

Core training exercises should form part of your daily training routine as an advanced player.

EXERCISE: *Superman*
Lie face-down on a mat with your arms stretched out in front above your head (like 'Superman'). For a period of six seconds, you must lift both legs and arms off the ground as high as possible. To increase the difficulty, try to move your arms and legs up and down as fast as you can.

This exercise will work both the front and back of your core muscle groups.

EXERCISE: *The Plank 1*

In the push-up position on the floor, bend your elbows 90 degrees to rest your weight on your forearms. Your elbows should be positioned directly beneath your shoulders and your body should be held in a straight line from head to foot. Hold this position for upto two minutes. Keep your back straight.

You can increase the demand on your core with the following exercise:

EXERCISE: *The Plank 2*

As for Plank 1, but raise one leg or arm in the air and try to hold the position for between two and five minutes.

Here is a similar, but even more demanding exercise for advanced players. Don't try this unless you are confident of being able to use the Swiss ball correctly.

EXERCISE: *The Plank 3*

As for Plank 1, but rest your feet or forearms on a Swiss ball for more than two minutes.

Plank 3 will require your core to work very hard to stabilize your body and stop the ball from rolling away.

To work the sides of your core muscle groups, you should also execute 'the side-plank'.

EXERCISE: *The Side Plank 1*

Lay on the floor on your left side with your legs straight. Prop up your upper body on your left elbow and forearm. Position your elbow under your shoulder. Brace your core by contracting your abs forcefully (as if you were about to be punched in the stomach). Raise your hips until your body forms a straight line from your ankles to your shoulders, keeping your head in line with your body.

Hold this position for 60 seconds, then relax and repeat on the other side.

This exercise can be varied slightly to make it more difficult:

EXERCISE: *The Side Plank 2*
As for the Side Plank 1, but lift up your top arm and point to the sky.
You must complete the sideways plank on both sides.

This following exercise wil help improve your lower core:

EXERCISE: *Leg Holds – Lower Core*
Lie on your back with your legs together. Slowly lift up your legs to the
top before gradually lowering them back down until they are a couple of
inches off the floor. At this point, take your legs up to the top before
bringing them back down. Repeat this 'up and down' motion eight times.

Crunches (or 'sit-ups', as they are more commonly known) are another
great way to develop core strength. Advanced players can practise crunches
with an added weight by holding it to their chest.

Early-Stage Plyometrics ('Counter Movement Hops')

Developed by Russian scientist Yuri Verkhoshansky in 1964, advanced
plyometrics training was a considerable factor behind the incredible
Olympic success of the Soviet Bloc countries throughout 1960s and
1970s. Unlike the regular strength exercises involving long, slow movements, plyometrics use quick movements to develop an explosive release
of power and strength.

In its most scientific form, plyometrics training requires incredible levels
of strength because it actually involves fully stretching the muscle followed
by full power acceleration to shorten it. While 'there are no tennis players
who are strong enough to complete full-on plyometrics in the strict sense,
early-stage plyometrics exercises are an important element of tennis
training,' says Jez Green, Andy Murray's former fitness trainer. As detailed
below, this involves small jumps and counter-movement hops.

The benefits of these exercises to tennis players are numerous. By its very
nature, tennis requires a unique blend of short, explosive movement patterns
involving the rapid release of speed and power. With this in mind, Jez Green
believes that the benefits of plyometrics can be seen in three areas of the game:

- The storage and release of elastic energy between the back swing and
  forward swing of stroke production
- Leg drive into the strokes
- The development of the crucial 'first step' towards the ball.

Research also indicates that the benefits of plyometrics spread to the central nervous system. Every time you contract a muscle, a signal is sent from the brain to the muscle via the neuromuscular system. The speed at which these muscles contract will naturally become faster if speed of the signal increases, which in turn will develop the speed and power of the athlete. Plyometrics exercises are shown to boost the efficiency at which these signals are sent.

The number of plyometrics exercises is infinite, but look to select those that mimic the movement and patterns of the sport. Here are some exercises to help improve your lower body.

Each exercise should be performed with maximum effort and each set should last no longer than six seconds. It is also important that you allow yourself sufficient time to fully recover between sets.

The number of sets and repetitions is very player dependent and it is best to first consult a fitness professional because this type of training does place your tendons and muscles under great strain. In any case, you should not attempt any of these exercises without having built up your strength and flexibility with cardiovascular or weight training.

EXERCISE: *Squat Jumps*

Lower yourself into the squat position (see page 168) before exploding upwards to jump as high as you can. Repeat once again.

When performing squat jumps your arms should rise above your head on the jump *before* you land and return to the squat position *before* you repeat the jump.

EXERCISE: *Box Jumps*

Stand by the side of a bench or a box, approximately 10 inches (25 cm) high. Lower yourself down into the squat position, then explode and jump onto the box. Balance and then step down.

EXERCISE: *Sideways Box Jumps*

Stand to the side of a bench or a box, approximately 10 inches (25 cm) high. Start with your right leg on the box and left leg on the floor before you explode upwards and land on the other side with your left foot on the box and your right foot on the floor. Now repeat the process in the other direction.

Upper body plyometrics exercises should focus on generating explosive power from the core and shoulders.

EXERCISE: *Medicine Ball Throws – Shoulder and Core 1*
Stand in the forehand/backhand position and hold a medicine ball at chest height. Then explode and throw the ball against a wall or to a partner/coach. Repeat.

To develop explosiveness in your shoulders, use the following exercise:

EXERCISE: *Medicine Ball Throws – Shoulder and Core 2*
Hold the medicine ball above your head and throw the ball down rapidly onto the floor in front of you. Repeat.

You can develop the rotational explosiveness required for power on your groundstrokes by using the Russian Twist exercise with a medicine ball.

EXERCISE: *The Russian Twist with Medicine Ball*
Sit with your back at a 45-degree angle to the floor, keeping your knees bent and together. Now rotate your upper body to move the ball from side to side.

To increase the difficulty of this exercise, lift your feet off the floor and try to balance.

Endurance
While tennis does not require you to run long distances across the court, you are required to have a good level of aerobic fitness in order to recover between points. For this reason, endurance training is an important element of the fitness training routine for the advanced tennis player. Agassi was known to run a 320-yard course between eight and fourteen times to develop leg-strength and develop aerobic fitness.

As with all physical training plans, the amount of focus spent on this aspect of performance will depend upon you and your game style. 'If I was working with David Ferrer, a baseline retriever, I would incorporate lots of long-distance running because this endurance is so crucial to his game-style,' says Jez Green. 'But if I was working with Milos [Raonic], I wouldn't do any long-distance running because his points are limited to about four shots.'

Developing players are advised to do a certain amount of long-distance running (i.e. 10 km) 'but, it is important that players do not base their whole training around endurance training because this does not lend itself to the requirements of the game,' says Green.

Endurance training can consist of swimming, cycling or running.

The 'X' drill works to develop the 'first step' and is effective in increasing your cardiovascular endurance – essential for those long baseline rallies.

EXERCISE: *The 'X' Drill*

Begin by standing at the middle of the baseline (point X) in the middle of five cones. Run to each cone in any order, plant your feet, execute a shadow shot with your racket in hand. Then return to point X, split-step and push off to the next cone.

In this exercise focus on (1) accelerating in your movements to the cones and (2) accelerating after execution of the shadow shot. Make a note of your timings and aim to improve on these.

The 'X' drill

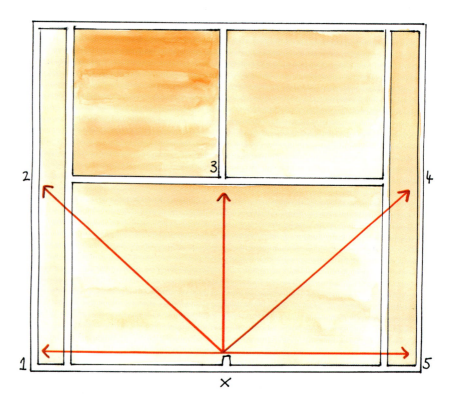

Periodization of Tennis Strength Training

The growing physicality of the game is causing more and more enthusiastic juniors to storm into the gym and hit the weights. Their assumption is that the more work they do inside, the better they will become, and they will grind themselves into the ground in an attempt to develop themselves physically.

Recovery, however, is an important part of conditioning and the benefits of any gym sessions will only reveal themselves once you learn that your body needs time to recover. 'Players need to rest and feed the muscle after stimulating its development,' says Terry Longmore, former Director of Fitness at Dukes Meadows Tennis Academy.

Developed in the 1960s by Matveyev, a Russian culture expert, periodization is a means of organizing and managing training to attain the best performance possible and minimize fatigue. It is simply not possible for an athlete to enjoy peak performance over the course of the whole calendar year and the concept works by establishing cycles of training activity and rest to allow the athlete to reach peak performance at certain times of the season.

Traditional models of periodization involve structuring the season into distinct training blocks in which an athlete will focus on developing a clearly identified area of physical fitness while other areas are maintained. The timing of these training blocks is normally carefully scheduled to allow the athlete to be at their peak for a certain event or tournament. While this works for sports with a short season, it is far less effective for sports like tennis where the season is long and highly unpredictable.

During the season, therefore, tennis players will actually adopt a *non-linear* model of periodization. This requires you to focus on more than one physiological quality at a time, while varying the volume and intensity of this training over shorter periods within your competition calendar. You will, however, normally revert to a more linear model in the December 'off-season' during which you will be able to work on developing a clearly identified area of your conditioning over a longer period of time.

Building a periodization plan for yourself is actually quite simple. The basic concept is to plan sufficient overload time to produce change, whilst avoiding levels of fatigue that can decrease performance and lead to overtraining and, eventually, injuries. This you can do by adapting the volume, intensity and skill of the exercise at hand.

The most simplistic periodization model will include a preparation phase designed to develop a base level of fitness and strength, followed by a pre-competitive phase in which training becomes more intense and the goals become sport-specific, i.e. by improving consistency, power and speed across the court. Science says that a minimum of six weeks is required to make substantial changes so physical training should begin approximately six weeks before the event. During the competition phase, the goal becomes basic maintenance of the specific body conditioning. The competition phase will always be followed by an active rest phase, which will last between one and four weeks.

Even with the most advanced periodization model in place, training too hard or too long can lead to both mental and physical problems that can decrease performance and can often lead to a prolonged period off the court. You should be aware of any signs of overtraining, the most common markers being a feeling of excessive fatigue, disrupted sleep patterns, reduced coordination and an elevated heart rate. It is also common to lose a passion for the game. Overtraining must be followed by a period of extensive rest to allow your body, mind and soul to recover fully.

The Role of Conditioning in Injury Prevention

❝ Andy's [Murray] is put under tremendous stress over the course of a match and it is important that injury prevention/compensation exercises are done every single day! ❞

JEZ GREEN, *former fitness trainer to Andy Murray*

Highly repetitive as it is, long-term tennis play has been shown to cause adaptations in flexibility, strength and balance in certain areas of the body. While these imbalances themselves will rarely cause pain or suffering, they will lead to small changes in body mechanics and techniques which can result in reduced performance or even serious injury.

Only approximately one third of tennis injuries are a direct result of an acute event and, as such, cannot be readily prevented by proper physical conditioning. These injuries are just natural consequences of the game and normally occur as a result of falling down or over-stretching in pursuit of a ball.

Two thirds of tennis injuries, however, are directly related to alterations in the athlete's musculoskeletal system as a result of overusing certain muscles in the body. It is here that an effective strength and conditioning programme must be used to compensate for this repetition ('compensatory exercises'), to improve a player's maximal force and reduce incidence of injuries.

Injury Prevention Exercises

The following exercises should form a part of all players' fitness routines. Alongside core stability work and low-intensity maintenance exercises, elite players will execute these exercises on a daily basis because they are not overly stressful on the body.

ELBOWS AND WRISTS

Resulting in pain just below the outside of the elbow, 'lateral Epicondylitis' – better known as 'tennis elbow' – is one of the most common tennis injuries. The injury arises when the muscles in the elbow joint, which move the elbow, wrist and fingers, become overused.

Preventing 'tennis elbow' is almost impossible, but strengthening exercises and a proper warm-up routine have been shown to prepare the muscles around the forearm for the stresses and strain of the game. Here are two exercises that are effective in strengthening these important muscles:

EXERCISE: *Elbows/Wrists 1*
Squeeze and release a tennis ball as tightly as possible ten times. Rest, then repeat.

EXERCISE: *Elbows/Wrists 2*
Hold a weighted object in the palm of your hand and complete small circles in the air with your wrist.

THE SHOULDER

Made up of four muscles, the rotator cuff helps position the shoulder in the shoulder socket. As you become fatigued, this allows for some increased 'play' of the ball in the socket, which in turn irritates the tissue in and around this area, thus causing pain when executing the stroke. You can prevent this by strengthening your four rotator cuff muscles with the aid of a shoulder exercise band. These exercises are described below in relation to 'Warm-Up' (see page 185).

Another common tennis-related injury arises from an imbalance in the shoulder blades and lower back. Executing a tennis stroke requires you to internally rotate and rapidly protract your shoulders, which inevitably leads to weaknesses in the muscles that retract the shoulders. In many cases, this will cause the shoulder blades to 'float' away from the spine in a phenomenon known as 'scapular winging'. You can test this by getting your coach or practice partner to see if your shoulder blades are visibly poking out of the upper back when you stand with your arms by your side.

The following compensation exercises should be executed regularly to counteract this imbalance:

EXERCISE: *Opposite Arm/Leg Raises*
Lying face-down on the floor with your arms above your head, lift your right arm and left leg, tightening your back and bottom muscles as you lift. Keep your knees and elbows straight at all times, and hold each position for four seconds before returning to the start position and repeating with your left arm and right leg.

Repeat this exercise ten times on each side.

EXERCISE: *Ys, Ts and Is*

Lie face-down on the floor and use your arms to execute three body positions: 'Y', 'T', and 'I'. Start in the 'I' position before moving on to the 'T' position, up to the 'Y' position before returning to 'I' and repeating. Your arms must not touch the floor at any point.

Hold the position at each point and move the arms up and down in rapid, short motions for five seconds before moving to the next position.

KNEES

The fast and sudden changes of direction can put your ankles and knees under great amounts of pressure, and injuries can be prevented by developing the appropriate muscles in and around these areas. This can be done with a stability disk.

A stability disk provides an unstable surface. You should begin by standing on the disk with one leg and working towards achieving this with your eyes closed and arms by your sides.

To further strengthen these key areas, you can then begin practising single leg squats with or without dumb-bells.

An ancillary benefit of these exercises is that these will train 'proprioception', i.e. your unconscious perception of movement and spatial orientation, which is a key component of balance and coordination.

Good Technique is the Best Injury Prevention

Despite its punctiliousness, the official tennis rulebook does not detail how players must, or should, hit the ball from one side of the court to the other. Indeed, from a purely biomechanical standpoint, there are actually an infinite number of different combinations of body movement, muscle activation and joint position that a player can use, none of which are more correct than any other.

The execution of a tennis stroke requires your joints and muscles to provide a mechanism to transfer energy throughout your body. What happens in one part of the body will have direct impact on the forces and loads experienced by the rest of your body because all body segments are linked to each other. In this way, a technically efficient tennis stroke will put less stress on your body as a whole because it requires less muscle activation.

Conversely, an inefficient transfer of energy through the kinetic chain forces body parts later in the chain to compensate if performance levels are to be maintained. This, in turn, increases the load placed on the other body segments to achieve the desired result and this increases the risk of injury. Alternatively, you must accept a lower level of performance.

With this in mind, you should be aware that while injury prevention exercises most certainly play an important role in any advanced tennis programme, in no way do they represent an excuse for failing to iron-out any technical flaws in stroke mechanics. You are strongly advised to work in unison with a qualified coach to address your technical flaws and to increase the efficiency of your kinetic chain (see pages 137–8). This, right here, is the single most effective method of injury prevention.

The Warm-Up

It is easy to be fooled into thinking that the top players come onto court, head straight to the baseline, hit some forehands, some backhands, some volleys, and a few serves before starting a match at full intensity. Nothing could be further from the truth.

Behind the scenes – and what is not shown on our TV screens – is that the top players will be very diligent with their pre-match preparation by completing a full, rigorous warm-up in the players' gym or on the practice courts prior to beginning the actual training session or match. 'Do five minutes of light jogging or stationary cycling to ease your body into activity and raise your heart rate,' says Novak Djokovic in his book entitled *Serve to Win*, before suggesting ten dynamic stretching routines.

To learn more about this, I spoke with Richard Gasquet and Laura Robson. 'If I have my match at two o'clock, I complete a long warm-up and practice at about eleven,' says Gasquet. 'I will then rest before heading to the gym for twenty minutes for a warm-up before I go on court.' And Robson's preparations are very similar: 'I will always have a hit a couple of hours before my match,' she says, 'and then half an hour before I go on court, I will then start warming up with fast feet, training bands and some light jogging.'

In order to prepare yourself for the physical and mental exertions asso-ciated with high-performance tennis, you should only start playing tennis on completion of a full body warm-up.

The Importance of the Warm-Up

Your warm-up routines are completed to maximize your performance on court. You should aim to generate heat and raise the core temperature of your body to prepare your muscles, ligaments and tendons for more vigorous activity. This increases your muscle efficiency and improves reac-tion time by allowing your muscles to contract and relax more rapidly.

Your warm-up also plays an important role in injury prevention. The idea is quite simple: an elastic band will snap very easily when it has not been stretched for some time. If the elastic band is stretched and the rubber is warmed, the band is then capable of stretching a lot further without snap-ping. The same applies to muscles and tendons: they are far more likely to be pulled or ruptured when cold.

In addition to this, the warm-up also 'opens up the neurological path-ways allowing the player to enter the court with the maximum coordination and the basic motor skills prepared for the task at hand,' says Terry Long-more, former Director of Fitness at Dukes.

Finding a Warm-up Routine

It is highly unlikely that any two warm-up routines will be identical because players' personal preferences will vary. Some players will undergo a far more rigorous and extended warm-up regime than others, and a pre-training session warm-up will normally be different to a warm-up before a competitive match.

The timing of the warm-up session will also vary; some players will feel more comfortable entering the match having broken a sweat after a high-intensity warm-up session; others will prefer a high-intensity warm-up completed hours before the match, followed by a brief, low-intensity session prior to the match.

That said, there are some important stages of the warm-up process that should form part of your pre-match routine.

The Important Phases: Warm-Up

THE PASSIVE/ACTIVE WARM-UP

You should begin with a passive warm-up, the goal of which is to raise your core body temperature. The passive warm-up requires your body temperature to be raised by some external means and this can be done by wearing extra layers of clothing or having a warm shower. The passive warm-up is an important step before commencing a more active warm-up.

Now move into the 'active' stage of your warm-up, which is focused on raising your heart rate and body temperature with body movements. The 'active' warm-up should consist of two types of exercise: 'general' and 'specific'.

GENERAL EXERCISES

'General' exercises are low intensity movements focused on raising core body temperature but do not actually mirror the specific actions involved in the sport of tennis. They will normally be followed with a series of 'specific' warm-up exercises that mimic specific movements required by the game.

'The active part of the warm-up should begin with some gentle cardio-vascular activity such a jogging or cycling,' says Terry Longmore. 'Running, at this stage, is too intense,' he says, 'but players can begin to speed things up very gradually as the muscles warm up.' The goal of this exercise is to loosen up the muscles and raise core temperature. It should take no more than ten minutes.

Longmore then advises that players increase the intensity of their warm-up routine with some light skipping. 'The idea is to maintain a high enough intensity to break a gentle sweat. This shows that the core body temperature has risen and that heat is being generated,' he says. Skipping also begins to loosen up the key muscles and activate the motor skills required to coordinate the feet on court.

SPECIFIC EXERCISES

After some gentle cardiovascular exercises, your core temperature should be high enough to move onto some more specific warm-up exercises. 'The advantage of these specific exercises is that they will be far more efficient in creating heat in the specific body part being used,' says Longmore.

EXERCISE: *Tic-Tac Baseline Footwork*
Stand on the baseline and switch from standing on your right foot to your left foot as fast as you can. Your feet should not come more than a few inches off the ground. You should maintain maximum intensity for a period of thirty seconds.

This exercise should be completed four times with thirty-second intervals between each set. This will activate the fast-twitch muscle fibres in your upper and lower legs.

Next, you can prepare your body for short bursts of explosive energy using shuttle sprints.

EXERCISE: *Shuttle Sprints/Directional Running*
Starting off with fast-feet on the baseline, sprint from the baseline to the service line and push off backwards to the baseline, facing the net at all times.

You should sprint to the service line and net, returning backwards to the baseline after each sprint forward. This should be completed three times. To finish the exercise off, side-step across the baseline and back to the middle to prepare your muscles for sideways movement.

'The final stage of the lower body warm-up is igniting the explosiveness in the legs,' says Longmore. 'The "first step" towards the ball in tennis is vitally important in moving across the court efficiently.'

During this exercise it '... is important to push back off one leg to incorporate hip rotations,' says Terry Longmore, 'this is an important step in injury prevention.'

EXERCISE: *Tramline Leaps*

To execute tramline leaps, position yourself on the outside tramline at the net, facing towards the baseline. Exploding forwards and right off the outside (left) leg, you should land on your alternate (right) leg on the inside tramline.

Repeat the jump, exploding off your right leg onto the outside tramline. Jump across and forward, maintaining balance on landing through activation of the core muscles. The idea is to arrive at the baseline in as few jumps as possible. Repeat this exercise four times.

These lunges, highly recommended by Longmore, are another great way to warm up the leg muscles.

EXERCISE: *Rotational Lunges*

Begin on the doubles sideline facing across the court. Lift your right knee, pull it towards your chest with both hands and rise up onto the ball of your left foot. Now release your right leg, take a large step forward and lower your body into the lunge position. Do not allow your front knee to pass over the end of your leading foot.

Holding the lunge position with your core activated, rotate at the core to face the direction of your leading leg. If your right leg is forward, rotate to the right; if your left is forward, rotate to the left. Go from tramline to tramline and back, holding each lunge for four seconds.

Throughout this exercise make sure that your head remains up and your back is straight.

Used by almost all players, including Andy Murray, resistance bands should form part of your warm-up routine

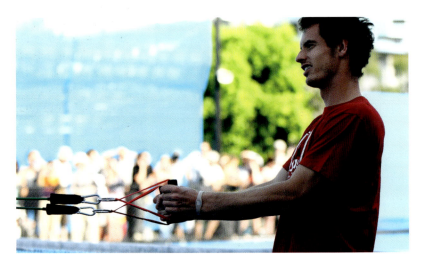

Head down to any practice court at a professional tennis event and almost every single player will use elastic shoulder resistance bands at some point in their warm-up routine. They are particularly useful for travelling players who have no access to a gym or weight-training facilities because they are light, easy to use and can be used as part of a strength and conditioning/injury prevention programme as well a warm-up routine.

The following specific exercises can be used to warm up your upper body.

EXERCISE: *Rotator Cuff Internal Shoulder Rotation – Horizontal*

Secure the band to the wall at a medium height to your side. Then grab the handle of the resistance band in front of your body with the palm of your closest hand facing sideways. Your elbow should be bent and pressed against your body at abdomen level.

Rotating at the shoulder, pull the handle of the band across your abdomen before allowing it to slowly return to the original position after a short pause. Your elbow must not move from the side of the abdomen.

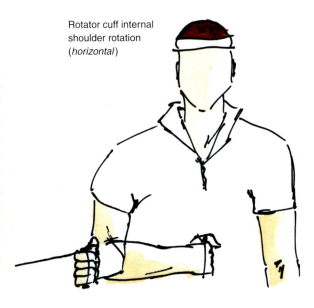

Rotator cuff internal shoulder rotation (*horizontal*)

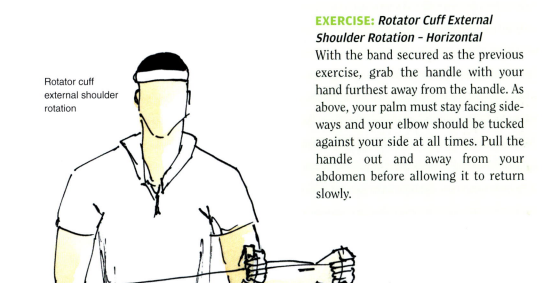

Rotator cuff external shoulder rotation

EXERCISE: *Rotator Cuff External Shoulder Rotation – Horizontal*

With the band secured as the previous exercise, grab the handle with your hand furthest away from the handle. As above, your palm must stay facing sideways and your elbow should be tucked against your side at all times. Pull the handle out and away from your abdomen before allowing it to return slowly.

EXERCISE: *External Shoulder Rotations – Vertical*

Warm the muscles you use for vertical shoulder movements by standing on the middle of the resistance band and holding each side in front of your body with elbows bent at a 90-degree angle and your palms facing the floor.

Pull the handles upwards over a 90-degree angle until your palms are now facing forwards, before slowly allowing the handles to return to the original position.

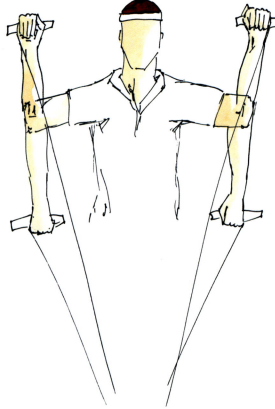

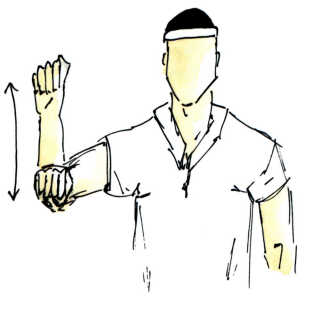

EXERCISE: *Internal Shoulder Rotations – Vertical*

Begin with one end of the band securely attached to the wall behind you at shoulder height.

Bend your elbow at a 90-degree angle out to the side of your body at shoulder level, palms facing straight. Grab the band and pull downwards, rotating the forearm inwards until it is ahead parallel to the ground.

During this exercise your elbow must remain at 90 degrees at all times and your upper arm (bicep) must remain parallel to the ground.

Dynamic Stretching

❝ Players should finish the warm up with some dynamic stretches to loosen up and stretch the major muscle groups. ❞
TERRY LONGMORE

Dynamic stretches focus on stretching muscle groups through normal movement patterns while increasing your body temperature and heart rate. Little guidance exists on how many repetitions of each stretch are optimal, but each player will have individual needs. Performing multiple repetitions of each movement is recommended, with more movements recommended in cooler temperatures and during tournaments where frequent matches and overtraining may increase stiffness between sessions.

EXERCISE: *Straight Leg Swing*
Standing next to the net-post for support, swing one leg forward as high as possible before swinging backwards as high as possible. It is important that you keep your knee straight at all times. You should feel a stretch in the hamstring.

EXERCISE: *Toe/Heel Walks*
Walk from the baseline to the net on your heels and then return on your toes. This will stretch your calf muscles.

EXERCISE: *Hip Flexors*
Begin on the tramline and bring your right knee up to your chest. From the chest, rotate that leg outwards until you feel a stretch on the inner thigh. At this point, return your leg to the floor before repeating with the left leg.
Complete the stretch approximately three times on each leg.

EXERCISE: *Cross-over High Stretch*
Facing the net, cross your left leg over your right leg and push your right hip out until you feel a light stretch on the outside of the hip. As soon as you feel this, release your leg and repeat across the court from tramline to tramline before returning in the opposite direction to stretch the left hip.

EXERCISE: *High Knees/Bum Kicks*
To complete your lower body dynamic stretches, jog across the court while bringing your knees up to your chest. On returning, kick your heels up to your buttocks.

Designed to activate your nervous system, shadowing is the final stage of the dynamic stretching routine and involves mimicking the specific on-court movements.

EXERCISE: *Shadow Shots*
Perform shadowing for three minutes, alternating between forehand, backhand, overhead, or smash and volleys. The intensity of your shadowing should increase gradually.

Your warm-up can be completed with a couple of on-court exercises designed to activate the basic motor skills and co-ordination skills while you continue to prepare your muscles by mirroring the specific movements required on court.

YouTube is littered with videos of Djokovic, Nadal and Murray all playing tennis football because it is a fun and effective exercise to warm-up. The game does not actually require rackets and is very simple.

EXERCISE: *Tennis–Football*
Within the service boxes, kick the ball, returning it back over the net into your opponent's court using any body part except your arms and hands. There is no limit to the number of times the ball can bounce on your side, but you must touch the ball after each bounce, i.e. if the ball bounces in the court twice without you making contact, you forfeit the point. The point begins with you 'feeding' the ball to your opponent with an underarm throw. Play a seven-point tie-breaker.

Tennis Specific Exercises

The next stage of your on-court preparation is a series of tennis-specific exercises designed to stimulate your neural pathways and further aid motor unit activation for the strokes and movements required. The final segment, hitting from the baseline, normally represents the official match warm-up as seen on the television screens at the major events.

Work your way to the baseline with the following stages.

SERVICE BOX RALLYING

Service-box rallying is common at all levels of tennis, but many players fail to see the real reason behind it. The exercise is actually very important in activating the co-ordination required to play tennis and gives your brain time to attune to the speed, ball height and 'feel' of the surface before moving to the baseline where these calculations will need to be even more advanced. At all times, you should be hitting with purpose, control and intensity in your footwork.

Begin by hitting into the service boxes with 'slice', even if you are a predominantly topspin player. 'Slice' does not require you to aggressively cut the ball; the idea is to control the ball and place it back close to your partner on the other side of the net. This requires you to have an 'open' racket face on contact.

After a few minutes of hitting with a controlled slice, you can then begin to work on controlled topspin in the service box. Your swing should be a long and fluid motion completed with both feet in position and yourself balanced. Look to manipulate the ball, relaxing your wrist and shoulder to maximize the 'feeling' on the strings. The intensity can be increased as the control and 'feeling' develop. If you have difficulty maintaining a rally in the service box, extend this stage to develop the necessary 'touch' and control. Only then should you move to the baseline.

Even at the baseline, your brain is not yet ready to track the ball and make the high speed calculations necessary to strike the ball with accuracy and conviction at full pace. You cannot go from first to fifth gear in a car and the same principle applies on a tennis court. You should begin slowly from the baseline, developing touch, 'feel' and control on the groundstrokes before gradually upping the pace.

'The best players I have worked with have hit with discipline and control from the baseline, slowly working their way up to 100 per cent intensity after approximately 30 minutes,' says Juan Carlos Báguena, former coach of Sergi Brugera (French Open Champion 1993 and 1994) and María Antonia Sánchez Lorenzo (1 WTA singles, 9 ITF). 'Some [players] will need more [time] than others – but it is important not to rush,' he says.

The Cool-Down

After coming off court, it is easy to be fooled into thinking that Andy Murray or Maria Sharapova simply complete their on-court interviews, shower and head home. But what really happens is that the players will prioritize a proper cool-down routine ahead of any pre-existing media obligation, whatever the result of their match. 'Recovery is the ultimate goal,' says Novak Djokovic in his book, *Serve to Win*.[1] The cool-down is the first part of a player's recovery from intense exercise and will form a vital element of any performance player's training regime.

Over the course of a training sessions or a match, your body's systems become maximally stressed, which leads to an increase in body temperature, heart rate and blood pressure. Your body begins to release hormones such as adrenaline and endorphins into the circulatory system to increase cardiac output, blood pressure, and the rate at which the muscles break down glycogen. There is normally also a build-up of waste products (creatine, myoglobin) in the muscles.

High levels of circulating adrenaline will lead to a feeling of restlessness if these are not washed out of the system. The waste products in the muscles can cause post-exercise stiffness and tiredness, and any rapid decrease in body temperature and/or heart rate can have serious consequences. An active cool-down works to remove these hormones from the system which, in turn, facilitates recovery.

An active cool-down is also designed to remove muscle lactate. As your body performs strenuous exercise, you begin to breathe faster in an attempt to shuttle more oxygen to your working muscles. Your body prefers to generate most of its energy using aerobic methods. Sometimes, however, in high-intensity training routines, your body will require energy production faster than your body can adequately deliver oxygen. In these situations, your working muscles must generate energy anaerobically in a process known as *glycolysis*, the by-product of which is lactate which increases the acidity of the muscle cells and results in a burning sensation. By maintaining a high blood flow through your body and increasing the rate at which your muscles use the lactate, an active cool-down session helps to return your lactate levels to resting values.

Ancillary benefits of the cool-down include a reduction in muscle stiffness and an increase in muscle flexibility. 'It is important that players maintain muscle plasticity,' says Terry Longmore. 'Muscle contraction causes muscles to shorten so the cool-down is important to relax the body, lengthen the muscles and maintain this flexibility. This, in turn, facilitates recovery,' he says. An active cool-down session allows your body to gradually lower its temperature and return to homeostasis.

Completion of an effective cool-down routine will be the last thing you want to do after a high-intensity session on the court. However, young players should always be encouraged to complete a cool-down routine so it becomes a natural part of their tennis routine as they begin competition.

There are two stages to the cool-down routine: cardio and stretching.

Stage 1 - Cardio: Low-intensity cardio keeps the blood flowing around your body, flushes out your muscles and allows your body temperature to gradually come down to a comfortable level. Cardio should be carried for approximately 5–10 minutes, lowering the intensity over the course of this period.

Your heart rate should be taken down to approximately 100 beats per minute and you should finish by kicking your arms and legs out, loosening them ready for stretching.

Stage 2 – Stretching: A complete cool-down should be completed with a stretching routine. When muscles contract, they become shorter and you will need flexibility and a wide range of motion if you are to return those hard-to-reach balls. The benefits of stretching include:

- Lengthening your muscles back to their original length after contraction
- Reducing the effects of muscle tightness
- Releasing muscle tension, which helps take pressure away from your joints
- Improving your flexibility and assisting joint mobility

Whereas dynamic stretching will be used in the warm-up routine, static stretching – stretching without movement – will be incorporated in the cool-down routine. It is important that your muscles are warm for static stretching so aim to complete the cool-down as soon as possible after leaving the court.

Each stretch should be held for at least twenty seconds and repeated three times.

Important! At no point should stretching hurt, and you should stop and hold the stretch when the tension in the muscle is felt. It is important to avoid jumpy or bouncing movements and you should inhale as you begin the stretch before exhaling as you perform the stretch.

A word of warning: please note that the following list of stretches is not exhaustive and, as an advanced player, you are strongly advised to consult a qualified fitness professional for a physical stretching routine that is specific to your needs.

The hamstring muscle runs along the back of your upper leg. Here is a common exercise used to stretch hamstrings.

EXERCISE: *Hamstrings*
Sit on the floor with both legs stretched out straight. Extend your arms and reach forward by bending at the waist to touch your toes. Keep your legs straight at all times.

The hamstrings exercise will also begin to stretch your lower back and calf muscles.

EXERCISE: *Lower Back*

While lying on your back, rotate at the waist to cross your left leg over your right leg and onto the floor on the other side. Both shoulder blades must remain in contact with the floor at all times and you should turn at the neck to face in the opposite direction to the stretch, i.e. to the left.

Hold the position for twenty seconds before reversing the stretch by bringing your right leg over your left leg and rotating at the neck to face right.

Lie on your back and bring both knees up to your chest, knotting your hands over your knees to pull them closer into your chest. With your knees tightly in position, you should feel a stretch in your lower back.

To really push this stretch, ask your coach/practice partner to push down on your legs.

The quadricep is the muscle on the front of your thigh.

EXERCISE: *Quadriceps 1*

Stand near a wall or a piece of equipment for support. Bring your heel up to your lower back by bending at the knee. The stretch should be completed by grabbing the top of your foot to pull your heel further into your buttocks.

A greater stretch can be felt using the following exercise.

EXERCISE: *Quadriceps 2*

Stand in the upright position, both feet shoulder-width apart, then take a large step forward with your right leg and bend at the knee. Your back leg (left) should be straight while your right knee should be in line and directly above your toes. From this position, drop your left knee to the floor and use your left hand to grab your left foot from behind, pulling your left foot up towards your buttocks.

The calf muscle runs down the back of the lower leg and can be stretched very easily.

EXERCISE: *Calf Stretch*

Stand with your feet shoulder-width apart, hands on your hips and with a slight bend in your knee. Initiate the stretch by taking one step back with your right foot and leaning forward at the waist, keeping your back foot on the floor at all times.

Hold the stretch for twenty seconds before changing legs by stepping back with your left foot.

The glutes, also known as gluteus maximus, are two muscles located in the buttocks and are common causes of leg pain when not stretched. They can cause an uneven distribution of forces on the knee and have been known to be cause back pain when they become tight.

EXERCISE: *The 'Pretzel' Stretch*

Lie flat on your back with both knees bent. Bring your right leg over your left leg so as to place your right foot on top of your left knee. Initiate the stretch by bringing both knees towards your chest and gently pulling your uncrossed leg upwards until you can feel a stretch in your right buttock. Now reverse the position to stretch your left buttock.

EXERCISE: *Shoulder Stretch*

Stand with your feet shoulder-width apart. Initiate the stretch by pulling your left arm across your body with your right arm, pulling your left elbow in as far as possible until the fingertips of your left hand can reach around your right shoulder and touch your right shoulder blade.

Stretching the chest requires an open door frame or an object with which you can form a 90-degree angle with your arms. This can be a tree, or piece of gym equipment or anything about shoulder height, which will provide support.

EXERCISE: *Chest Stretch*
Stand with one palm positioned against the upright object at shoulder height, before slowly rotating at the trunk of your body to push your fixed arm backwards until you can feel a slight stretch in your front shoulder region.

Most professional players will conclude their recovery with a massage, but this will not normally be affordable for those at the lower levels of the competitive ladder. A more economical alternative is the foam roller, which is available from most sporting shops. 'You foam-roll by rolling different parts of your body over the tube, in effect giving yourself a massage,' explains Djokovic in *Serve to Win*.

Physical conditioning has rapidly become one of the cornerstones of the modern game. Besides its well-documented role in injury prevention, proper physical conditioning also allows players to hit the ball harder and play for longer than ever before, and it is simply not possible to succeed at any advanced level without it.

It is so common for an uninformed player to neglect this aspect of performance, focusing instead on technical developments on court. With this chapter you should now have the information required to begin physical conditioning, together with an understanding of it.

CHAPTER EIGHT

Developing the Mindset of a Champion

❛ The game looks like it takes place between the lines on the court,
but really it takes place between your ears. ❜
NOVAK DJOKOVIC [1]

Exhausted. Frustrated. Disappointed. I sat there, my mother beside me, quietly whispering 'point by point' as she tried to support her bewildered son. I just didn't know how to explain it. While I could happily beat highly ranked players in practice, I struggled when it really mattered. Something deep in my psychology seemed to prevent me from being able to take that final step. I was failing in my matches when my game was put to the severest test. Not technically, but mentally, emotionally and psychologically. How could I be winning a match 6–2, 5–1 and still leave with a great big 'L' beside my name?

And it did not end there. Playing the German leagues after a string of bad results, I fought desperately to find the confidence to hit the ball with any conviction. I double-faulted. I framed balls. I missed shots. And I lost matches. While I knew what to do, my mind just would not allow it. As the number one seed, I asked to compete on the 'outside' courts away from the big crowds. I was frustrated; my memories of my previous results were influencing my performance in the present. It was like one big vicious circle from which I could not escape.

I was aware of my psychological flaw. I could feel it each and every time I stepped out on to court under pressure. I felt uncomfortable. Nervous. Twitchy. Out of my comfort zone. But I did not know what I could do about it. I was led to believe that you were either born with mental strength or you were not – and I was just not one of those lucky few. It really was that simple. As much as it hurt, I accepted it.

How wrong I was.

Roger Federer won fewer points than Andre Agassi in his 2004 US Open quarterfinal victory; Federer won. Rafael Nadal won fewer points than Federer in his 2009 Wimbledon triumph; Nadal won, too. But how?

'Break point', 'game point', 'set point', and 'match point' – the scoring system in tennis creates a situation where some points hold more or less

Roger Federer's mental strength has been a fundamental factor behind the Swiss' unparalleled success in the game

'weight' than others. The top players have an ability to hone in on this mental strength to keep total focus when these points emerge, and this allows them to triumph even though they don't always lead in the statistics of aces and winners. Roger Federer and Rafael Nadal won their respective encounters because they won when it really mattered – they won the 'big' points.

Although players will torture themselves with long hours of hard work on the court or in the gym, few do anything to condition their minds for competition, and yet the physical game is only a small part of the battle. On average, the tennis ball is 'in play' for just fifteen minutes of every hour. What about the other forty-five minutes of that hour? What about when players towel off, take on board some fluids? What happens at the change of ends? It is during these times that your mind can begin to wander. This is the mental element and it is here that matches are won or lost. You must train your mind accurately and consistently to properly use those forty-five minutes of thought control. And it is this skill to control your mind that will determine what you do during the fifteen minutes of actual battle.

Almost robotic in his ballet-like movements across the baseline, the Roger Federer of today is calmness personified. He is, with little doubt, the greatest player ever, but the athletic talent and mental strength with which he has wooed the world was not always as natural as it may seem. 'I used to throw my racket around like you can't imagine,' he once confessed, 'I was getting kicked out of practice sessions non-stop when I was sixteen.'

At the age of seventeen, the great Swiss decided to see a sports psychologist to help mask these emotions, but the real turning point came on

1 August 2002 when his childhood coach, Peter Carter, was tragically killed in a car accident near Kruger National Park. In the wake of the funeral, Federer returned to court for a Davis Cup match against Morocco with a new sense of determination. The death of a close friend taught him the value of tennis; there was the gentle realization that it is only a game, and this allowed him to move forward with a new sense of calm and perspective that was so glaringly absent in his early years.

'When something like this happens,' he said, 'you see how really unimportant tennis is.' His mother agreed: 'It was the first death Roger had to deal with and it was a deep shock for him,' she said, 'but it has also made him stronger.'[2]

Each and every January, Federer invites Carter's parents, Bob and Diana, as his guests of honour for the year's first Grand Slam at Melbourne Park. It is testament to the man that Federer has become and a beautiful illustration of his gratitude for Peter's work in moulding the seventeen-time Grand Slam Champion into the greatest the game has seen.

The term 'mental toughness' means different things to different people. For Federer it means keeping calm on the court and allowing his sublime talents to do the talking. For others, it is persistence: the ability to keep on fighting whatever the score may be. For some it is the ability to maintain focus throughout the duration of the match.

To learn more about mental toughness, I spoke at length with Peter Gilmour, an International Mental Performance Coach. According to Peter, there are four identifiable cornerstones to mental strength in sport: belief, self-confidence, focus and motivation.

The Cornerstones to Mental Strength

Belief

> If you think you can or if you think you can't, you are right.
> HENRY FORD

Following her first-round loss to Virginie Razzano at the 2012 French Open, many thought this was the beginning of the end for Serena Williams. It was, after all, a bizarre loss; one that reflected a player with a distinct lack of direction, bereft of ideas and focus. Just twelve months later, a transformed Williams returned to Paris to lift her second title on the dirt of Roland Garros, playing the best tennis of her illustrious career.

The difference came in the shape of Patrick Mouratoglou, her coach and mentor, to whom she turned in a desperate attempt to channel her incredible talents that lay deep within. Under Mouratoglou's guidance, Williams went on to achieve unprecedented things, including a 34-match winning streak, a Wimbledon title, an Olympic Gold Medal and the US Open Championships. But what exactly did Mouratoglou change?

Patrick Mouratoglou (*left*) gave Serena Williams the belief that she could again rise to the top of the women's game

'Belief,' says Mouratoglou. 'We have worked on a lot of technical and tactical things together, but the difference has been the mental side,' he adds in our conversations.

'Before [we started working together], Serena never believed she was capable of achieving great things. She was not consistent and she could only find her best level on the big occasion. She had to learn to believe that she could win week after week. She accepted losing too much. Under me she has started to refuse to lose.'

Following her loss in Paris, Williams asked Mouratoglou to work with her during the Wimbledon fortnight. In discussions leading up the event, Mouratoglou recalls that he had to explain to Serena that there was absolutely no reason why she should lose matches if they work together in the right way. 'I remember seeing her face [when I told her she was not going to lose],' he says, 'I was really serious. I really believed it. And from then on it clicked [with her]. From then on she started to think differently.'

The power of belief can be seen at the very top of the men's game. For many a year, Rafael Nadal and Roger Federer were the leading men in a drama that captured a huge global audience. Murray and Djokovic were just extras, standing in the wings, maturing until they were ready to break the duopoly. The young Serb broke this historic stranglehold first with his breakthrough year of 2011, before Murray earned the right to walk along-

Serena Williams won the 2012 Wimbledon title just weeks after she began working with Patrick Mouratoglou

Murray's new-found belief and mental strength took him to the US Open title in 2012

side these greats with his 2012 victory at Flushing Meadows. Neither player drastically changed their games; they simply began to believe that they too had the ability to compete at the highest level in world tennis.

Murray, of course, began working with the great Ivan Lendl, the catalyst in an astounding mental development deep within Murray's psyche that pushed him over the line on the lawns of SW19 that bright summer's afternoon in July 2013. But as much as the Scot's relationship with Lendl was celebrated, lauded by the world's media, Novak Djokovic's transformation happened behind the scenes, far from the public eye. And it all started with a phone call.

After watching Djokovic surrender a two-set lead to Frenchman Jo-Wilfried Tsonga at the 2010 Australian Open, Dr Igor Cetojevic, an expert in alternative medicines with no interest in tennis, reached out to offer his help in curing the Serb's breathing difficulties that had so regularly prevented him from realizing his prolific talent.

Following an initial consultation, it was agreed that Cetojevic would travel with the Djokovic team to provide physical, mental, emotional and spiritual guidance. Besides installing a set of strict dietary requirements into Djokovic's routine, Cetojevic worked to develop certain areas of Djokovic's psyche through counselling, colour therapy, meditation, and visualization. The Serb was encouraged to read New Age spiritualist books, including *The Four Agreements* – something Cetojevic believed would help as Djokovic tried to break the Federer–Nadal stranglehold. 'He was focusing on their strength and power and losing his centre,' says Cetojevic in an interview with ESPN. 'I helped him focus on his inner strength.'[3]

The results were there for us all to see. Following a string of magnificent victories towards the end of 2010, a faster, fitter Djokovic finally reached the very pinnacle of his beloved game defeating Nadal on the lawns of SW19 in 2011. Showcased to the world was a calmer player on court, more mature and more in control of his emotions than ever before. 'I learned to believe,'[4] said Djokovic following a 2011 press conference, showing thanks to Cetovojic as 'the great doctor' who had cured him of his demons.

It can be very difficult to commit to something when the reward is so uncertain, but all the great players believe themselves to be so before they actually become so. Following his 2009 Wimbledon victory, Roger Federer described how he did not enjoy success in his career until he first began believing in himself. He realized that in order to become a champion, he first had to believe himself to be one.

It's the chicken or the egg scenario: many players believe that they must win the matches before they believe, but it is actually the other way round – you *must* believe in order to win matches. The difficulty comes with finding the belief in the first place, and this is where mental training can be highly effective.

Belief can be distinguished from self-confidence because it is not related to the environment or external influences. You can have belief in your abilities on the training court yet lack self-confidence under the pressures of a competitive match situation.

Self-Confidence

Novak Djokovic showed incredible mental resolve to win the 2014 Wimbledon title

❝ Losing is not my enemy; fear of losing is the enemy. ❞
RAFAEL NADAL[5]

He was 30–15 down at 3–5 in the fifth set of the 2011 US Open semi-final against Roger Federer when Novak Djokovic netted a basic backhand return into the net. To all the world, it appeared that the despondent Serb was heading for another premature exit, frowning to the cameras as he made his way across the court, questioning the expectant crowd's allegiance. But what followed was simply spectacular.

Under intense pressure at match point down, Djokovic hit a cross-court forehand return that simply defied all logic. Branded as 'one of the greatest all-time shots' by John McEnroe, it was also reflective of a player with complete confidence in his abilities, and it is this extraordinary self-confidence that has given Novak Djokovic the upper hand in so many of his matches.

The Serb just exudes confidence even when behind in a match; he always believes that his superior technical ability will prevail sooner or later. As Nadal explained after the 2011 US Open final, 'I think his [Djokovic's] forehand is not more painful than before; his backhand is not more painful than before; he serves the same.' So what has changed? 'He's having less mistakes than before,' explained Nadal. 'He is confident enough in every moment in one more ball, one more ball.'

The power of self-confidence is also illustrated by Stanislas Wawrinka's rise from a steady 'Top Ten' player to one of the game's elite regularly challenging for Grand Slam titles. The Swiss, as is evident watching him terrorize opponents with the most splendid of one-handed backhands, has always had the ability, but the breakthrough only came once his confidence caught up with his undeniable talent.

'Why this year, why last year? It's just my time. I'm twenty-eight, I'm more mature, I understand better when I win or when I lose and why,' he said on the Monday morning following his maiden Grand Slam Title in Melbourne. 'Everything last year came with the self-confidence and now I know that I can beat everybody on the big stage at a Grand Slam, it doesn't matter if it's the final, semi-final, quarter-final. That changed everything because when you have that confidence in yourself then you can win a Grand Slam.'

According to Patrick Mouratoglou, this self-confidence – or 'ego,' as he so aptly describes – is a key ingredient in the success of the game's elite. 'The top players have a perception of themselves that is high enough that they refuse to lose to others players,' he says. 'Their mental attitude is different. They believe in their abilities and know that they are not going to lose to this opponent even though the opponent is playing the best tennis of their career and they are playing their worst match of the year. They just do not accept losing and because of this, they constantly look for solutions to find a way to win.'

Whether it be pre-match nerves against an opponent they have never previously beaten or on-court before the 'big' points, mentally untrained players can begin to doubt their abilities to win. Thoughts like 'I can't win this' or 'I am going to miss this shot' reign supreme, and what the mind envisages, the body does. Mentally strong players do not have self-confidence because they win the big points – they win the big points *because* they are confident.

In his book, *Prime Tennis: Triumph of the Mental Game*,[6] Dr Jim Taylor acknowledges the existence of two types of negative thinking. Negative thinking, according to Taylor, can be good if tailored to produce feelings of energy and being psyched up. He uses the example of 'I am so mad that I am going to work twice as hard in practice next week', to illustrate the negative thoughts being used to promote better future performance. Taylor also recognizes the negative thoughts associated with feelings of depression and helplessness, which hurt confidence, focus and motivation. It is these types of negative thoughts that must be targeted by mental training.

Focus

> ❝ [Tennis players] do not have the luxury of thinking cumulatively. ❞
> ARTHUR ASHE, *winner of three Grand Slams*

In 2013 Serena Williams lifted her second French Open title, eleven years on from her maiden Grand Slam on the dirt of Roland Garros. It was an emotional victory, her first-round loss just twelve months earlier, making it perhaps more meaningful than many of the titles that had come before. In the wake of the victory, just twenty minutes after she had fired down her tenth ace of the day to seize the title from Maria Sharapova, she stood on court stretching with her team. But Williams did not allow herself to revel in her success: she immediately told her team that she now wanted to go and win Wimbledon.

According to Mouratoglou, this focus is common amongst all those players who find success in the game. 'All the top players have goals, but when they achieve something they immediately forget and focus on the next target when other players will be happy with what they have achieved.' As Mouratoglou points out, Williams' focus on that day in Paris bears a striking resemblance to when Rafael Nadal told the world he wanted to go and win Wimbledon just days after lifting the French Open title as a fresh-faced nineteen-year-old. And this focus off-court will also be reflected on-court, both in match-play and practice. 'The best players in the world are more focused and more intense during practice than the others,' continues Mouratoglou.

However, this does not paint the whole picture. In order to really understand the psyche of success, we must also consider what focus is. To answer this, I spoke with Dick Gould, former Head of Stanford University Men's Tennis, two-time ITA-Wilson 'Coach of the Decade' and winner of seventeen NCAA titles. In his time at Stanford, Gould moulded the games of many of the world's leading players, including John McEnroe, Roscoe Tanner and the Bryan brothers.

According to Gould, players must enter the court with a very specific goal in mind – but this goal must not be to win because this puts too much pressure on the athlete. 'My greatest quality as a coach was removing the pressure to win,' he says. 'Very rarely did I talk about winning. I always encouraged my players to go out there and play their best. Winning was never the goal: it was the result of my players playing their best on the court.'

To really analyse your opponent, or to really improve a specific area of your game, you must be completely immersed in the court – in the 'zone' – and be concentrating enough to register the idiosyncrasies of the game. You will fail to notice these if your focus is continually distracted by off-court stimuli.

The difficulty with tennis is that it is so hard to measure improvement. In athletics, for example, an athlete might never actually win an event but will always feel good about himself when he has bettered his own time, even though he finished last. But in tennis it is all about results; who beats whom. On the professional tour it is slightly different because improvement can be measured by ranking, which is based on an accumulation of results, but at lower levels of tennis there is an onus on particular results. This pressure makes the mental aspect so incredibly important. Players can apply unnecessary pressure on themselves because they are thinking about the result, and not the point itself.

In tennis, therefore, focus means keeping your mind in the present moment, hence the old tennis cliché 'point by point'. You must avoid focusing on future points – 'thinking cumulatively,' says Ashe – or previous points, both of which lie outside the scope of your control. The conscious mind loves to look outside the court; it loves to review points already played, and it loves to predict the future, but success requires you to focus the mind on the ball during the point and things you can control outside of it.

Legendary Stanford coach Dick Gould (*left*) says players must focus on performance rather than the result

Emotional Stability

Closely related to focus, emotional stability is an important aspect of mental strength. As humans, we all have our emotions, which are controlled by our surroundings. These emotions can play a huge part in the outcome of the match and you must learn to manage them if they are to maximize your performance.

Under the guidance of Ivan Lendl, Andy Murray, a notorious perfectionist, channelled the frustrations that had held him back for so long, and was able to maintain a more resolute focus on the pressure points in matches. Only by cutting out these small lapses in concentration was the Scot able to bring an end to Britain's seventy-seven-year wait for a Wimbledon Men's Champion.

Not all players will deal with their emotions on court in the same way. Some – John McEnroe, for example – used emotion as a source of motivation; anger got his blood pumping and tuned him into the match. For the majority, however, including Roger Federer, emotional stability is about not giving anything away. All top players will sometimes need to vent their frustration, but the emotional stability showed by almost all the top players is simply astounding. Very rarely do you see them moping around the court, head down or showing negative body language – and if they do, the match is already over.

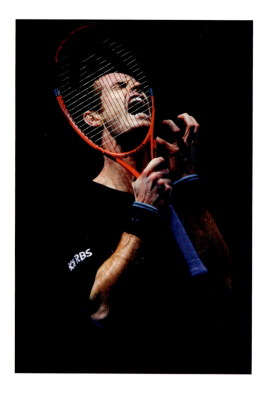

While hitting a winner gives you a 'natural high' and a feeling of fluidity and confidence, getting angry has both mental and biological consequences. Adrenaline can actually benefit your performance by speeding up your reactions when secreted in the right amounts, but anger will normally result in the constriction of your muscles as they become flooded. As a result, you begin to feel tense, losing that fluidity. That's when the errors begin to rack up.

Any display of anger or frustration also sends a message to your opponent that they are winning the mental battle, and in turn this lifts their self-confidence. On the other hand, appearing positive is indicative of confidence and control rather fear and vulnerability. Positive body language sends out a very important message to your opponent that you are not ready to roll over and accept defeat.

Under the guidance of the great Ivan Lendl, Andy Murray (*above*) learned to channel those emotions that had so often held him back

Jordi Arrese, 1992 Olympic Silver Medallist, believes that showing emotion on court is not necessarily a bad thing, as long as it is not done in a negative way. 'Negative energy is bad for performance and players must not keep this anger and frustration inside them. Some players will break rackets. I think that is fine if it allows them to refocus. The important thing is that the player develops control of their emotions.'

Andy Murray celebrates his 2013 Wimbledon victory

For many, this emotional stability will develop naturally as they mature, without the need for any mental training. David Ferrer, for example, describes himself as 'a very angry player' as a junior. When he was younger, his coach, Javier Piles, who still works with him today, would lock him in a broom cupboard at their local tennis club for hours on end when he was not giving his best on the court. At one stage, so disillusioned with what was expected of him in training, the Spaniard even quit the game to pursue a career in bricklaying – a decision that lasted less than a week.

How things have changed. Ferrer has now matured to become one of the most focused and dedicated performers in the sport. During the off-season he practises with the much heavier Basque wooden bat used in pelota to build strength in his upper body and goes on 60-mile bike rides to work on his endurance. The answer, he said, was time.

'When you're young, it's difficult, because you don't have any experience. Now I know that I have to control my frustration in practice and matches, but as a teenager it's not always easy to stay focused and disciplined so you need your coach to be strong and keep you on track.'[7]

Other players will benefit from specific techniques. Research has shown that smiling actually relaxes the body, lowering stress hormones and improving regulation of the adrenal glands and leads to secretion of endorphins. How you carry yourself is largely influential on how you feel emotionally. If your body language is positive, head up high, chest out, then it is hard to feel angry and negative.

Finding Prime Intensity

As the Rafa–Roger rivalry of the mid-noughties encapsulates so perfectly, different players compete and train at different intensities. While the Spaniard has based his illustrious career on unparalleled levels of grit, determination and intensity, the great Swiss appears to glide across a tennis court with the greatest of ease.

Closely linked to this idea of 'match tightness' is mistake management. All players make mistakes, but focus and mental stability will determine when these mistake are made. The top players have all developed the ability to hone in on the match at the most important moments, shutting the door on unforced errors to win the 'big' points. Very rarely do top players make mistakes in bunches.

This ability is perhaps best illustrated through the success of these players on tie-breakers, a point in all matches where errors are at their most costly. Statistics indicate that Djokovic wins over 65 per cent of his tie-breakers (although this went down in the 2013 season) and Federer wins almost 66 per cent of his. The reason for this is quite simple: the best players manage their errors to stop them from occurring at the important stages of a match. Instead, most of their errors will come towards the beginning of the set when the points will have less influence on the outcome of the match.

As with emotional control, mistake management can actually be practised without any specific techniques. A great exercise to develop this skill is for you to rally with an opponent on a full or half court. Neither you or your opponent should be looking to be overly aggressive but the tempo must remain high at all times. One player will eventually make a mistake and when they do, they must then hit x number of balls before another mistake is made. The value of x will depend on the level of the players. The premise of the exercise is to encourage you to mentally raise your focus where necessary to prevent a second error occurring.

Motivation

If 2010 was about crowning Rafael Nadal as the new King of Tennis, 2011 represented the rise of the 'Djoker'. The Serb began his career in promising fashion, setting tennis tongues wagging when he pushed Federer in the 2007 US Open final at the age of twenty. Djokovic's performance was befitting of a champion, but Federer's experience and mental fortitude allowed him to close out the sets where the inexperienced Serb could not.

Not until 2011 did Djokovic really make his mark on the game. The Serb's defeat to Jurgen Melzer in the 2010 French Open quarter-final is not remembered as a great match, but what happened shaped the men's game forever. As the third seed taking on the World Number 27, Djokovic was the overwhelming favourite, but the Serb let the match slip away despite leading by two sets and a break. 'That was the turnaround, mentally,' said his coach and mentor at the time, Marián Vajda.[8] 'After the defeat, he convinced himself he had to work harder,' he added. 'It did change things,' Djokovic said.

A similar showcase of sheer dedication and motivation can be illustrated by Thomas Muster. In 1989, in Miami, Muster seriously injured his leg when he was knocked down on the side of the road by a drunken driver. For many, this would be just cause to rest and take time away from the court – but not for Muster. The great Austrian proceeded to spend hours honing his strokes from a specially designed wheelchair with his leg in a cast.

There is little glamour in training to be a professional tennis player and this motivation is a key ingredient in success. The top players have to be so disciplined and dedicated to continue working to make gradual improvements each and every day if they are to develop as a tennis player and this only stems from a deep-lying motivation for success. Jez Green, the former fitness trainer of Andy Murray, notes how it is the Scot's incredible dedication and commitment to get up each morning to put in the hours in the gym and on the practice court that have allowed him to reach the pinnacle of the game. It would simply be impossible to put these hours in and make these sorts of sacrifices without being highly self-motivated.

And make no mistake – this motivation will also show itself on the court. Djokovic was match point down four times in his fourth set at the French Open quarter-final against Tsonga in 2012. Djokovic won. He was two sets down to Federer at the 2012 US Open. Djokovic won. And there are many more examples. Nobody does 'match point down' as well as the great Serb, and it is his highly motivated nature that allows him to come back where others would roll over and accept defeat. Similarly, just six years after his accident, Thomas Muster became the World Number One player. Highly motivated players will fight back with great grit and determination, and mental training can help develop this skill.

Developing Mental Strength: Some Effective Techniques

‘ There is a misconception that players are either born with mental strength or they will never have it. That could not be more incorrect. It is possible to manufacture mental strength; it does take time but players can build it up. ’

PETER GILMOUR, *International Mental Performance Coach*

Only a fortunate few are born with the mental fortitude required for sporting success. For the vast majority, it will take time for these psychological attributes to develop and players can spend years upon years looking for that secret ingredient that makes all the difference in their performance.

The following techniques can all be used to help you overcome the mental hurdles that the game presents. It is common for players to use a combination of these rather than just one technique on its own, so mix and match to suit your development.

Novak Djokovic's self-confidence and belief in his own game have taken him to the very pinnacle of the game

- Visualization
- Routines
- Relaxation
- Trigger Words
- Hypnosis
- Emotional Freedom Technique (EFT) or 'tapping'

Before we begin, however, it is important to note that techniques to develop mental strength are very player-specific and, while the following information will offer you a detailed insight into which techniques are available and how they can be practised effectively, you are strongly advised to consult with a qualified sports psychologist before attempting any of the following disciplines.

Visualization

As far as sporting success goes, it is hard to match that enjoyed by Bob and Mike Bryan. After turning professional upon their graduation from Stanford University in 1998, they have gone on to hold the World Number One doubles ranking for longer than anyone else in the history of the game, accumulating over forty-six Grand Slam titles between them along the way. But how does the greatest doubles pair of all time mentally prepare for their successes?

'We use visualization all the time,' they said when I met them in Australia. 'We imagine the crowd, the stadium, and winning the match. It really helps us to feel comfortable out there on the court.'

Visualization involves the mental creation or re-creation of an action or event in the mind. Otherwise referred to as 'guided imagery', visualization requires you to imagine the event as vividly as possible, employing your

Visualization forms a key part of the Bryan brothers' pre-match preparations

visual senses along with your sense of taste, touch, smell and sound. It can be used to both calm your pre-match nerves and fill you with confidence.

On his capture and incarceration in solitary confinement by the Vietnamese, Colonel George Hall would spend time each day imagining himself playing a round of golf to maintain his sanity while locked away. Upon his release, he was able to play to the same handicap as before his capture, despite not having held a golf club for close to a decade.

There is more overwhelming scientific and anecdotal evidence to support the powers of visualization and its benefits in performance maximization, but Australian psychologist Alan Richardson's study with a group of basketball players remains the most powerful.

Richardson divided a group of basketball players into three groups and tested their respective abilities to shoot free-throws. The first group were then instructed to practise twenty minutes a day, the second would only visualize themselves making free throws, and the third group would do neither. After one week of practice, group two had improved the most and shot numbers as good as, if not better than, the group who had actually practised. But why does it work?

The basis of visualization is the lesser-known 'Carpenter effect'. Research indicates that the observer of a tennis match experiences high levels of activity in the brain and muscles that are actually activated in the physical execution of the action being witnessed. This develops neuromuscular programming, which assists the observer to execute the actions observed at a later date.

In this way, players watching a high-level player hitting will actually unconsciously learn to hit those strokes through the 'Carpenter effect'. The most famous example of this effect is Pete Sampras learning his strokes by observing Rod Laver tapes all throughout his development. While the 'Carpenter' effect is effective in its own right, visualization takes this phenomenon to a new level.

In his book, *The Inner Game of Tennis*,[9] W. Timothy Gallwey describes how all humans have two selves: 'Self One' and 'Self Two'. 'Self One', according to Gallwey, is the conscious, telling self, and 'Self Two' is the subconscious, 'doing' self. To communicate with 'Self Two', Gallwey explains that 'Self One' (the conscious mind) must communicate in vivid imagery because 'Self Two', the sub-conscious, does not understand words or phrases. By imagining, therefore, 'Self One' is telling 'Self Two' what to do. In other words, by imagining, the player is giving the body instructions. As a result, the specific action visualized in the mind is then executed.

Executing any action – a tennis serve, for example – requires a specific programme of neuromuscular circuits, which in turn activate the muscles to move the body. Studies have shown that simply visualizing the action results in a micro-muscular stimulation in the same muscles used to actually execute the serve in 'reality'. In other words, visualization has a physiological effect on the body and, from a neurological perspective, the body cannot tell the difference between a 'real' experience and a vividly imagined one.

While undoubtedly a highly important aspect of mental preparation and performance maximization, it is important to recognize that visualization does have limits. In reality, visualization and actual execution must complement each other instead of being used as alternatives to one another. In other words, visualization cannot make you a champion, but it is a very powerful tool to accelerate development towards you becoming one. It is very difficult to accurately imagine hitting a groundstroke without actually having hit one.

HOW TO USE VISUALIZATION

Relax: Visualization requires high levels of concentration, so you should try to be as relaxed as possible. This will prevent your mind from switching to other thoughts and will maximize the imprint on your neurological pathways.

Imagine: Place yourself in the very environment where the action is happening. Imagine the sights, the sounds and the smells with as much detail as possible – the more detailed your imagination, the better your results will be. It is now that you will visualize the action itself.

As an observer to external stimuli, you can observe in two different modes: (1) where you are a spectator, disassociated from the actual action being observed, and (2) from a first-person perspective. Visualization requires you to observe in Mode (2), i.e. as if you are actually executing the action, or shot, being observed.

You should picture yourself executing the action clearly in your mind. If you are visualizing to improve a stroke, you must imagine the feel of the ball on the strings, the emotions as the ball goes in and the sounds of the crowd applauding your skill. How exactly does it sound? How exactly does it feel? You must imagine executing the action as vividly as possible.

Cool-down: Visualization sessions will normally last between twenty and thirty minutes, and can be brought to a close by finishing the imaginations and relaxing your mind. You can begin to bring yourself out of the first person and back into reality.

WHEN TO USE VISUALIZATION

Pre-Match: Almost all major tennis events have private rooms available for players where they can get their bodies prepped and focus their minds using techniques that include visualization. 'I have used visualization before,' says Laura Robson, the former British Number One. 'For the hours leading up to the match I'll be by myself imagining what I am going to do in certain situations,' she says. 'It helps me to relax.' Visualization should be used as part of every player's warm-up routine.

The pre-match stress and nervousness that you will almost inevitably feel before you step out on court can actually work to improve your performance. Nervousness is only negative when it interrupts the healthy state of equilibrium of the nervous system. When your nervous system becomes overwhelmed, you experience a heightened state of readiness ('fight or flight') as chemicals flood your body. This, in turn, contracts your muscles and prevents a fluid, relaxed on-court performance. In these situations, you can use visualization and relaxation techniques to return your body and mind to a state of equilibrium.

In effect, visualization allows you to play the match out in your head before you even step onto the court. You can imagine yourself feeling calm and steady at different points in the match, visualize yourself winning and feeling the glory on match point; if you have 'done' it *before* the match, there will be less pressure to 'do' it *during* the match. In this way, your coach can play a role in assisting you in your pre-match visualization routines. Most coaches will go through a detailed plan with their players about how to approach the match from a tactical standpoint, and this can give you a lot of confidence.

'Once you explain how the opponent is going to play and what they are going to do, and how your player is going to beat him, your player can then visualize how exactly he is going to win,' says Patrick Mouratoglou, a believer in the positive effects of visualization. 'It is always important to have a plan,' he says. This will minimize nerves and promote a strong, confident performance.

In-Match Visualization: There is not enough time for visualization in-play, but the twenty-five seconds between points and the ninety seconds during changeovers will rarely be wasted by the game's elite. As they sit there, eyes glazed over in a state of trance, many players are actually visualizing the upcoming points. They may visualize the serve or return they are going to hit before they actually execute it, and many will even play out the point in their heads before the ball is in play, imagining the combination of shots they intend to use.

Visualization can perhaps be used most effectively on the serve, the single shot over which the player has complete control. Maria Sharapova, the queen of routine, can actually be seen visualizing the serving motion between points, trying to maintain focus and playing out the points in her head.

To visualize the serve, you should imagine your service preparation, visualizing a well-placed ball toss followed by a smooth, controlled racket swing and a perfect connection with the ball. You should imagine the sound of the ball hitting the strings and fizzing through the air to the direct target area on the other side of the net. As above, you should stand ready, focused, relaxed, imagining the swing and how it will feel on the strings. Only after this drawn out visualization routine should you actually complete the serve.

Visualization is also a very effective tool for you as the returner, especially where you can 'read' where the serve is going to be placed.

VISUALIZATION IN STROKE DEVELOPMENT AND MAINTENANCE

You can also use visualization off-court to develop or maintain a stroke. Just as you might repeatedly practise your backhand and volley on court, you can visualize yourself executing these shots in your mind's eye to reinforce or fine-tune certain elements of the technique.

'NEGATIVE' VISUALIZATION

Jeffrey Hodges, Performance Consultant to elite athletes, describes how human beings are like 'guided missiles'[10] in that 'we move in the direction of our regular and consistent thoughts and imaginings; we move towards the picture we have in our mind like a magnetic attraction.'[11] If we can imagine it, we can do it. According to Hodges, therefore, visualization can also have *negative* effects if the player imagines a negative outcome.

To elaborate on his point, Hodges uses the example of a tennis player double-faulting because he has imagined missing his second serve. Despite the player repeating to himself not to double fault, the error occurs because it has been visualized; or, to use Gallwey's theory, 'Self One' has instructed 'Self Two' to double-fault through visual imagery. 'Self Two' does not understand the internal dialogue and executes the actions as seen in the imagery. You must, therefore, be aware of the negative effects of visualization and try to maintain a positive mindset in the knowledge that any negative imagery will damage your performance.

Routines

In their 2013 meeting at the Monte Carlo Masters, Marinko Matosevic walked over to Rafael Nadal's bench on the changeover and intentionally knocked over his meticulously placed water bottles in the hope that this would throw the almost-robotic Spaniard out of rhythm.

By any measure, Nadal's routine is the model of precision and accuracy. He walks onto the court with a single racket before sprinting to the baseline following the coin toss. At the change of ends, he steps in front of the line with his right foot and takes a sip from each his two water bottles, one neatly behind the other, both of which have been positioned perfectly to ensure that the labels face diagonally at the court. Before each serve, he straightens his socks, pulls at his shorts and brushes his hair behind his ear. It is only then that he is ready to play.

But Nadal is not alone: Maria Sharapova clears her hair from her face, completes some hop-skips and bounces the ball once before serving. John Isner always bounces the ball between his legs when serving and Richard Gasquet re-grips his racket at almost every change of ends. The routines of 2013 Wimbledon Champion Marian Bartoli changed over the course of her

As part of his pre-match routine, Rafael Nadal meticulously places his water bottles so that their labels face the baseline

career, ranging from numerous 'dry-swings' to full-squat jumps before each and every point.

Superstition may certainly be a factor, but pre-match and on-court routines are encouraged because they clear the mind and help the player to achieve optimal concentration. 'Some call it superstition, but it's not. If it were superstition, why would I keep doing the same thing over and over whether I win or lose?' asks Nadal. 'It's a way of placing myself in a match, ordering my surroundings to match the order I seek in my head.'[12]

Players begin to believe that this obsessive succession of actions will work for them because it has worked for them before. It offers security and regularity in a sport where certainty is at its most absent. Past research has shown the positive effects of pre-performance routines in various sports, and this is particularly true when it comes to 'closed' skills such as the serve.

It is also important to note that these routines will regularly stretch well-beyond the boundaries of the court. From booking a practice court to sleeping schedules and foods eaten, players will all have a very specific pre-match and post-match routine they will follow along with the specific on-court routines. Continuing with Rafael Nadal as an example, his pre-match ritual consists of a obsessively precise six-hour routine involving a cold-shower, re-gripping each of the six rackets he takes on to court and running water carefully through his hair.

Routines should not be forced; they will occur naturally as you experiment with your preparations and on-court rhythms.

Relaxation: Breathing and Music

As natural as nervousness and anxiety are, they can be distracting and hinder performance if they are not channelled in the correct way. According to David Ranney, author of *Tennis: Play the Mental Game*,[13] when the player is focused and the muscles are relaxed, they are being controlled by the 'other than conscious mind', and this 'other than conscious mind' knows how to hit a ball far better than the 'conscious mind'.

For this reason, you must learn to relax your mind if you are to perform to the best of your capability.

Breathing: Breathing techniques are taught in many physical disciplines but they are particularly beneficial in tennis where being relaxed is an important aspect of performance. Knowing the importance of breathing is one thing, but it is important that you learn the correct breathing techniques. Oxygen is required for muscles to function efficiently and you can loosen up your muscles by taking long, deep breaths. Research indicates that players should inhale through their nose and exhale slowly through the mouth, extending each breath for about ten seconds. You can do this between the change of ends, prior to a match or even between points as part of an on-court routine.

Another great breathing technique used to bring thoughts back into the present moment is to exhale all the way out and empty your lungs. Hold this position without inhaling for a couple of seconds to immediately refocus your brain on the present moment, escaping those fears, doubts and insecurities that can so regularly hold back your performance.

Music: Not strictly part of mental training, but nevertheless an important aspect of match preparation and mental relaxation is music. The vast majority of modern-day athletes will listen to music at some point during their pre-match preparations as a way of helping them to relax, relieve anxiety and de-stress. Jelena Gencic, who worked with a young Novak Djokovic, spoke to the *New York Times* about how the Serb thinks about Tchaikovsky's 1812 Overture to refocus and inspire himself during matches. Still today, Djokovic is known to use classical music as part of his pre-match preparations.

Research suggests that different music has varying effects on different people, so you must find the music that puts you in the right frame of mind to play to the best of your ability. And your choice of music may well change over the course of your preparations. You, for example, may use relaxed, low tempo music to calm yourself and prevent distraction earlier in the day before switching to a more upbeat track as a source of inspiration before going onto the court.

Studies also indicate that music with a tempo of sixty beats per minute (e.g. classical symphonies or slow piano melodies) works in synchrony with the human heartbeat and creates a relaxing effect. It slows down your heart rate, breathing rate and thinking rate, allowing you to enter into a state of rest and calm. '[Listening to music] sharpens that sense of flow, removes me further from my surroundings,' says Rafael Nadal.[14]

'Trigger' Words'

'Trigger' words are simply reminders that trigger a certain response from the player to instantly regain concentration on the goal. That response normally brings the player back into the present, but trigger words can also be used to remind the player of a certain aspect of technique. Many players will actually write these trigger words on the throat of their rackets or even keep reminders in their tennis bags to read during the changeover.

While 'trigger' words might appear to be nothing more than a waste of time, they can be highly effective. The mind cannot focus simultaneously on two different things and, because of this, players can control their thoughts by thinking of a 'trigger' word instead of anything negative, for example. To give an example, it is impossible for a player to think about losing at the same as thinking of the word 'Focus'.

Studies also indicate a link between key words and muscle memory, suggesting that certain words will actually trigger certain responses within the body itself. Players can therefore 'hit harder', 'load up' or 'swing-through' simply by saying these words out loud.

'Trigger' words must be kept short and simple if they are to be effective.

Hypnosis

The Russian Olympic team was assisted by eleven hypnotists during the 1956 Melbourne Olympics, and boxer Steve Collins famously hired Dr Tony Quinn, a renowned hypnotherapist, to assist him in overcoming rival Chris Eubank.

Hypnosis has been used in sport for many years but even today it is perceived by many as a magical form of mind mastery that conjures up images of innocent audience members behaving out of the ordinary as soon as the onstage magician clicks his fingers. As a result, there is a 'great reluctance' of many coaches to accept hypnotherapy as a legitimate form of mental conditioning, notes Peter Gilmour, an International Mental Performance Coach.

The truth is that hypnosis can be a great method for players of all abilities to improve their on-court performance and many of the world's top athletes have been known to use hypnosis prior to competition to maximize their performance and enter a state of heightened concentration.

Tiger Woods, for example, has been known to enter a self-hypnotic trance before hitting each golf shot. Not only does this help him focus on the goal at hand, it also helps him quieten his mind, release his anxiety and work from his sub-conscious, which knows how to hit the shot far better than the conscious mind.

Hypnosis is a trance-like state of heightened awareness, intense focus and relaxation. The subject is alert at all times and is most often compared to daydreaming or 'losing oneself' in a book or movie. All the regular doubts, fears and worries of the conscious minds are tuned out as the subject becomes engrossed with whatever they are focused upon.

Hypnosis works because of the 'conscious' and 'sub-conscious' mind. The sub-conscious mind is the driving-force for the majority of beliefs and behaviours, taking control of all the actions we do automatically: breathing, walking, blinking, etc. It is deep within the sub-conscious that most of our thinking is done, and it is here that all the blueprints for tennis strokes are maintained. The information here is pure and untarnished by the doubts and fears generated in the conscious part of the mind. When players train, players are enhancing the blueprint of the tennis action or stroke deep within their sub-conscious.

Most players, however, are only aware of their conscious mind: choosing the words we speak, or what to do on the weekend. Although the conscious mind represents very little of what we do, it works very closely with the sub-conscious.

Self-hypnosis allows players to perform from the sub-conscious where they will execute actions automatically with heightened awareness and intense focus. The conscious mind is out of the way and has a less active role in the thinking process. The athlete is acting directly from original action blueprints without the influence of the conscious mind. As a result, the action will be what we have spent hours on the court training without all of those doubts, fears and worries that often arise in a pressurized match situation.

As a method of communicating with the sub-conscious, the control panel of the brain, hypnosis also allows players to positively programme certain reactions and responses from the player to certain external stimuli. Jeffrey Hodges, Performance Consultant to elite athletes, notes that unconscious confidence is a result of parental and social conditioning and that hypnosis can be used to replace any negative conditioning by 'filling in the gaps where there was no positive encouragement, and to enhance and amplify the existing positive conditioning.'[15] In this way, hypnosis can be used to raise your confidence and overcome issues of self-doubt or pre-game nerves that may have prevented you from maximizing your athletic potential.

EFT Tapping

Named 'tapping' because it involves speaking aloud while 'tapping' on one of the hundreds of acupoints located at junctions along the invisible energy pathways that run through our bodies, EFT (Emotional Freedom Technique) Tapping was first developed by Gary Craig as an abbreviation of the methods used in TFT (Thought Field Therapy), an earlier Energy Psychology method.

By tapping on these specific parts of the body, you can liberate yourself of negative emotions like anger, depression, stress fears and anxiety. This then allows you to play with heightened awareness, working from the sub-conscious mind with high levels of confidence and belief.

Many athletes from a variety of sports have been known to incorporate EFT into their training programmes, but the reasons for its success continue to remain unproven. The leading belief is that the tapping is targeted on the thirteen 'energy meridians', which are used in ancient Chinese acupuncture.

EFT is best learned via a qualified mental performance coach.

How to Begin Mental Training

‘ I can categorically state that beginning mental training will improve a
player's on-court performance. ’

PETER GILMOUR, *International Mental Performance Coach*

So, it's simple, right? Start mental training and your performance will
improve. But just how, exactly, do you begin mental training?

Andy Murray's 2012 Wimbledon victory was considered a great day for
British tennis. But the momentous occasion only proved to highlight the
numerous deficiencies that lie within the heart of the LTA, which, with an
annual budget close to £60 million, has not helped any of Britain's last three
tennis champions: Greg Rusedski, Tim Henman and Andy Murray – all of
whom developed outside the LTA pathway.

Peter Gilmour has long noted an inherent psychological flaw in British
players that has been highly influential in the country's underachievement
over the past decade. According to Gilmour, 'From a very early age in the
UK especially, players are fed self-limiting beliefs,' he says. 'Ask top juniors
in the UK about their athletic goals and most will say "Top 50" [in the world
rankings] or "Top 100". Go to Spain and the top juniors as early as fourteen
will say they want to win a Grand Slam or be Number One in the world,'
adds Gilmour. 'These limiting beliefs hold players back from maximizing
their potential and they either quit at an early age or work hard to overcome
these thoughts. Mental training can help players do this,' he says.

There has long been a fear within the LTA to fully accept the significance
of the mental game and Gilmour 'has little doubt that the state of British
tennis would improve drastically were more emphasis placed on this aspect
of performance.'

Although the high-performance players in the LTA programme do now
have access to mental training, it can be difficult for those outside of this
system to overcome these problems by finding a qualified sports psychologist themselves and footing the bill. Techniques to develop mental strength
are best practised following consultation with a specialist sports psychologist and, for now, at least, it is best to discuss the issue with your coach
who can advise you on finding a psychologist fit for your needs.

However, while there are thousands of qualified tennis coaches established on British shores, until the LTA formally recognizes the value of
sports psychology in performance maximization and makes it more accessible to elite players, British tennis will continue to under-perform.

It really becomes quite simple: once the techniques and benefits are
understood and the apparent air of mystery around it is removed, mental
training for tennis becomes one of the most fundamental ways in which
any player can take his or her performance to the next level.

CHAPTER NINE

Taking the Next Step to Success

What a wonderful experience it has been to delve back into the world of tennis to investigate and answer the questions that puzzled me for so many years. For me, it is perhaps too late, but taking all this information on board and applying the practical elements will allow players like you to jump over hurdles and make quick, informed decisions at important times in your career where others will struggle. Time really is of the essence in high-level sport and I can only wish that this material had been made readily available when I was competing.

That is not to say that I look back at my time in the game with any sense of regret. Without doubt, there are decisions I would have made differently had I had the means of seeing the benefits of each choice – I would, for example, have taken the scholarship to the USA and I would also have spent more time focusing on my mental conditioning – but I made the decisions based on all the information that was readily available to me at the time and I cannot criticize myself for that.

While I certainly cannot say I achieved anything close to what I had intended, I do believe that my experiences in the sport gave me far more than I ever could have imagined, including three foreign languages, a plethora of wonderful experiences and friends all across the world. I also developed a strong sense of self-survival and a greater depth to my character than if I had not pursued it to such lengths. For this alone, I am happy to have had the opportunity to have played the game at all.

Tennis really is a wonderful game and it is important that if you have the desire, you push yourself in the sport to see where it can take you. At times in life, it can be so easy to put so much focus on career and education that any sporting aspirations become crowded out by school or university studies. This single dilemma – law or tennis? – is something that shaped my progression as a junior, but only by pursuing the sport have I finally been able to happily commit to practising the law, something that had always interested me, but which seemed only to obstruct my pathway in tennis.

Make no mistake: the experiences and skills learned during my time have already and will continue to help my further career successes. Life on the tennis circuit is finite, and very few talented players will be fortunate enough to make a career from playing the game, but that is not to say you should not try; the beauty is in the journey.

For now, this is where I will leave it. For those players reading this book: commit to your development and embrace the opportunity that you have. Tennis competition can open up so many wonderful doors and pathways to those who do choose to pursue it and it is important to appreciate that this opportunity will not stay open for long. Challenge yourself, push yourself and see where it takes you. But most importantly, enjoy the journey.

This book should help you to do just that.

Endnotes

Chapter 3 A Guide to Competing on the Tour

[1] Extracts from BBC Sport website (17 April 2009). Article reproduced by kind permission of BBC Sport

[2] Extracts from *Guardian* Sports Friday (26 April 2013). Article reproduced by kind permission of *Guardian* Sport

[3] Ibid.

[4] Please note that as from early 2016, the US$15,000 category is abolished with the view that these tournaments will offer $25,000 in prize money. In 2017 these levels of prize money will rise again to between $15,000 and $125,000, ahead of further proposed increases in 2018. See page 51 for further details.

Chapter 4 Adapting Effectively to the Court

[1] Reproduced with the kind permission of *Grantland*

[2] *Science for Tennis Players*, Howard Brody (University of Pennsylvania Press, 1987)

[3] Extracts from BBC Sport's coverage of the 2014 Wimbledon Championships kindly reproduced by kind permission of BBC Sport

[4] Ibid.

Chapter 5 Choosing the Right Equipment

[1] *A Champion's Mind: Lessons from Life of a Tennis Player*, Pete Sampras (Three Rivers Press, 2009)

Chapter 6 Improving Your Technical Game

[1] Translated this means 'Aggression starts in the legs'

[2] *Tennis for Life*, Peter Burwash (Times Books, 1981)

Chapter 7 Fitness Training for Tennis

[1] *Serve to Win: The 14-Day Gluten-Free Plan for Physical and Mental Excellence*, Novak Djokovic (Zinc Ink, 2013)

Chapter 8 Developing the Mindset of a Champion

[1] *Serve to Win: The 14-Day Gluten-Free Plan for Physical and Mental Excellence*, Novak Djokovic (Zinc Ink, 2013)

[2] *The Roger Federer Story: Quest for Perfection*, Rene Stauffer (New Chapter Press, 1997)

[3] 'Freak of Nature: How Novak Djokovic Harnessed the Untapped Powers of His Body', Eli Saslow (*ESPN* magazine, 13 July 2012)

[4] Ibid.

[5] *Rafa: My Story*, Rafa Nadal and John Carlin (Sphere, 2012)

[6] *Prime Tennis: Triumph of the Mental Game*, Dr Jim Taylor (Writers Club Press, 20 August 2000)

[7] Reproduced with the kind permission of *Tennis Australia* magazine (January 2014)

[8] Extracts from *The Daily Telegraph*. Interview and article reproduced with kind permission of *The Telegraph* Sport (27 January 2013)

[9] *The Inner Game of Tennis*, W. Timothy Gallwey (Pan, 1986)

[10] Reproduced from www.sportsmind.com.au, with kind permission of Jeffrey Hodges B.Sc, M.Sc. (Hons), B. Ed.

[11] Ibid.

[12] *Rafa: My Story*, Rafa Nadal and John Carlin (Sphere, 2012)

[13] *Tennis: Play the Mental Game*, David Ranney (Night Lotus Productions, 2006)

[14] *Rafa: My Story*, Rafa Nadal and John Carlin (Sphere, 2012)

[15] Reproduced from www.sportsmind.com.au, with kind permission of Jeffrey Hodges B.Sc, M.Sc. (Hons), B. Ed.

Picture Credits

The author and publishers wish to thank the following individuals and organizations for permission to reproduce their images (page numbers are given in **bold**):

© Patrick Mouratoglou Tennis Academy [**18** (*top*); **41**; **43** (*top & bottom*); **44**; **128**; and **198** (*top*)]

© Ella Ling [**18** (*bottom*); **23**; **70**; **71** (*bottom*); **73**; **74** (*top & bottom*); **78** (*top*); **89**; **151**; **162** (*top & bottom*); **163** (*top & bottom*); **165**; **184**; **196**; **199**; **200**; **204** (*top & bottom*); **207**; **208**; and **213**]

© Matthew McNulty [**78** (*bottom*); **81** (*bottom*); **83**; and **198** (*bottom*)]

© Raito Ray Hino [**19** (*top & bottom*); **142** (*bottom*); **143**; and **154** (*top*)]

Jordi Arrese (**49**)

© Dick Gould [**20** (*top & middle*); **22** (*bottom*); **24** (*bottom*); and **203**]

© Stanford University Athletics [(**20** (*bottom*); **24** (*top*)]

© The University of Virginia [**21**; **22** (*top*); **32** (*left & right*); **38** (*top & bottom*); and **39** (*top & bottom*)]

© Rubin Statham [**119**]

© Wilson Tennis [**104** (*top & bottom*); **105**; and **107**]

Unless otherwise stated, all illustrations drawn by Tara Wallace.

All other images supplied by the author.

Index